棠树文丛
—代表作—

法概念的跨语际旅行

从意义单位到翻译单位

宋丽珏 著

创于1897
The Commercial Press
商务印书馆
The Commercial Press

本书受上海市高水平地方高校建设项目资助，
系上海市哲学社会科学规划青年课题
"语料库驱动下的汉英立法文本翻译单位研究"
（2016EYY004）的研究成果

总　序

　　学术研究是高校非常重要的一项功能,也是衡量一所大学综合实力、核心竞争力的主要指标。开展学术活动、产出学术成果、培养学术人才是高校完成人才培养、科学研究、社会服务等使命的主要手段。大学之所以成为大学,学术的兴盛正是主要的标志之一,只有学术水平提高了,才能更好地完成培养人才和服务社会的目标。

　　党的十八大以来,以习近平同志为核心的党中央高度重视哲学社会科学工作,从改革发展稳定、治党治国治军的高度,肯定了哲学社会科学的重要意义。习近平总书记在 2016 年 5 月 17 日召开的"哲学社会科学工作座谈会"上指出,"要加大科研投入,提高经费使用效率。要建立科学权威、公开透明的哲学社会科学成果评价体系,建立优秀成果推介制度,把优秀研究成果真正评出来、推广开",为新时期哲学社会科学的发展指明了方向。学术专著是广大教师平时研究成果的精心积累,出版则是优秀研究成果推广的重要手段。做好学术著作的组织出版能够提高教师科研活动的积极性,弘扬优秀学术,开拓创新,也能为学校的科研事业做出应有的贡献。

　　华东政法大学全面贯彻党的教育方针,落实立德树人根本任务,围绕上海教育中长期规划纲要的总体目标,按照建设"双一流"高水平多科性教学研究型特色大学的战略要求,遵循科研发展规律,加强管理,精益求精,在科研方面取得了不俗的成绩。近年来,学校的优秀学术成果持续增多,学术影响力有所提升,学校科研工作日攀新高。

　　法学是华东政法大学的主要学科,也是我校的知名品牌。推介法学研究成果是科研管理部门的服务项目和重要职责。这次推出的"棠树文丛"就是以华东政法大学法学领域的优秀成果为主,兼顾其他学科的优秀成果。"棠树"出自《诗经》。《诗经·甘棠》云:"蔽芾甘棠,勿翦勿伐。"这是说周初召伯巡行理政,在甘棠树下听讼决狱,断案公正无私,其事流芳后世,歌诗以载。法平如水,民心所向,古今无异,故以"棠树"为本丛书命名。这次组织出版"棠树文丛",可以促进华政的学术研究水平,提升法学等学科的影响力,为实现依法治国的宏伟目标和弘扬法律的公平正义添砖加瓦。

高层次优秀科研成果的出版是教师和科研管理部门共同追求的目标,也是我们贯彻落实《华东政法大学学术专著出版资助管理办法》的举措。我们希望通过这次学术专著推进活动,规范学校图书出版工作,进一步激发我校教师多出优秀成果的科研积极性,展现华政学术风采。

华东政法大学科研处

2022 年 4 月

目　录

第一章
法概念的语言学与超语言学意义

第一节　法概念及意义的跨语际实践

　　翻译活动中客体和主体相遇,必须借助语言生成和实现。概念作为语言表达的基本工具,是对客观事物的抽象概括,并以人所获得的概念为出发点,赋予事物指称及意义。法概念便是具有法律意义的社会事实或社会现象通过概括性表达而形成的术语或其他意义单位。宏观地看,概念的"跨语际"就是考察新的词语、意义、话语以及表述的模式,在继受方语言与传播方语言的接触、冲突过程中,在继受方语言中兴起、流通并获得合法性的过程。因此,当概念从传播方语言走向继受方语言时,其意义与其说发生了"改变",不如说是在继受方语言的本土环境中发明创造出来的。这个过程与文化历史差异、社会发展、民族精神等等有着密不可分的关联,属于宏观"意义单位"。微观地看,在法律语境下的意义单位需要通过具体语词或话语来实现。

　　法概念在一种语境中承载的意义单位,寻找在另一种语言中的对应单位,从而形成翻译单位的过程,便是一种概念的旅行。在此过程中,涉及对语言层面的各级意义单位,包括术语、法律用语、篇章句式、语篇、话语的研究;在超语言层面,则涉及国家主义、历史主义、文化主义、本质主义等方面。我们在探讨法律翻译单位之时,不可避免地要采用"立体"视角,即在宏观、中观和微观多维度展开讨论。在语言层面和超语言层面的讨论都是法律翻译单位研究的重要面向和组成部分。

以往的相关研究集中在语言学、翻译学、史学和法学领域内,但成果存在各行其是、互不为谋的现象。以改革开放(1978 年)以来的研究成果为例:一、汉译外国法律名著丛书,包括世界法学汉译名著 4 种(如边沁著《立法理论:刑法典原理》),外国法律文库 32 种(如詹宁斯、瓦茨修订《奥本海国际法》),罗马法民法大全翻译系列 10 种(如桑德罗·斯奇巴尼选编《婚姻·家庭和遗产继承》),当代法学名著译丛 10 种(如波斯纳著《法理学问题》),宪政译丛 11 种(如詹宁斯著《法与宪法》),外国法典译丛 20 种(如《当代外国破产法》),司法文丛 5 种(如史蒂文·J. 伯顿著《法律和法律推理导论》),公法名著译丛 20 种(如肯尼斯·卡尔普·戴维斯著《裁量正义》),丹宁著作 6 种等等,共计 416 种;二、外译中国法律法规规章系列丛书,包括中华人民共和国法律/汇编(英文版)系列 15 种,中华人民共和国专门法(中英对照)系列 50 种,双语对照法规系列 6 种,中英对照法规系列 7 种,法律法规(中英文)系列 59 种等等,共计约 200 种;三、法律翻译类,包括笔译类 40 种,口译 10 种,翻译理论类 4 种等等,共计超过 60 种。

具言之,自 1978 年以来,国内法律译介与外译工作已取得全面发展,尤其在中国法外译方面取得突出成绩,并特别体现在外译文本的类型更具针对性,以更好地回应国家战略发展方向以及中国法治话语"自塑"的需要。进入千禧年以来,我国对外开放政策得到良好贯彻,国内企业"走出去"和国外企业"引进来"的数量明显增加,对外经贸合作取得新进展,对外开放逐渐深化。国家出台促进进出口稳增长、调结构的政策措施,也推动了相关法律翻译文件的外译,而外译文本也进一步地推动了政策的实施和发展,为对外开放保驾护航。

　　同时,随着法律翻译数据平台的建立和法律翻译专门人才培养的加强,法律翻译效率得到显著提高,译者可以获得更充足的时间对法律文本进行选择,并对翻译结果进行甄别。其中,基于社会环境选择翻译什么类型的法律文件体现了针对性的特点。于法律翻译而言,"翻译生态环境"就是社会发展大方向,即国家政策等纲领性文件及其思想。自中国于2001年加入世界贸易组织(WTO)至今,经济贸易方面的法律外译工作得到特别重视。2015年更是我国全面推进依法治国的开局之年,《中华人民共和国英文法规大系(法律编)》也适时出版,在一定程度上反映了国家需求与文本选择间的直接关系。

　　2013年以后的中国法律外译文本的翻译工作主体逐步确定为专门机构,而回顾法律译者这个群体,不难发现:译者主体从传教士、法学家到专门译者团体,其变迁体现了法律翻译影响社会阶层的范围。同时从等效性上考量,不同时代赋予了不同人群以法律翻译的权力。作为翻译过程中最具主观能动性的存在,译者需要面对具体的翻译生态环境,无时无刻不受社会、文化、历史、专业领域等方面的制约和影响。而不同的译者主体会呈现不同类型的法律文本,这将对社会发展产生不同的影响。以当代中国为例,如《2012年中国政府白皮书汇编》由中华人民共和国国务院新闻办公室发布,《中华人民共和国知识产权局公报》由国家知识产权局办公室编著。可见我国当下法律翻译对专业性的要求极高。之所以如此,除法律知识的专业性要求之外,更重要的是翻译团队中具备双语背景与专业知识框架的专业人士能够提高译文的可读性和实际操作可行性,使其为外文读者所接受、理解和使用。

　　法律翻译涉及国家上层建筑,为国家发展作出引导性建议。故此,法律翻译一旦发布,往往伴随着广泛而深刻的社会影响。这种强引导性恰是一把双刃剑,若翻译不当,便有阻碍对外开放与交流之危险。因此,把握好法律翻译的引导性是至关重要的一环,而"把握好"则体现在法律外译文本服务国家战略要求和适应社会大环境,并符合"通情达理"的标准等方面。所谓"通情达理",指的是译者能够通晓双方国情,在做到专业层面不失误之余,讲好中国故事,便于外方理解意义,推动对外开放与交流。为达到以上目的,译者需要在译前明确翻译目的,根据基于国家发展需要制定的翻译目标进行译文内容的选择。从2013—2020年间的法律翻译文本外译情况来看,涉及知识产权、进出口税则、出入境管理方面的文本偏多,如2013—2017年《中华人民共和国国家知识产权局公报》、2014年《中华人民共和国出境入境管理法(汉英对照)》、2018年《中华人民共和国海关进出口税则及申报指南(汉英对照)》等。这些法律外译文本为对外开放过程中可能遇到的类似知识产权权益保障、出入境管理和进出口税率等实际问题作出明确说明。同时,法律外译文件的类型也逐渐细化,由宏观层面的出入境管理和进出口税则拓展到更为具体的中外合资方面的法律文件,比如2015年的《中外合资法律文件(中英文对照)》和《中外合资经营企业合同与章程(中英文对照)》。也正是在这一时期,相关市场主体在境内外合作方面的力度大大加强。由此可见,法律翻译的引导性与社会发展是相互影响的。

诚如前述,法律翻译影响深远且服务于国家战略发展,所以从事法律翻译的个人与团队是经过国家机制层层筛选得到的,因此可以说是社会大环境孕育了译者主体,译者本身就体现了国家发展或准备发展的大方向。而若确定了译者主体在法律翻译中的能动地位,则需要聚焦法律翻译人才培养。展望未来法律翻译人才培养即译者主体培养,我们需要根据国家战略发展方向制订人才培养计划,并在计划中明确政、产、学、研四者之间互通有无的原则和方式。同时,法律翻译的政治属性和社会属性决定了其强引导性。这种引导性涉及社会各个方面，译者应跳出翻译研究的二元对立，如"直译和意译""形式和内容""忠诚和叛逆""规划和异化"等，从社会历史文化的总体框架中去考察整个翻译过程和翻译结果。① 通过将法律翻译过程分为译前、译中、译后三个部分，并在适应选择论的指导下对翻译涉及主体与其他主体的关系进行整理，可以得到以下关系图：

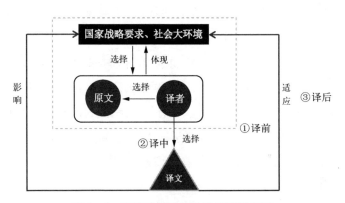

图 1－1　适应选择论下的法律翻译机制

第二节　汉英法律翻译面临的挑战

语言与法律的关系一直是吸引众多学者目光的重点研究领域，语言不仅仅是法律权力借以展开运作的工具，在许多至关重要的方面，语

---

① 参见刘云虹、许钧主编：《翻译批评研究之路：理论、方法与途径》，南京大学出版社 2015 年版。同时参见蔡新乐：《文化史就是翻译史——陈寅恪的历史发现与其翻译观初探》，《外语与外语教学》2006 年第 10 期。

言本身就是法律权力。克罗地亚里耶卡大学荣休教授、法学家、翻译学家苏珊·萨尔切维奇（Susan Šarčević）曾提出："被我们称作权力的那个抽象之物是每天在法律制度的各个层面发生、无数个语言互动的即刻原因和结果。权力因此既由法律实践的语言细节所决定，也决定着法律实践的语言细节。"①相应地，近20年来法律翻译类文章和法律翻译类著述中，国内学者们从法学出发探讨法律语言本体（如法律语言的总体特征、法律语言的词汇和句法特点、法律语言的简明原则等），如陈中绳、傅明华、王佳等学者从比较法角度著有《英文法律词典概说》等文章，另有贺卫方、邓正来、朱苏力、徐国栋、米健、方流芳、何家弘、杨玉圣、王健、潘琪等均对法律术语相关研究有所探讨，并著有《法学翻译与中国法的现代化》②等。也有学者从语言学、翻译学角度探讨法律文本翻译、法律翻译理论（包括翻译理论、可译性、译者主体性等）以及其他领域（如法庭翻译、争鸣与商榷、综述与回顾、因特网与法律翻译、人物评价及书评等）进行了讨论，如杜金榜、张新红、廖美珍、刘蔚铭、宋雷、王振华、赵军峰、张法连、屈文生等，均对法律翻译这一主题有多角度的探评，著有《从词典出发：法律术语译名统一与规范化的翻译史研究》（上海人民出版社2013年版）等作品。但需要指出的是，尽管我国的法律翻译研究已经取得了一些成就，却也仍然存在着一些亟待解决的问题。加之由于法律法规属于专业性极强的一种文体，而且属于意识形态的组成部分，其中难免有不少属于各国特色的表述，而该类表述在其他语言文本中难以找到完全对等的表达，故对法律法规名称（包括条款名称）等等的翻译极为棘手。基于上述原因，虽然自我国

① Susan Šarčević, *New Approach to Legal Translation*, The Hague: Kluwer Law International, 1997, p. 18.

② 《美国法律文库》会务组编：《法学翻译与中国法的现代化——"美国法律文库暨法学翻译与法律变迁"研讨会纪实》，中国政法大学出版社2005年版。

加入世界贸易组织后,法律法规的英译已成为中国对外法律交流和贸易活动的重要环节,目前我国很多法律也都有了其英文版,但其中的译文质量往往参差不齐,不尽如人意,例如:

表1-1 中国法律名称英译情况举例

原文	英译	译文勘误
中华人民共和国执业医师法	Law on Licensed Doctors of the People's Republic of China	修饰语误用。译文的限定关系是"中华人民共和国(的)执业医师的法律",与原文差异较大,实则为:制定主体-中华人民共和国,修饰主体-法律,修饰语-(有关)执业医师的。故此,译文应为:Law of People's Republic of China on Practicing Doctors 或 Practicing Doctors Law of the People's Republic of China(注:用 Licensed Doctors 对译"执业医师"比较准确,但也可用更为易懂的 Practicing Doctors)。
中华人民共和国专属经济区和大陆架法	Law of the People's Republic of China in the Exclusive Economic Zone and the Continental Shelf	介词误用。译文中的介词 in 后可接具体地点(如此处的专属经济区),而本法中所指是有关"专属经济区和大陆架"地点及管辖权等等相关内容,故此本法译名应为:Law of the People's Republic of China on the Exclusive Economic Zone and the Continental Shelf。
出口食品生产企业卫生注册登记管理规定(已废除)	Regulations on Administrate Registration and Enrollment on the Establishment of Food for Export	特定指称表达不当。管理规定属于行政法规类,应将"管理"提至"规定"之前,[...] administrative regulations on [...]。而"出口食品"也绝非"为了出口的食品"(food for export),export food 即可准确表达意义。故此,该法规可译为:Administrative Provisions on the Sanitation Registration and List Entry of Export Food Manufacturing Enterprises。

这里简单把存在的问题归纳为下列几点原因：

首先，法规翻译的英译存在缺陷和不足。"入世"后，我国陆续出版了各项法律法规的英译本。尽管国务院办公厅早在2003年已发布《做好行政法规英文正式译本翻译、审定工作的通知》，但法律、法规翻译版本中仍大量存在：拼写和语法错误；省译、增译和望文生义；语言修养欠佳；文体不当；多法律术语翻译方面存在错误；对原文理解不透；由法律文化差异所造成的错误；等等。

其次，法律法规翻译理论及策略研究并不完善。法律翻译实践缺乏系统性的理论做指导，目前学界研究法律语言和法律文本者居多，对翻译理论的探讨远远滞后于其他研究范畴。由于缺乏一个清晰明确的理论视角，研究者对法律翻译的原则和策略等所做的分类也较为混乱。而且，目前多数学者均是笼统地对法律语言的翻译原则和策略进行探讨，未对法律法规的词汇、句子以及语篇各层面区别对待并提出相应的翻译原则和策略——事实上，这方面的强弱与否在很大程度上直接决定了这一学科的发展空间和深度。总的来说，目前我国该领域的多数成果仅仅局限于对某些翻译实例的总结性描述或心得体会。

再次，翻译研究的范围尚不够全面。目前研究英译汉者居多，只有少数学者论及法律法规的汉译英，而且其讨论也只限于某些层面，缺乏系统、全面的研究。目前探讨法律英语语言层面的居多，很少有人论及法律汉语的特点及法律规范本身固有的特点，对法律法规（法律法规的名称、宏观结构、逻辑结构等）也缺乏进行系统的研究。由于汉语与英语分属汉藏语系和日耳曼语族，加之中国法属于大陆法系，而英、美等国的法律属于英美法系，故而中国法律法规与英美立法在法律概念、法律结构以及法律法规的术语、句式及语篇上均存在较大的差异。就信息理论而言，立法文本乃是作者与读者（包括首要读者和次要读者）

之间进行语言交际的信息语境,因而在翻译过程中,译者应对作为一种语言信息的原文是否恰当地体现在目的语中进行衡量,以决定是否对有关目的进行调整。因此,可采用 K. 赖斯(K. Reiss)和 H. 维米尔(H. Vermeer)的翻译目的论,尤其是其中的功能(functionality)和忠实(loyalty)原则,以保证源语信息在目的语中的再现,①并根据读者的不同需求在目的语文本中对原文的句式、语篇表达等结构做适当的调整。就法律文本的功能角度而言,法律法规属于规定性法律文件,其效力源于合法的制定程序,故文本承载的信息具有约束力。尽管译语文本是译者翻译活动的成果而并不具有类似的约束力,但在词汇选择、句式表达和篇章结构安排上均应反映出法律法规的庄严正式和具有施为性的特点,并相应地应遵循译名同一性、精炼性、语言规范化、准确性等翻译基本要求。

第三节　法律翻译的智能实现

在大力统筹推进国内法治和涉外法治的大背景下,从立法领域到司法领域,从法律实践到法学理论都离不开法律翻译活动。无论是学界专家或译界实践先锋都对中外法律交涉/法律翻译有着较为一致的认识,即法律翻译并非词语对等,而是从语义、功能对等到法律概念的等价。法律翻译也不仅是词语的鏖战,更是一场宏大的跨语际旅行。文本之外不同国家的民族意志、历史积淀、国家主义等因素都以独特的

---

① K. Reis, H. Vermeer, *Groundwork for a General Theory of Translation*, Berlin: Walter de Gruyter, 1984.

姿态进入了世界舞台。同时，当下兴旺的互联网、数字化催生了"虚拟-现实"的双重世界，使得数字生产的方方面面都受到了前所未有的冲击与变革。

基于此，本书围绕着法律概念、法律翻译、新技术方法三个核心主题展开，试图在数字时代找到法律概念由原文中的"意义单位"外化为"翻译单位"后，进入不同法系再次内化为"意义单位"的过程。全书以笔者主持的上海市哲学社科规划项目（青年项目）"语料库驱动下的汉英立法文本翻译单位研究"的相关研究为基础写作完成，该项目的核心内容即通过数据采集，创建高质量法律翻译语料库：项目通过网络采集香港律政司所颁布的权威双语立法文本（共计22万句对，约600万词频），另收集整理全国人大法工委组织开展的《中华人民共和国民法典》英译、上海市司法局行政法制研究所汉英《上海城市法规全书》（《上海城市法典》）、上海市高级人民法院委托的汉英"金融商事审判白皮书"（包括《2020年度上海法院金融商事审判情况通报》《2016—2020年上海法院涉地方金融组织纠纷案件审判情况通报》以及《2020年度上海法院金融商事审判十大案例》）等高质量双语文本作为入库数据。在此基础上，笔者所在上述项目团队采用术语提取技术，整理出《重要汉英民法术语及扩展翻译单位列表》（见附录），可作为后续翻译实践的重要参考，并形成术语库。

值得注意的是，项目创建的语料库中所包含的大量双语句对，绝大部分没有被标注具体类别（如司法、立法、法学或具体部门法），剩下的一些句对虽然被标注了类别，但不精确，被准确标注的句对只占相当少的一部分。考虑到任何数据平台上的语料检索、内容分发与路由都依赖于准确的语料类别标注，因而对于这样大量的（千万量级）双语句对语料，项目主要基于Tmxmall平台架构，采用卷积神经网络（CNN）训练分类器模型,实现对所有现有的语料数据进行分类,并把分类器模型包装成 web 服务,对新增语料数据进行实时的分类。项目团队创新使用"四步"语料库建设方法,分别为:1. 文件解析过滤器。2. 调整段落对齐。3. 对齐算法自动完成句句对齐。4. 微调句-句对齐结果。其中,需要设计技术操作层面包括对齐算法的调整及检索功能的实现。以英语对齐为例:(1) 以段落为单位进行对齐,将中文和英文通过断句规则进行断句。断句后可以得到中文和英文的句子个数。(2) 计算中文句子的排列组合情况,根据中文句子的每种排列,使用插空法求解每种排列对应的英文句子排列组合,再计算每种中英文排列组合的对应句子相似度,从而挑选出相似度最大的中文和英文的排列组合,即为最终的对齐结果。项目中涉及的语料库建设原理、方法与成果构成了本书的基干部分,在第二章、第三章中都有具体论述,包括以下三个方面:

其一,是关于法律翻译对应单位研究的成果,包括:1. 实现了汉英法律术语识别与提取。为最大程度保证术语库建设的质量和效率,项目组采取了基于多语种平行语料库的自动化术语抽取方法,通过与专业词典(如《元照英美法词典》)的词条进行匹配完成提取,并结合规则及统计模型以多种方法互补的模式进行操作。2. 实现术语分类、聚类与相关性分析。首先采用三个步骤实现文本分类/聚类:(1) 文本表示;(2) 分类/聚类算法选择或设计;(3) 分类/聚类评估。在此基础上,项目组采取计算词语相似度的方法进行术语相关度分析,测算词与词的属性向量间的距离;使用词语空间和关系空间结构化存储词语与其上下文之间的统计信息,为词语相似度的计算提供数据支持。3. 设计术语库的数据库结构,并搭建相应的检索系统,提供应用接口(API)以便计算机辅助翻译软件或其他机器翻译系统调用。

其二,提出"共选理论视角下的汉英法律翻译研究及扩展意义单位"这一语料库驱动的短语学工作模型。根据辛克莱(J. Sinclair)的观点,扩展意义单位共有 5 个构成成分,分别是节点词、语义韵、搭配、语义趋向和类联接。其中,类联接是节点词语法关系的抽象,是其共现于的语法或结构类型,而语义趋向是对搭配词语义特征的抽象,在分析比较研究对象及其英文对应语时应考虑这两个因素。基于此,本书分析了中国特色社会主义表达在扩展语义单位框架下的英译实现,引入阿尔滕贝格(B. Altenberg)提出的相互对应率概念及算法来处理出数据,通过分析意义单位与翻译单位(均基于短语型式)的相互对应率确定最终译文。此项研究可为机器翻译提供重要参考。

其三,是法律词汇化句干聚类分析及汉英翻译对应研究,并形成基于句对齐算法的研究成果。句对齐是翻译语料库建设的重点和难点,通常先以段落为单位进行对齐,将中文和英文通过断句规则进行断句,得到中文和英文的句子个数,在此基础上根据中文句子的每种排列,使用插空法求解每种排列对应的英文句子排列组合,再计算每种中英文排列组合的对应句子相似度,从而挑选出相似度最大的中文和英文的排列组合,即为最终的对齐结果。本书在回顾现有语料对齐技术的基础上,对最新的在线语料对齐方案进行介绍和探讨。

第四章是关于语料库驱动下民法术语变迁及其英译的研究(1978—2020),是在上述语料库建设研究基础上的具体应用成果,亦为项目最终成果的重要组成。无论我们的法律思想、制度如何变化,表达法律的方式始终不变。语言作为法律的载体,是法治精神的具体体现。故此,在以上研究内容之外,笔者从民法语言的历时变化入手,回望社会变革和制度变迁,并从语言层面跃至跨语言层面,以"要求—请求""社会公共利益—公序良俗""其他组织—非法人组织"等法律语言的变迁为例,在话语变化中梳理历史演进的线索,并从以上表达的翻译形式中发现问题、找寻对策。

　　第五章主要探讨了智能时代法律与语言的学理交融推进,通过引介法律与语言交叉学科的新研究方向——法律和语料库语言学(LCL)的诞生与发展,进而分析了语料库语言学作为法律意义测量工具的可能性。在论述过程中,笔者梳理了在美国司法领域应用语料库语言学分析的经典案例,探寻了利用语料库语言学方法可以打破基于词典、法官常识判断的弊端,更加适用于法律解释领域。同时,本书还探讨了法律与语言结合的未来方案,并以法律知识图谱构建为例释,为法律解释学发展提供了一条新路径。

第二章
汉英法律翻译原则与翻译单位

第一节　传统法律文本翻译原则

规范性法律文本翻译的总体原则是法律对等。所谓法律对等,即在翻译过程中以保持法律概念、法律规范、法律传统、法律效力与法律效果等法律因素的对等为首要考虑因素,而将语言方面的对等作为次要考虑因素。当然,这并不是说语言因素不重要:如果法律词汇和术语等基本语言因素的对等都无法保障,又谈何法律对等? 实际上,语言对等是实现法律对等的前提条件。立法文本翻译的法律对等是一个抽象的原则,其实现必然在语言层次上操作,因而要坚持翻译的准确与精确原则、一致与同一原则、简洁清晰原则、使用术语与专业表达原则以及套用法律套语原则。翻译的第一步一般是先分析原文的句子结构,以便更好地进行翻译工作。无论是人工翻译还是计算机辅助翻译,首要步骤都是分析句子结构,以下列句子为例:

原文为:

（1）如买方所订船只到达装港后,卖方不能按买方所通知的时间如期装船时,则空舱费及滞期费等一切费用和后果均由卖方负担。(2) 如船只因临时撤换、延期或退关等情况而未能及时通知卖方停止发货者,在装港发生的栈租及保险费损失的计算,应以代理通知之装船日期(如货物晚于船代理通知之装船日期抵达装港,应以货物抵港日期)为准,在港口免费堆存期满后第16天起应由买方负担,人力不可抗拒的情况除外。(3) 但卖方仍负有载货船只到达装港后立即将货物装船之义务并担负费用及风险。(4) 前述各有关费用均凭原始单据核实支付。(《国际货物买卖合同》,2011 年)

上述条款有四个句子,每个句子可拆分为以下成分:

(1)

　　(a) 费用和后果(subject of the main clause)

　　(b) 由……负担(passive predicate)

　　(c) 空舱费及滞期费等(adjective qualifier)

　　(d) 如……(adverbial of condition)

　　　　卖方(subject of the clause)

　　　　不能装船(predicate)

　　　　船只到达……后(adverbial of time)

(2)

　　(a) 计算(subject of the main clause)

　　(b) 以……为准(passive predicate)

　　(c) 由……负担(passive predicate)

　　(d) 栈租及保险费损失(adjective qualifier)

　　(e) 在装港发生的(adjective qualifier)

　　(f) 如……晚于(adverbial of condition)

(g) 如……(adverbial of condition)

船只(subject of the clause)

撤换、延期或退关(passive predicate)

卖方(subject of passive voice verb)

通知(passive predicate)

在……后第……天(adverbial of time)

除外(adverbial of condition)

(3)

(a) 卖方(subject of the sentence)

(b) 负有……之义务,并担负……(predicate)

(c) 船只(subject of the clause)

(d) 到达(predicate of the clause)

(e) ……后(adverbial of time)

(4)

(a) 费用(subject of the sentence)

(b) 核实支付(passive predicate)

(c) 凭……(adverbial)

汉语和英语的句法结构非常不同,翻译时应注意选用英语的词语和句型结构,避免逐字翻译。而英语并非汉语译者的母语,汉英在翻译时比英汉更具难度(本节主要探讨汉英人工翻译句子分析的原则和技巧,故例句均为汉英翻译),应该综合利用各种翻译技巧。试比较以上汉语法律条款的英译文:

Should the Sellers fail to load the goods within the time as notified by the Buyers, on board the vessel booked by the Buyers after its arrival at the port of shipment, all expenses such as dead freight, demurrage, etc., and consequences thereof shall be borne by the Sellers. Should the vessel be withdrawn or replaced or delayed eventually or the cargo be shut out etc., and the Sellers are not informed in good time to stop delivery, the calculation of loss for storage expenses and insurance premium thus sustained at the loading port shall be based on the loading date notified by the agent to the Sellers (or based on the date of the arrival of the cargo at the loading port in case the cargo should arrive there later than the notified loading date). The above-mentioned loss to be calculated from the 16th day after expiry of the free storage time at port shall be borne by the Buyers with the exception of Force Majeure. However, the Sellers shall undertake to load the cargo immediately upon the carrying vessel's arrival at the loading port at their own risks and expenses. The payment of the aforesaid expenses shall be effected against presentation of the original vouchers after being checked.

又如,原文为:

(1) 精神病人在不能辨认或者不能控制自己行为的时候造成危害结果,经法定程序鉴定确认的,不负刑事责任。(2) 但是应当责令他的家属或者监护人严加看管和医疗;在必要的时候,由政府强制医疗。(3) 间歇性的精神病人在精神正常的时候犯罪,应当负刑事责任。……(4) 醉酒的人犯罪,应当负刑事责任。(《中华人民共和国刑法》第十八条)

上述条款有四个句子,下面来分析每个句子的组成成分:

(1) 精神病人(subject of the sentence)

　　不负……责任(predicate)

　　在……时候(adverbial of time)

　　不能……(predicate of adverbial clause)

　　造成……(predicate of the clause)

(2) 家属或者监护人(subject of passive voice)

　　责令……(passive predicate)

　　严加看管和医疗(complement)

(3) 精神病人(subject of the sentence)

　　间歇性的(attribute of the subject)

　　应当负……责任(predicate)

　　在……时候(adverbial of time)

　　犯罪(predicate of the clause)

(4) 醉酒的人(subject of the sentence)

　　应当负……责任(predicate)

以上汉语法律条款的英译文为:

A mentally ill person who causes dangerous consequences at a time when he is unable to recognize or unable to control his own conduct is not to bear criminal responsibility after being established through accreditation of legal procedures; but his family or guardian shall be ordered to subject him to strict surveillance and arrange for his medical treatment. When necessary, he will be given compulsory medical treatment by the government. A person whose mental illness is of an intermittent nature shall bear criminal responsibility if he commits a crime during a period of mental normality... An intoxicated person who commits a crime shall bear criminal responsibility. [①]

第二节　汉英平行语料库与翻译

一般认为,平行语料库(parallel corpora)和可比语料库(comparable corpora)都可用于对比研究,[②]但二者的优劣明显不同。[③] 前者既包含原语文本,又包含了与原语文本对应的另一语言的文本,即译语文本。由于双语文本在词语、句子或段落层级上对齐,词语和结构的跨语言对应数据已可观察。但译文语言难免受到原语文本的影响,显示的并非自然语言使用的原本特征。[④] 而后者,即可比语料库,由两种不同语言或不同语言变体的文本构成,所含均为原语文本,反映了自然语言使用的模板或真实特征。但是可比语料库中的双语文本间未建立任何连

①　本节示例均选自李克光、张新红:《法律文本与法律翻译》,中国对外翻译出版公司 2006 年版,第 228—253 页。

②　S. Johansson,"Contrastive Linguistics and Corpora", in S. Granger, L. Jacques, P. T. Stephaine (eds.), *Corpus Based Approaches to Contrastive Linguistics and Translation Studies*, Amsterdam & New York: Rodopi, 2003, pp. 38-40.

③　S. Granger, "The Corpus Approach: A Common Way Forward for Contrastive Linguistics and Translationstudies?", in S. Granger, J. Lerot, S. Petch-Tyson (eds.), *Corpus-based Approaches to Contrastive Linguistics and Translation Studie*, Amsterdam & New York: Rodopi, 2003, pp. 17-30.

④　R. Xiao, L. He & M. Yue, "In Pursuit of the Third Code: Using the ZJU Corpus of Translational Chinese in Translation Studies", in R. Xiao (ed.), *Using Corpora in Contrastive and Translation Studies*, Newcastle: Cambridge Scholars Publishing, 2010, pp. 182-214.

接,无从观察词语对应并确定彼此对象,况且严格意义上的可比语料库至今仍鲜有报道。[①] 因此,利用平行语料库显示的翻译对等开展对比、研究仍是目前相关领域研究切实可行的出发点,而复现翻译对等(recurrent translation equivalent)体现了翻译社团的双语知识、交际策略和共识,从一个侧面揭示了双语词语的对等关系,因此是最重要的对比依据。[②] 在对比短语研究中,将搭配序列作为研究单位是必要的策略,搭配序列的异同对比直接指向双语短语单位的对应关系。只有当被比单位的形式、意义和功能特征都相同或相似时,它们才可能具有最大程度上的对等。

基于平行语料库的翻译研究是从平行语料库显示的复现翻译对等出发的,因此接下来将考察它们在双向翻译过程中的互译数据,计算相互对应率,从而评估词语的跨语言对等。结合使用平行语料库和本族语单语语料库,并且通过对比语料库的验证,可以找到翻译对等与典型搭配之间的对应关系。

第三节 对比短语学概念

在实际翻译过程中经常遇到的一种现象是:A 语言的单词可能对应于 B 语言的短语,反之亦然。探讨跨语言词语单位的对应关系是对

---

① 卫乃兴、陆军等:《对比短语学探索——来自语料库的证据》,外语教学与研究出版社 2014 年版。

② W. Teubert, "Directions in Corpus Linguistics", in M. Halliday, W. Teubert, C. Yalop & A. Germakova (eds.), *Lexicology & Corpus Linguistics*, London & New York: Continuum, 2004, pp. 113-165.

比短语学的基本内容之一,有助于发现双语交际过程中的意义单位与词汇选择策略。本章提出一个研究一般词语单位对应关系的工作方法,该方法从翻译过程中产生的复现翻译对等出发,利用阿尔滕贝格提出的相互对应率计算两个词语之间的互译概率,以探讨对应关系。具体的方法由三个步骤组成:第一步,考察语言 A 译为语言 B 过程中词汇 X 产生的复现翻译对等 Y 及其概率;第二步,考察 Y 在语言 B 译为语言 A 过程中产生的翻译对等 X 及其概率;第三步,利用相互对应率公式计算 X 与 Y 的对应程度,考察并确定对应关系。[①]

其中,相互对应率是阿尔滕贝格提出的概念,指双向翻译语料库中语法结构或词汇相互被译的程度。其基本思想如下:如果语言 A 中的词语 X 总是被译为语言 B 中的词语 Y,同样,语言 B 中的词语 Y 总是被译为语言 A 中的词语 X,那么这两个词语的相互对应率为 100%;反之,如果二者总是不被互译,相互对应率则为 0。相互对应率越高,被比对象就越有可能是跨语言对应单位。相互对应率的计算公式如下:

$$MC = \frac{(A_t + B_t) \times 100\%}{A_s + B_s}$$

其中,MC 即相互对应率,A_t 和 B_t 分别代表词语 A 和词语 B 在译文文本中出现的频数,A_s 和 B_s 分别代表词语 A 和词语 B 在原文文本中出现频数。辛克莱认为,语言使用中的词语选择具有某种趋向,可以称之为短语趋向(phraseological tendency)和术语趋向(terminological tendency)。[②] 前者正如图伯特(W. Teubert)所言:"翻译单位的对应物

---

① B. Altenberg, "Adverbial Connectors in English and Swedish: Semantic and Lexical Correspondences", in H. Hasselgård, S. Oksefjell (eds.), *Out of Corpora: Studies in Honour of Stig Johansson*, New York: Rodopi, 1999, p. 254.

② J. Sinclair, "The Search for Units of Meaning", *Textus*, No. 9, 1996, pp. 75-106; J. Sinclair, *Trust the Text*, London: Routledge, 2004, pp. 159,168,170.

并非形而上学的实体，而是翻译活动产生的偶然结果。"①根据这样的概念，结合冯志伟对香港 BLIS② 进行的穷尽术语挖掘，得出下面结果：

在对 BLIS 中的法律术语进行了全面的穷尽和调查汇总后，发现其中除了大量的指称事物的名词性术语之外，还有为数可观的指称行为、状态、数量、属性、时间、空间、关系的动词性术语、数词性术语、形容词性术语、副词性术语、时间词性术语、方位词性术语，甚至还有表示关系的介词性术语、连接词性术语等。③ 举例如下：

动词性术语：BLIS 中的法律术语要表达行为和状态，因此随便浏览一下 BLIS 的法律英文文本，就马上可以发现大量的英语动词术语（包括在上下文中产生了形态变化的词形）。例如 abolished（废除，撤销），acknowledge（承认），acquiesced（默认），adjourn（延期，延审），administering（管理，执行），admit（承认），applies（请求，申请），apply to（提交），appoint（指定，任命），appointed（任命），ascertain（查清，判明），authorized（委任，批准），be deemed （应当），be appointed（任命），be authorized（委任），be claimed（索赔，索取），be forfeited（没收，惩罚），be granted（批准，授予），be heard（审判，审理，聆讯），be issued（发布），certify（确认），certified（确认），claimed（索取），commit（犯法，羁押），confirm（确认，认证），declare（宣布），deduct（扣除），defend（辩护，答辩），defended（辩护），delegate（委派、代理），deliver（交付，移交），discharged（清偿，解除），disclaim（放弃，卸弃），dismiss（驳回，免职），dissolved（解除，抵消），distrain （扣押），effected（生效），enabling（授

---

① W. Teubert, "Corpus Linguistics and Lexicography", *International Journal of Corpus Linguistics*, 2001（Special Issue）, pp. 126-153.

② 香港的"双语法例资料系统"（Bilingual Laws Information System, 简称 BLIS）收录了所有现时实施的香港法律的主体条例及附属法例的中文文本和英文文本。

③ 冯志伟:《语言与数学》,世界图书出版公司 2011 年版。

权),enact(颁布,制定),enforce(强制,强迫实施),exclude(豁除),endorsed(背书,认可),execute(执行),expanded(扩充),falsifies(伪造),incurred(承担债务),indicate(指出),inspect(审查),is acknowledged(承认),is aggrieved(受害),is exhibited(提供物证),is rejected(驳回),is summoned(传唤,传讯),issue(发布,发放),levied(征收,征税),make an order(命令,裁定),nominated(任命,指定),pawn(当押),prejudiced(危害),presume(假定),prohibiting(查禁,禁止),proves(证明),provide(提供),punish(惩治,制裁),reject(拒绝),remove(免任),sealed(盖章,查封),served(送达),shall rank(排序),substituted(代替),sue(控告,提起诉讼),summoned(传唤,传讯),surrender(让步),to commit(羁押),to lapse(权力终止,遗赠失效),to release(释放,豁免),unsworn(未宣誓),verified(证实),withdraw(撤销),等等。

数词性术语:BLIS中的法律术语要表达数量的大小,因此,法律术语中有不少的数词性术语。例如,State Immunity Act 1978(《1978年国家豁免权法令》)中,"1978"指明了本法令是在1978年这个特定的年份颁布的国家豁免权法令,具有特定的意义,"State Immunity Act 1978"也因此成为一个含有数词"1978"的多词型术语。

形容词性术语:BLIS中的法律术语还要表达事物的属性,因此法律术语中同时存在很多形容词。例如consistent(一致的),defamatory(诽谤性的),deferred(递延的),derivative(衍生的),designated(指定的),duly(正式的),eligible(在法律上合格的),empowering(赋权的),enforceable(强制性的),excusable(可宽宥的),exempt(可豁免的,可免除的),false(假的),frivolous(琐屑无聊的),genuine(真实的),guilty(犯罪的,有罪的),honest(诚实的),impracticable(不可行的),improper(不当的,不正当的),liable(负债的,有责任的),licensed(有执照的),

liquidated(已清算的,已清偿的),onerous(繁苛的),permissible(许可的),prescribe(订明的),punishable(可处罚的),recoverable(可追回的),spent(失效的),terminate(有期限的),undue(不当的),unterminate(无期限的),unliquidated(未清偿的),unseasonable(无理的),vacant(空缺的,无人继承的),vexatious(纠缠诉讼的),voluntary(自愿的)。

副词性术语:当法律术语要表达行为和状态的方式时,副词的使用也就不可或缺。例如 accordingly(相应地),concurrently(并行地),conditionally(有条件地),fraudulently(欺诈地),improperly(不当地,不正当地),knowingly(明知故犯地),lawfully(合法地),maliciously(恶意地,蓄意地),persistently(一贯地,固执地),personally(当面地),reasonably(合情合理地),respectively(各自的),retroactively(可追溯地),truly(真实地),willfully(蓄意地,故意地)。

时间词性术语:时间是由过去、现在和将来构成的连绵不断的系统,它是物体运动和变化的持续性的表现,是物质存在的一种客观形式。BLIS 中的法律术语要描述时间,因此术语中有不少表示时间的词语。例如 calendar-month(公历月),first instance(一审,原讼),retired age(退休年龄)。

方位词性术语:空间是事物及其运动存在的另一种客观形式,它在不同的维度上延伸。BLIS 中的法律术语要描述空间或方位,因此,法律术语中有不少表示空间的词语。例如 habitual residence(惯常居住地),area of the waters of Hong Kong(香港水域)。

复合介词或者介词短语性术语:BLIS 中的法律术语要确切地描述或表示关系,因此法律术语中还有复合介词或者介词短语。例如 hereinafter(从此处以下),notwithstanding(尽管),without prejudice to(无侵害,不侵害),the said(该),therein(在那里,在其中),thereof(在其中,由此）,thereunder(在此之下,根据)。

由此可见,从知识本体(ontology)的角度看来,术语不仅仅是名词或名词短语,也可以是动词、数词、形容词、副词、时间词、方位词、复合介词、介词短语。传统术语学把术语仅仅看成名词或者名词词组的观点,具有很大局限性。

诚如冯志伟在《现代术语学引论》①一书中提到的那样,术语学应当建立在完整的知识本体的理论基础之上。客体除了包括客观的实体之外,还可以包括活动(activity)、数量(quantity)、属性(attribute)、时间(time)、空间(space)和关系(relation)。

由于网络技术的发展,在信息检索(information retrieval)和信息抽取(information extraction)中,都需要从网络的文本中进行术语的自动抽取(term extract)和自动标引(term indexing)。术语的抽取和标引都是在具体的文本中进行的,是建立在语料库的基础之上的,它深深依赖于语料库,因此都要依靠文本的"上下文"(context)或者"富语境"(rich context)。"上下文"可以分为"词汇上下文"(lexical context)和"文本上下文"(textual context)。一个语言单位的词汇上下文可以定义为:在一个句法结构中,具有同样给定依存关系的单词、术语或候选术语的集合。例如,一个名词的词汇上下文可以定义为与该名词关联而构成复合名词的其他所有名词的集合。词汇上下文根据语言的"联想轴"(paradigmatic axis)把相关的单词、术语或候选术语聚合在一起。一个语言单位的文本上下文是在原文本的句子或固定长度的窗口中,在该语言单位前后同现的单词、术语或候选术语的集合。文本上下文根据语言的"语段轴"(syntagmatic axis)把相态的单词、术语或候选术语聚合在一起。

---

① 冯志伟:《现代术语学引论》,语文出版社1997年版。

这样一来,术语的研究就不能只局限在"词汇"的狭小范围之内了,术语必须到实际法律文本的语料库中去提取,术语学在法律领域的体现必须考虑在不同上下文语境中的各种"术语变体"(term variation)。

结合前人的研究成果,在"术语"概念上达成的共识基本集中在以下几点:

1. 无歧义,即精确翻译让人信服、一看就懂,不至于产生混淆。一个术语在一个场合只代表一个概念,其译名应与概念所承载的信息吻合,法律术语涉及多种法律体制的借鉴和转换,更加要求达到精确、有效,如force majeure(不可抗力)、corporate personality(法人人格)。但在实际翻译操作中,这种理想状态很难达到,即便范围仅仅圈定在法律语体中,如Civil Law(民法/大陆法)就有两种内涵,具体需要考虑其上下文的意义。

2. 行业规范性强。科技、法律、政经文章的语言一般较规范,这是由"其描述客观事物必须准确无误这一要求所决定的"[1]。因此,术语在被精确翻译后往往能彰显其特有的规范性。

3. 权威性强。术语如不能得到精确翻译,则会使译文的说服力大打折扣,即损失其权威性;加之"术语的译名应尽可能采用国际通用的术语和符号,以便国际间的学术交流"[2],因此对术语的精确翻译十分重要。只有做到翻译精确,一词一义,才能极大地方便人们对信息的收集整理和查找搜寻。

根据短语学理论并综合前人研究结果,法律术语翻译应在理论指导下开展实证研究,即建设大型法律翻译语料库→利用工具+人工干预→获得术语→通过翻译语料库中检索复现率获得汉英对应形式→译文检查校准。

---

① 冯志杰:《汉英科技翻译指要》,中国对外翻译出版公司 1998 年版,第 11 页。
② 周亚祥:《科技术语译名的统一问题》,《中国科技期刊研究》2001 年第 4 期。

第四节　立法文本中程式语的法律逻辑及语言元功能聚类

　　"法律语言"是指存在法律文本中或司法过程中的语言应用,又可分为"立法语言"及"司法语言"。常见的法律文本包括宪法、合同、契约、判决、法令或遗嘱等等。[①] 不同类型的法律语言均具有清晰、严谨、规范的特征。其中,法律程式语作为普遍存在法律文本中的语言表达型式,是指在不同类型法律文本中使用的一系列特殊的语言表达型式。其一方面伴随着法律文本的规范性使用而发展,另一方面慢慢具备了相对固定的内涵和功能。本节根据短语学理论中程式语概念,基于功能语言学理论,利用语料实证进行程式语法律逻辑及语言元功能的聚类研究。

一、相关概念及研究背景

(一) 程式语概念

　　程式语作为普遍存在的语言使用特征,是指按照一定型式,整体存储在大脑内的固定或半固定的语言表达。埃尔曼(B. Erman)和沃伦

---

　　① P. Tiersma, "A Message in a Bottle: Text, Autonomy, and Statutory Interpretation", *Tulane Law Review*, Vol. 76, No. 2, 2001, p. 431.

(B. Warren)对程式语的研究表明,英语口语中存在 58.6% 的程式语使用,书面语篇中也存在 52.3% 的程式语使用。① 比伯(D. Biber)也曾指出,在学术论文写作中,超过 50% 的语言使用都是固化词串或半固化词串及内部变体的表述(也就是说由 2—3 个固定词素和 1—2 个插入词素组成)。② 程式语的使用渗透在各个语体、语域中,除上面提到的学术论文外,还包括法律语篇在内的各类专门用途语篇。但是,对于程式语概念的界定、划分标准及功能分析,目前仍存在较大争议。

因此,对于程式语进行研究的最大困难是缺乏内涵和外延判定的标准。在对程式语开展研究的 40 余年中,学者们尝试用不同术语去命名"程式"这一语义内涵,其中包括"语块""词串""公式化语言"等等。雷(A. Wray)和帕金斯(M. Perkins)首次提出"程式语"(formulaic frequences)这一术语,指出其本质为"整体储存在大脑中,使用时整体提取"的多词单位。③ 此后,一批学者尝试对程式语概念作出进一步规范,虽然定义各有侧重,但是语言学界关于程式语特性的认知是一致的。④

学界一般认为程式语分为狭义和广义两种概念。在狭义理解上,考伊(A. P. Cowie)认为程式语是指固定或相对固定的,可以表达相

---

①　B. Erman, B. Warren, "The Idiom Principle and the Open Choice Principle", *Text*, Vol. 20, No. 1, 2000, pp. 29-62.

②　D. Biber, "A Corpus-driven Approach to Formulaic Language in English: Multi-word Patterns in Speech and Writing", *International Journal of Corpus Linguistics*, Vol. 14, No. 3, 2009, pp. 275-311.

③　A. Wray, M. Perkins, "The Functions of Formulaic Language: An Integrated Model", *Language and Communication*, Vol. 20, No. 1, 2000, pp. 1-28.

④　See K. Conklin, N. Schmitt, "Formulaic Sequences: Are They Processed More Quickly than Nonformulaic Language by Native and Nonnative Speakers?", *Applied Linguistics*, Vol. 29, No. 1, 2008, pp. 72-89.

遇、赞美或邀请等等话语行为的结构。① 随后考伊又进一步规范了狭义程式语的描述："程式语是用于语篇中,可以表达说话者的态度,并等同话语标记语功能的固化表达结构。"②显然,这样的定义仍不令人满意。随后,广义程式语的概念由雷提出,其表述内容如下:

> (程序语是)存储在人脑中的词语序列(sequence),由连续或是非连续词语(有时无意义)及其他元素组成。程式语具有"整体使用"的特征,也就是在存储或使用时经常以"整体"形式出现的短语结构,而并非依据语法分析得来。③

上述表述的最大问题是其过分宏观的定义将一些并不具有语言意义的单位都纳入其中。不过同时,也正是在这种情况下,语料库检索中的词串复现频率可以作为判定程式语最有效的途径,在此基础上结合人工筛选,便可获得较为准确的程式语型式,这也是本节所采用的研究方法。基于以上原因,文中采用广义程式语定义对其概念进行限定。

(二) 法律程式语的相关研究

法律语言作为专业技术性语言有别于日常语言,这样的差异使得法律语言在使用上更加具有法律本身的严谨、规范和制约性。因而与其他文类相比,程式语的使用数量在法律文类中显得尤为突出,这种特

---

① A. P. Cowie, *Phraseology: Theory, Analysis, and Application*, Oxford: Clarendo Press, 1998, p. 133.

② A. P. Cowie, "Speech Formulae in English: Problems of Analysis and Dictionary Treatment", in G. Meer, A. Meulen (eds.), *Making Sense: From Lexeme to Discourse*, Centre for Language and Cognition, 2001.

③ A. Wray, *Formulaic Language and the Lexicon*, Cambridge: Cambridge University Press, 2002, p. 9.

殊性吸引了众多学者的关注,法律程式语的研究与表述应运而生。

法律程式语可以被视为一种法律实践中固定下来,具有语义、语用功能的结构,其使用贯穿了整个立法、司法过程。在定义方面,方瑛提出:"法律程式语包括在法律活动应用中形成的规范、严谨、统一的词汇或句式结构。"①虽然此种归纳本身缺乏理论支持,加之词汇与句式分属语法中的两个层面,很难统称为程式语(实则分别为程式语[词]及型式句),但是考虑到目前相关定义的缺乏,因此在此暂且将其归入广义法律程式语内涵之内进行探讨。

从语言学角度来看,法律程式语的价值主要体现在语用功能及实际法务操作中,包括表达法律概念或在法律社团中表达相应的语篇功能。这样看来,复杂但不具备实际功能的结构不属于本节考察范围之内。在发掘高频法律程式语型式的同时,归纳程式语型式和语义的对应同样非常重要。由于本族语法律程式语和其英文对应型式研究对于法律英语教学和法律翻译都具有积极意义,为了更好地描述法律程式语的使用分布和功能,下文主要采用双语例释。

二、问题意识与研究设计

(一) 研究问题

本研究试图解决下列问题:(1)法律高频程式语有哪些型式?(2)除法律专门术语外,程式语(词)在立法文本中有何主要语言功能及法律逻辑功能?(3)如何对以上功能进行聚类分析?

----

① 方瑛:《法律程式化语言研究》,江西农业大学 2011 年硕士学位论文,第 3 页。

（二）研究对象

本部分以法律汉语作为研究对象，结合法律语篇进行整体考量。由于立法语言的特征具有比司法语言更加规范、正规的特点，本部分主要的研究对象集中在立法文本中。以基本达成一致的程式语定义作为基础概念，即在语篇中可以担当语用和/或语篇结构功能，并且被认为是整体储存在头脑中的多词语结构。① 限于篇幅，法律程式语在文中只限于词语层面，并不包括句式结构。由于汉语及英语在语系和结构上存在根本差异，在法律汉语中语义内涵和功能变体都需要被考虑进来。

（三）研究工具与研究步骤

立法文本的收集以大陆地区现行的法规为准，基于《中华人民共和国法律法规汇编》（中英文版），建立库容为 213 万词的平行语料库，其中汉语部分约为 103 万字，对照英文部分约为 110 万词。语料库收集内容涵盖十个部门法（宪法、行政法、民法、商法、经济法、社会和劳动保障法、环境法、刑法、诉讼程序法、军事法）的主体部分。运用"中国法律法规汉英平行语料库"（PCCLD）②作为观察库，结合双向研究体例（形式如图 2 - 1）来保证研究的效度和信度。研究运用 AntConc 3.2.1 作为文本分析工具，用于生成词丛、关键词和搭配。

---

① See A. Wray, *Formulaic Language and the Lexicon*, Cambridge：Cambridge University Press, 2002；S. De Cock, "A Recurrent Word Combination Approach to the Study of Formulae in the Speech of Native and Non-Native Speakers of English", *International Journal of Corpus Linguistics*, Vol. 3, No. 1, 1998, pp. 59-80.

② 中国法律法规汉英平行语料库（大陆），http://corpus. usx. edu. cn/lawcorpus1/index. asp。

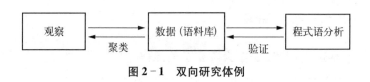

图 2－1　双向研究体例

主要研究步骤是:(1)对选取的语料进行预观察。根据法律常识,手工标出一些高频出现的程式语。(2)在语料库中进行检索,对高频程式语进行自动抽取,并对照人工筛选结果。同时,根据法律文本的一般特征(简洁、具体),剔除不具有实际意义的词串或词。(3)以高频程式语为节点语词,采用随机抽样法,分别从自建语料库及 PCCLD 抽取 100 条符合要求的索引行,逐一进行观察并确定其主要搭配形式,归纳关键词出现的型式特征,结合句子环境进行功能性的聚类分析。

三、程式语的聚类功能分析

(一) 程式语的提取

根据上文所述自建小型语料库,首先运用 AntConc 3.2.1 的 n-gram 程序提取所有 $2<n<5$(n 为数量标记,个数)的程式语型式。根据研究目的,剔除不具备研究意义的或合并重复的多词结构。按照其显著性,提出频率最高的 9 种法律程式语(词)型式:

表 2－1　法律高频程式语

序号	高频程式语(词)	英文对应型式	出现频次
1	应当+v.	shall+v.	5936
2	不得/不可/不能……	may/shall/will not	1783
3	(凡)……的	description of different persons/ situations/ types	1034

序号	高频程式语(词)	英文对应形式	出现频次
4	有权	have the right to	723
5	(并)处(以)	at the same time, (commit money/ criminal punishments)	635
6	为了……/为……	in order to/ for purpose of...	142
7	本法所称/ 本法所说	in this Act/ refer to... this Act	111
8	在……的情况下	provided that the law is not contravened	102
9	具备(符合……) 以下条件	with... (quality)	67

(二) 立法文本的法律逻辑功能

乔治·库德(George Coode)于 1843 年撰写的题为《论立法表达》的备忘录中指出,各类法规的法律句子"包括四个组成部分:一、情况——句子生效的那种景况和场合;二、条件——使句子得以成立的作为和前提;三、法律主体——可以或必须施行法律行为的人;四、法律行为——法律主体可以或必须施行的行为"。这种四分法并非对句子的划分,而是一种逻辑分析,与中国法学界所言的法律规范的逻辑要素基本上是相同的。① 在法律语言学的不断演变中,我国法学界通常认为法律规范语言表达一般由"假定""处理"和"制裁"三个部分组成。② 其中"假定"与库德提出的"条件"和"情况"等同,是指明法律规范适用

---

① 参见郝铁川:《论逻辑思维与法律思维》,《现代法学》1997 年第 3 期。
② 潘庆云:《中国法律语言鉴衡》,汉语大词典出版社 2004 年版,第 276 页。

的条件、情况。① "处理"是指法律规范原则本身,即"允许怎样做""应当或禁止怎样做"。"制裁"是指违反法律规范的法律后果。一般的立法句中,都会包括的主体是"处理"部分或法律行为部分,主要功能是限制"法律主体"的权利或规定其"义务"。基于我国立法实践,普遍采用的逻辑句式为:条件+法律主体+法律行为(处理)+制裁。根据这样的逻辑结构可以有效地考察高频程式语(词)所处的句子环境,归纳其功能类型。

(三)程式语的法律逻辑功能聚类分析

程式语一,"应当+v."是"应当+(插入成分)+v."的简化型式,用以表示"义务性"规范,是指政府、机关或其他赋权部门应履行的相关义务,同时限定了其权利范围。因此,使用程式语一是针对法律主体,表达要求依照法律执行的某种或某些强制行为。语料库证据显示,其出现的逻辑型式为"法律主体+应当+条件/情况+VP(法律行为)",如:

(1)机关、单位对所产生的国家秘密事项,*应当*按照国家秘密及其密级的具体范围的规定*确定*密级,同时确定保密期限和知悉范围。[《保守国家秘密法》第十四条]

An organ or entity shall determine the classification legel of a state secret arising in the organ or entity pursuant to the provisions on the specific scope of state secrets and scopes of classification levels, as well as the secrecy period and access scope.

(2)保险人未及时履行前款规定义务的,除支付保险金外,*应*

---

① G. Coode, *On Legislative Expression or Language of Written Law*, Introduction to a *Digest of the Poor Laws*, Appendixed to the 1843 Report of the Poor Law Commission, 1843. Reproduced in Elmer A. Driedger, *The Composition of Legislation*, Ottawa: Queen's Printer and Controller of Stationery, 1957, pp. 34-67.

*当赔偿*被保险人或者受益人因此受到的损失。[《保险法》第二十三条]

If the insurer fails to fulfill the obligations specified in the preceding paragraph in a timely manner then, in addition to the payment of compensation, the insurer *shall compensate* the insured or the beneficiary for any damage incurred thereby.

程式语二,"不得"一般出现在禁止性规范立法句(占所有语料的63%)中,这是实体法表达的常见型式,其法律功能旨在限制和禁止某个或某些非法行为的发生,如:

(3) 清算期间,公司存续,但*不得*开展与清算无关的经营活动。公司财产在未依照前款规定清偿前,*不得*分配给股东。[《公司法》第一百八十六条]

During the liquidation period, a company *shall not* engage in business operations which are not related to the liquidation. Company assets *shall not be* distributed to the shareholders prior to settlement of the aforesaid liabilities.

另有37%的"不得"句出现在描述"条件"的分句中,充当使得立法句成立的前提,如:

(4) 立法会议事规则由立法会自行制定,但*不得*与本法相抵触。[《澳门特别行政区基本法》第七十七条]

The rules of procedure of the Legislative Council shall be made by the Council on its own, *provided that* they *do not* contravene this Law.

（5）定金的数额由当事人约定,但<u>不得</u>超过主合同标的额的百分之二十。[《担保法》第九十一条]

The amount of the deposit shall be stipulated by the parties, but it *shall not* exceed 20 percent of the amount of the principal contract.

观察发现,当"不得"分句表达法律条件时,一般由转折连词"但"带出,看似转折的关系其实表达条件、前提的语义内涵。例(4)中"不得与本法相抵触"及例(5)中"不得超过……百分之二十"实为两条法规实现的前提条件。

程式语三,"(凡)……的"是指形容一类拥有同质因素的集合,用来表达一类法律主体。也是对可能发生的情况进行假设描述,经常用来预测一些危害社会或违法的行为,如:

（6）(<u>凡</u>)有下列情形之一<u>的</u>,不得再次公开发行公司债券。[《证券法》第十七条]

No additional company bonds may be issued in any of the following circumstances.

根据语料库检索,除特别用法之外,"凡……的"承担的法律逻辑功能主要集中在法律条件(约占全部语料的43%)或法律主体(约占全部语料的27%)两类,是规定法律主体义务的功能的程式语表达。

程式语四,"……有权"后出现的高频搭配词依次为:要求(20%)、提起(申请)(15%)、了解(调查、查阅)(15%)等等。这类搭配动词均包含"主动""意愿"类意义。一般认为,其包含了赋予法律主体相应法律权利的语义内涵,即赋予法律主体一定的法律权利可以发生某种行为或不发生某种行为,①如:

(7) 对任意或非法的拘留、监禁,居民*有权*向法院申请颁发人身保护令。[《澳门特别行政区基本法》第二十八条]

In case of arbitrary or unlawful detention or imprisonment, Macao residents *have the right* to apply to the court for the issuance of a writ of habeas corpus.

(8) 受害的公民、法人和其他组织*有权*要求赔偿。[《国家赔偿法》第六条]

The aggrieved citizen, legal person and other organization shall *have the right* to claim compensation.

程序语五,"处(以)"一般出现在"(并)处(以)+……罚款"的型式搭配中(占全部语料的93%),用于刑法中附加刑或民法处罚的相关描述,后常接具体惩处措施的叙述前提或序曲,来强行限制非法行为,如:

(9) 情节严重或者拒绝改正的,可以中止供电,可以*并处*五万元以下的罚款。[《电力法》第六十五条]

If the case is serious or in case of refusing to make rectification, the administrative department of electric power may suspend their

---

① 封鹏程:《现代汉语法律语料库的建立及其词汇计量研究》,南京师范大学2005年硕士学位论文,第40页。

power supply and impose a fine of up to 50,000 yuan.

（10）……情节严重的，<u>处</u>五倍以上十倍以下罚款。[《动物防疫法》第一百条]

If the circumstances are serious, the offender may be concurrently finedno more than 5 times but less than ten times of the illegal gains.

根据具体语料库检索，"（并）处"分句属于法规的制裁部分，可以解释触犯某一具体法规后需要承担的法律后果。

程式语六，"为了……"或"为……"的使用一般出现在："V+（adv.）+P"的句法结构中，如：<u>为了</u>科学、有效地组织统计工作；<u>为了</u>促进和规范外国投资者来华投资；等等。使用位置上，其经常运用在法案或其他规范性材料的启示部分。节点词后面的高频搭配词依次为："规范"（27%）、"加强"（23%）、"保障"（13%）、"防止（制止）"（9%）及"适用"（1%）。不难看出，程式语六主要通过积极规范性语言搭配来实现阐述立法文本的目的和意义的功能。通过进一步考察，除宪法及其他个别特殊的法案外，此类程式语表达普遍出现在各类立法文本的第一条，如：

（11）<u>为了</u>规范保险活动，保护保险活动当事人的合法权益，加强对保险业的监督管理……促进保险事业的健康发展，制定本法。[《保险法》第一条]

This Law is formulated *with the purpose of* regulating insurance activities, protecting the legitimate rights and interests of the parties involved, strengthening supervision and regulation of the insurance industry and promoting its healthy development.

（12）<u>为了</u>发展教育事业，提高全民族的素质，促进社会主义物质文明和精神文明建设，根据宪法，制定本法。[《教育法》第一条]

This Law is enacted in accordance with the Constitution <u>*with a view to*</u> developing the cause of education, enhancing the quality of the entire nation and promoting the socialist material as well as cultural and ethical progress.

程式语七，"本法所称/本法所说"的基本法律逻辑型式为"本法所称+专有名词/专业名词……+是指"，用来表达对于某个或某类法律术语的诠释。其作用是进一步规范相应法律术语的内涵和外延。正如前文所述，在法律文本中出现的日常词汇使用都可能存在专业内涵表意，对于这些程式语的准确理解和使用就显得尤为重要。出于这样的考虑，程式语七主要用于阐明专业法律术语和概念的内涵，如：

（13）<u>本法所说</u>的父母，包括生父母、养父母和有扶养关系的继父母。[《继承法》第十条]

The "parents" <u>*referred to in this Law*</u> include natural parents and adoptive parents, as well as step-parents who supported or were supported by the decedent.

（14）<u>本法所称</u>价格包括商品价格和服务价格。[《物价法》第二条]

<u>*The term*</u> "price" used <u>*in the law*</u> *includes* prices of all kinds of merchandise and prices of all kinds of services.

程式语八,"在……的情况下"经常用来引导法律生效的前提,可以描述句子生效的情况或句子成立的条件,其功能是限制或制约当事人行为。一般出现在下列两种法律逻辑型式中:

表 2-2　程序语八常见的法律逻辑型式

法律逻辑型式	语料库例释
法律主体+情况+(法律行为)	*在*证据可能灭失或者以后难以取得的*情况下*,诉讼参加人可以向人民法院申请保全证据……(《行政诉讼法》第四十二条)
条件+法律主体+(法律行为)	……*在*违背真实意思的*情况下*订立的合同,受损害方有权请求……(《合同法》第五十四条)

程序语九,"具备(符合……)以下条件"一般用来描述一个或一些法律要求的条件,其法律逻辑型式为:"法律主体+条件+法律行为"。它的主要功能是在法规中限定具体情况,如:

(15)设立保险公司应当*具备*下列*条件*……[《保险法》第六十八条]

To establish an insurance company, the following are required.

(四) 立法文本的语言元功能特征

根据韩理德(M. Halliday)提出的语言元功能三分法,概念功能、人际功能和语篇功能是所有语言的基础功能,概莫能外。① 法律语言作为一种特殊语言类型,首先具有概念功能(ideational),能够反映各类

① M. Halliday, C. Matthiessen, *An Introduction to Functional Grammar*, London: Edward Arnold / Beijing: Foreign Language Teaching and Research Press, 1994/2000.

社会团体需求和运转的情况,提供人们需要遵循的规约和规范方面的信息,明确在社会生活领域各个方面中法人(或自然人)应承担义务和享受权利的具体内涵。其次,它具有人际功能(interpersonal),界定了人们在社会活动中承担义务和享受权利的范围,并且规定超越这一范围的行为即是违法行为①。最后,它具备语篇功能(textual)。法律语言特殊的社会功能,需要它严谨、明确、清晰,避免任何形式的歧义和不确定。法律程式语作为法律语言的具体组成部分,同样具备以上的功能特征。

1. 概念功能分析

限于法律语类特性,法律程式语功能基本集中在概念功能之下的及物性特征,及物性作为概念功能的语义系统,由六个主要过程组成,包括物质、心理、关系、行为、话语及存在过程。立法的目的是规范社会生活,而法律程式语这种语言型式主要通过关系过程来实现这一目的。关系过程按精密度细分为"集约类"(intensive)、"环境类"(circumstantial)和"属有类"(possessive);按方式分为"所属类"(attributive)和"识别类"(identifying)。程式语四"有权"在立法文本中表示法律主体拥有"做某事"的权利,即"有权"是对具体"权利"的修饰,体现"属有[识别]"的关系过程,如:

(16)澳门居民*有权*对行政部门和行政人员的行为向法院提起诉讼。[《澳门特别行政区基本法》第三十六条]

程式语七"本法所称"具有说明相关法规性质的功能,属于关系过程中"环境[识别]"表达,其语义延伸包含"什么是什么"的内涵,如:

---

① 张德禄:《语言的功能与文体》,高等教育出版社 2005 年版,第 244 页。

（17）<u>本法所称</u>循环经济,<u>是指</u>在生产、流通和消费等过程中进行的减量化、再利用、资源化活动的总称。[《循环经济促进法》第二条]

值得注意的是,及物系统中每一个过程均由"过程"(process)、"参与者"(participant)、"环境成分"(circumstantial element)三要素组成。程式语六"为了……"是表示"目的性"语义内涵的表达,不属于六个过程解释范围。根据它在句子中担当成分的特征,应属于环境成分,如:

（18）<u>为了</u>保护、建设和合理利用草原,改善生态环境,维护生物多样性,发展现代畜牧业,促进经济和社会可持续发展,制定本法。[《草原法》第一条]

当然,上文未提及的其他五种过程散见在立法文本中,限于篇幅以及与程式语功能的相关度,此不赘述。

2. 人际功能分析

系统功能语言学认为,人际功能描述了人与人之间的互动与协商关系,其中包括说话者要求听话者承担义务或对提议的赞成,主要通过语气及情态来实现。情态系统包括情态化(modalization)和意态(modulation)两个部分。情态化指在以交换信息为语义功能的命题中,说话人对命题可能性和经常性的判断,包括可能性(probability)和经常性(usuality)。意态指在以交换物品或服务为语义功能的提议句中,说话人对提议的态度,包括义务(obligation)和意愿(willingness)。[①] 立法

---

① M. Halliday, C. Matthiessen, *An Introduction to Functional Grammar*, London: Edward Arnold/Beijing: Foreign Language Teaching and Research Press, 1994/2000.

的目的是规范社会活动,主要通过规定法律主体的权利和义务来实现。可以认为,立法文本以意态表达(如程式语一"应当"、程式语二"不得")来反映国家意志和国家的法律行为,使"作为"与"不作为"这两个法律术语更具有实际意义,如:

(19)保险公司开展业务,<u>应当</u>遵循公平竞争的原则,<u>不得</u>从事不正当竞争。[《保险法》第一百一十五条]

同时,立法由于其特殊性,多用陈述语气及祈使语气进行具体法规的描述。例(19)中,"<u>不得</u>从事不正当竞争"就是祈使语气的具体实现。

3. 语篇功能分析

主位与述位是有效生成语篇的前提保障,同时能够通过主、述位调整实现相应的语篇效果。根据立法语句的逻辑结构,其在规定公民权利与义务的同时,也规定了相应的客观实现条件或情况。这就使得很多立法句的"条件"处于主位位置上,形成句项主位或无标记主位型式句。任何法规在规范相关法律主体权利、义务的同时,均须限定相应的客观前提条件,即程式语八"在……情况下"与程式语九"具备……以下条件"所表达的语义内涵。一般将这两类程式语表述的客观条件和因素放在受强调的主位,形成主位(凸显)-述位结构的语篇功能。

除此之外,语篇功能的衔接手段("替代""连接"等)也可以通过程式语表达得以实现。"替代"是指运用某种语言型式代替上下文中的一个或多个词语,即为了避免重复也可以衔接上下文。程式语三"(凡)……的"字结构是典型的替代手段(如:……<u>凡</u>构成犯罪<u>的</u>,给予相应处分……），即名物化手段，属于元语篇；"连接"是指语篇中表达各种逻辑关系的手段，程式语五"（并）处（以）"表达了概念意义上的延展（extension），主要体现了语篇功能下属的递进关系特征（如：……逾期未改正的，责令停产停业整顿，*并处*二万元以下的罚款……）。

五、研究启示

上文具体分析了高频出现的法律程式语具有的法律逻辑及语言元功能，根据立法语言的基本特征即"约束和规定法律主体的权利和义务"，可以认为，所有立法语句均归属于两大范式法律逻辑功能（即约束性和规定性）之下。结合上文各个程式语的功能分析，可以进一步将两大功能分化为 8 个小类。在将 9 个程式语的法律逻辑及语言元功能进行整合后，得到下图：

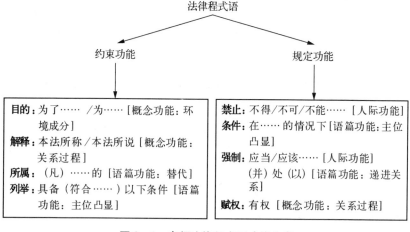

图 2-1　高频法律程式语功能分类

　　可以看出,在程式语中存在着法律逻辑功能,它体现了法律语言的特殊性,标识了法律语类的特征。同时,程式语中凝结着语言元功能,它体现了语言的普遍性,标识了法律语言中存在的语言共性。由此可见,法律逻辑功能与语言元功能共同存在并作用于程式语中,这既是法律语言普遍性与特殊性的统一,也是理论性与实践性的统一。

　　本节尝试运用短语学原理重新界定程式语概念。通过自建及参照语料库证据考察高频程式语构成特征的研究方法,继而从三大语言元功能的角度对程式语在立法文本中的功能进行探讨,可以发现其中涵盖了:概念功能中的关系过程;人际功能中的语气和情态系统;语篇功能中的主位(凸显)—述位结构、替代手段及递进关系连接;等等。最后,笔者运用法律逻辑功能的全新视角进行功能聚类分析,形成"高频法律程式语功能分类"结构。本节同时论述了程式语中法律逻辑及语言元功能之间的内在关系,并通过上述分析丰富了立法文本分析的研究方法,体现了程式语在立法文本中语言功能及法律逻辑功能的实践意义,对我国立法语言的形成及完善具有参照意义。

第五节　立法翻译文本中的
程式语搭配特征

　　如前所述,作为多词单位按照固定或半固定模式整体储存在大脑中的语言型式,①"程式语"(或"程序语序列")概念经常会与"整体""约定俗成"或"习惯用语"概念联系在一起。作为一种普遍存在的语言使用现象,程式语并不依靠语法规则生成,而是稳定存在的语言使用模式,"序列"同时暗示了其内部可辨别性特征。而立法文本是立法机关(全国人大或人大常委会)通过并颁布实施的各项法律法规,具有准确、规范、严谨的基础特性,因而在立法文本及其译文中普遍存在的程式语不但具有独特的搭配特征,而且具备一定的语义内涵和语用功能。本节通过对可比语料库的观察发现,程式语搭配型式和功能在源语文本及翻译文本中存在较大差别,主要体现在翻译文本中的简化、常规化和异常化并存现象,并针对此现象进一步展开研究。

一、"程式语"与"搭配"

(一) 程式语相关研究

如前所述,在 40 多年的研究中,虽然定义各有侧重,但是学界关于程式语特性的认知是一致的,如由于程式语"整存整取"的心理学内隐(implicit)特性极难把握,只有将语料库检索中的词串复现频率作为判定程式语有效途径,并结合人工筛选,才能获得较为准确的程式语型式,这也是本节所采用的研究方法。

针对不同语体的差异特征,学者们就专业语篇中的程式语进行了

---

① J. Sinclair, *Corpus*, *Concordance*, *Collocation*, Oxford: Oxford University Press, 1991; A. P. Cowie, *Phraseology*: *Theory*, *Analysis*, *and Application*, Oxford: Clarendo Press, 1998; A. Wray, *Formulaic Language and the Lexicon*, Cambridge: Cambridge University Press, 2002.

分类探讨,包括科技语篇①、新闻语篇②、文学语篇③及法律语篇④等等。作为反映人类社会、经济、生活等行为规范的语言载体,法律语言具有三个基本特点:复杂性、累赘性和保守性。与其他应用型或文学语言不同的是,法律语言(以立法语言为主体)中各个语域大部分都有比较稳定的模式,因而对其程式语研究更具现实意义。

其中,康传彪列举了"授权性的、义务性的、禁止性的和法律效力性的"四类翻译法律英语中的程式语。⑤方琰对法律汉语中的程式语做过比较详细的描述,她在调查中得出的法律汉语程式语分类,⑥对我们进行法律英语翻译研究具有参考价值。但对于法律程式语的研究目前均尚处于初始阶段,且仅仅集中在法律程式语的型式及分类两方面。显而易见,这样巨大的研究空间值得我们徜徉其中。

(二) 搭配概念相关研究

"搭配"(collocation)源自辛克莱共选理论的五要素概念之一,即"节点词""搭配""类联接""语义趋向"和"语义韵",⑦是语言学领域特别是语料库语言学最为重要的概念与研究内容之一。以弗斯

---

① 陆军、卫乃兴:《扩展意义单位模型下的英汉翻译对等型式构成研究》,《外语教学与研究》2012 年第 3 期。

② 邓瑛:《基于语料库的英国媒体关于中国制造报道的话语分析》,上海交通大学2011 年硕士学位论文。

③ 李更春:《程式语研究的理论突破及其对外语教学的启示》,《现代教育科学》2013年第 5 期。

④ 康传彪:《法律英语中程式化语言结构及其应用》,《湖北经济学院学报(人文社会科学版)》2006 年第 6 期。方琰:《法律程式化语言研究》,江西农业大学 2011 年硕士学位论文。

⑤ 康传彪:《法律英语中程式化语言结构及其应用》,《湖北经济学院学报(人文社会科学版)》2006 年第 6 期。

⑥ 方琰:《法律程式化语言研究》,江西农业大学 2011 年硕士学位论文。

⑦ J. Sinclair, et al. , *Collins COBUILD Grammar Patterns 1: Verbs*, London：Harper-Collins Publishers, 1996.

(J. Firth)为代表的众多语言学家一致认为"研究共现词汇之间关系"是搭配研究的实质,开展研究的前提是确定"中心词",观察文本中高频出现的多词搭配可以揭示语言运用倾向。一般认为,母语中和翻译文本中的搭配使用存在较大差异,恰当的搭配已成为区别母语与非母语的重要语言标志。① 值得注意的是,中心词可以是"单词",亦可以是"多词"。本节以程式语作为研究中心,即以"多词"作为中心词。

目前,翻译文本中的搭配研究主要集中在搭配范围、搭配常规和搭配异常化三个领域,②并以将翻译文本中相关中心词的搭配情况与目的语原文中的搭配进行对比的方式作为研究手段。在类似研究中存在的主要问题是:(1)翻译文本中存在搭配异化或常规化研究过泛,针对性较差,对于某一专门领域翻译文本的探讨不足。(2)以程式语结构作为中心词的搭配研究尚未开展。(3)研究中均是单向研究模式,即翻译文本(外语)→目的语(母语),缺乏对翻译文本的逆向研究。而一般情况下,非母语使用者对搭配的敏感度大大低于母语使用者,因而开展逆向研究可以发现同一语类中语言使用差异并进行纠正和规范。

可以看出,不论是关于程式语还是搭配的研究均已渐趋成熟,但针对程式语搭配的研究仍处于草创未就阶段。结合以上论述,本节集中在三个方面进行探讨:(1)探索立法文本中的程式语型式及其共现的搭配特征。(2)在参照语料库中考察相同程式语共现频率、相关搭配的使用情况并进行对比。(3)分析翻译文本与参照文本中使用程式语存在的差别,进行译文规范工作。

<hr />

① A. Cowie, "Phraseology", in R. Asher, *The Encyclopedia of Language and Linguistics*, Oxford: Oxford University Press, 1993, pp. 3168-3171;武光军:《基于语料库的翻译文本中的搭配特征研究:回顾与评价》,《北京第二外国语学院学报》2012 年第 10 期。
② 武光军、王克非:《基于英语类比语料库的翻译文本中的搭配特征研究》,《中国外语》2011 年第 5 期。

二、工作定义与研究设计

　　根据上文的论述,程式语的工作定义为"以预制模式固定或半固定储存在大脑中的多词结构"。由于本节主要采用语料库方法来进行实证研究,判定程式语的界定标准因而显得至关重要。根据常规研究标准,一般认为由"两个或更多的单词所构成的、出现频率很高且具有统计学同现趋势的多词序列"①才具有研究价值,本节的研究贯彻这一原则。

　　同时,根据研究所采用的自建翻译语料库库容(203 万词),结合法律文本的特征,文中将研究参数统一界定为频率大于 10 次/百万词,并且完整或片段具有各种语篇功能的 2、3、4、5 词结构作为研究对象。针对与相关程式语共现的搭配研究,主要将 MI>3(MI 代表词与词之间的共现率,即两个词或多个词同时出现的频率)作为显著搭配标准。根据不同程式语的出现频率,结合 MI 计算公式得到显著搭配的型式并进行进一步研究。

　　本节采用一个自建语料库及一个参照语料库开展研究。自建语料库文本来自国家权威机关颁布的法规及立法文案的英文翻译版本,文类包括行政法规、规范性文件、法案及法律评论的权威英文翻译版本。参照语料库是"英国国家语料库法律子库"(BNC Law)②,其 90% 的内容由立法文本组成,库容 200 万词,与自建库存在较高可比性。

---

　　①　D. Biber, S. Conrad & R. Reppen, *Corpus Linguistics: Investigating Language Structure and Use*, Cambridge: Cambridge University Press, 1998, p. 21.

　　②　BNC Law, http://www. lextutor. ca/concordancers/concord_e. html.

　　本节研究试图解决以下三个问题:(1)翻译语料库存在何种型式的高频程式语?(2)与原语语料库应用程式语搭配相比,翻译语料库中的程式语存在何种差异——简化、异常化或常规化?(3)相关搭配具备何种功能?

　　针对以上问题,本节采用的研究方法包括三个步骤:(1)利用语料库驱动方法,分别在自建库中检索 n 元序列(n-gram)为 2 词、3 词、4 词和 5 词结构。人工剔除不具备实际语义及语用功能的搭配(如 of not,any of the,等等)或替换重复出现的 n 元结构(如 in accordance,accordance with,in according with,等等)。(2)按照以每一程式语作为中心词随机提取 100 索引行的标准进行观察,分析程式语的语篇功能。(3)再参照语料库 BNC Law 将已提取的高频程式语作为中心词进行"上下文关键字"(KWIC)检索,进一步对比程式语相关搭配在自建库及参照库中型式和功能差别。

三、程式语搭配研究

(一)具体程式语的选择及搭配词提取

本部分针对上文提出的三个研究问题进行逐一解答及验证。

研究问题(1):翻译语料库存在何种型式的高频程式语?

根据自建小型语料库(self-built law corpus, SLC),首先运用 AntConc 3.2.1 的 n-gram 序列程序提取所有 2<n<5 的程式语型式。根据研究目的,剔除不具备研究意义的或合并重复的多词结构。[①] 按照

---

　　① 如 2 词结构中出现"in accordance",而 3 词结构中重复出现"in accordance with",根据语言使用惯性和重要性,统一在 3 词结构中处理该程式语。

其显著性,提出频率最高的 9 种法律程式语(词)型式。在 BNC Law 参照库中同时将 9 种程式语进行检索,得出表 2-3。为了研究方便,所有数据都已经过标准化处理。

表 2-3　具体程式语型式

序号	程序语型式	出现频率(自建库 SLC)次/百万词	出现频率(BNC Law)次/百万词	频次差
1	shall be	7882	234	7648
2	in accordance with	2286	177	2009
3	where the	1706	811	885
4	according to	1415	136	1279
5	be sentenced to	761	1	760
6	subject to	625	438	187
7	in violation of	413	3	205
8	approval of	304	18	205
9	have the right to	258	19	239

同时,针对学界普遍认为 MI 值大于 3 的搭配可视为显著搭配[①],但在目前常用的语料库计算软件中,尚无计算 n-gram 程式语 MI(相互信息值)的计算程序这一情况,本部分研究采用人工计算方式,根据 MI 计算公式[②],通过专业数学计算器将 MI>3 的显著搭配提取出来并进行观察。

---

① Kenneth Ward Church, Patrick Hanks, "Word Association Norms, Mutual Information, and Lexicography", *Computational Linguistics*, Vol. 16, No. 1, 1990, p. 24.

② 公式为:$MI = \log_2 \dfrac{f(n, c) \times T}{f(n) \times f(c)}$。

（二）语料分析

SLC 即为翻译英语库,BNC Law 作为可参照的原生英语库,在两个库中分别检索可以对比得出翻译英语与原生英语在同一程式语使用上的差异。下图是 9 个程式语在 SLC 及 BNC Law 中的搭配模式对比情况。

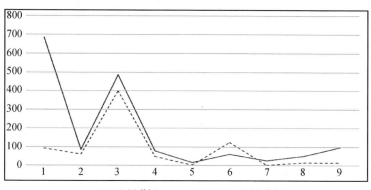

—— SLC翻译英语　------ BNC Law原生英语

图 2-2　节点程式语标准化搭配词数目对比折线图

其中,序号1—9分别代表程式语一至九。显而易见,9 个程式语中 8 个作为节点的程式语在 SLC 中的搭配词数目高于其在 BNC Law 中的搭配词数目。结合表 2-1 已检索出的程式语出现频数,我们计算了 9 个程式语在原生英语库中的搭配数目与其在翻译英语库中的搭配数目之间的差异,以确定其具有显著性,列表如下:

表 2-4　程式语搭配词数目差异的显著性检验

序号	程序语型式	SLC 中搭配 发生频数	BNC Law 中 搭配发生频数	卡方值
1	shall be	687	89	225[*]
2	in accordance with	84	59	271[*]
3	where the	488	396	60[*]

续表

序号	程序语型式	SLC 库中搭配发生频数	BNC Law 库中搭配发生频数	卡方值
4	according to	72	45	139*
5	be sentenced to	8	1	6**
6	subject to	66	125	56*
7	in violation of	30	3	23*
8	approval of	52	16	48*
9	have the right to	102	15	11*

　　注：* 表示 P<0.01。

　　　　** 表示 0.01<P<0.05。

　　根据上表及研究数据,下面集中解决前文提出的研究问题(2):与原语语料库应用程式语搭配相比,翻译语料库中的程式语存在何种差异——简化、异常化或常规化?

　　首先,相对于原语语料,翻译语料中的搭配模式是否出现简化现象?

　　卡方检验表明,9 个程式语在翻译立法英语中使用的搭配数目与原生语料中相同程式语的搭配词语数量存在显著差异,即翻译语料中程式语的搭配数目远远高于原生语料中出现的搭配数目。这与普遍认为在原生英语中搭配应高于翻译英语的设想相去甚远。以程式语一"shall be"为例,与之连接的主要搭配如下表所示:

表 2-5　"shall be"搭配的具体情况

类联接	SLC 中的具体搭配	BNC Law 中的具体搭配
Ved	sentenced; submitted; imposed; ordered; deemed; fined; formulated; determined; punished; investigated; paid; confiscated; handled; revoked; issued...borne; decided; governed; carried...etc (判处、承担、罚款、视为、惩罚、充公……)	deemed; treated; entitled; construed; taken; regarded; determined; brought; used; given; allowed; borne (认定、视为、承担、赋予……)

类联接	SLC 中的具体搭配	BNC Law 中的具体搭配
adj.	liable；responsible；applicable（有责任的、有义务的、可适用的）	liable；conclusive；guilty（有责任的、决定性的、有罪的）
art.	the	a；the
prep.	in	in；at；as

可以看出，无论是翻译语料中出现的类联接种类，或是搭配类符数目及所属的语义内涵范围，均高于原生语料中出现的情况。这与以往针对普遍翻译文本研究的结论——如翻译文本出现的搭配词具有以简化及常规化为主的特征——相悖，却与另外一条预测性结论不谋而合，即"有些翻译文本中的搭配可能比原生文本中的搭配还要丰富"[1]。根据以上论述，与原生文本相比，立法翻译文本中不存在简化问题。恰恰相反，由于搭配类符范围扩大，立法翻译文本中存在复杂化问题。

其次，相对于原语语料，翻译语料中的搭配模式是否呈常规化？

常规化是所有翻译文本追求的特质之一，翻译文本力求在语言使用上更加符合目标语的形式及使用风格[2]。但是过分追求常规化就会出现夸大的语言表达型式，比如翻译文本中会使用更长的句子结构及更多的功能词汇。由于法律文本本身具有的准确严谨特征，无论是在翻译还是原语文本中，长句的使用都是法律文本的特征之一，因而对此不做详细探讨。故而功能词汇的使用可以作为判定程式语搭配是否常规化的标准之一，如同样包含"根据"语义的程式语二及程式语四在SLC 中与功能词的搭配数（经过标准化处理，以百万词频为单位）分别

---

① 武光军、王克非：《基于英语类比语料库的翻译文本中的搭配特征研究》，《中国外语》2011 年第 5 期。

② M. Baker, "Corpus Linguistics and Translation Studies", in M. Baker, G. Francis & E. Tognini-Bonelli (eds.), *Text and Technology*, Amsterdam: John Benjamins, 1993, p. 11.

是 1503 及 754,而在 BNC Law 中的功能词搭配数为 57 及 29。可以看出,程式语二及程式语四在翻译文本中使用功能词汇的情况大大高于原生文本。这种搭配情况是否应用于所有程式语,需要进一步考察。根据语料统计,得出下表:

表 2-6 程式语搭配功能词显著性检验

程式语	卡方值	程式语	卡方值
1. shall be	29.6*	6. subject to	0
2. in accordance with	79.6*	7. in violation of	0.03
3. where the	0	8. approval of	0
4. according to	50.7*	9. have the right to	0
5. be sentenced to	0		

注:* 表示 P<0.01。

通过卡方检验可知,在 9 个程式语中,有 6 个程式语(占 67%)搭配功能词汇在 SLC 与 BNC Law 中并未出现显著差异。因此,我们可以判定法律翻译文本中(除个别情况外)程式语搭配整体上体现了常规化特征。

最后,相对于原语语料,翻译语料中的搭配模式是否出现异常化现象?

由于缺乏统一的判定标准,翻译异常化的判定是翻译研究中较难解决的问题。毛拉宁(A. Mauranen)发现,相对于原生目的语文本,翻译文本常存在着异常的词语组合,即非典型搭配亦存在此种情况,这使得译文缺乏规范性,造成译文语言令人匪夷所思、难以理解的情况出现。[①] 目前,判定译文是否出现异常化的最普遍方法仍然是依据人工

---

① A. Mauranen, "Strange Strings in Translated Language: A Study of Corpora", in M. Olohan (ed.), *Intercultural Faultlines: Research Models in Translation Studies I*, Manchester: St. Jerome, 2000, pp. 119-141.

判断和词典查询方式。本部分结合两者优势并加入对比语料库检索方式，进一步判定程式语搭配异常化的情况是否存在于立法文本中。

研究发现，在翻译文本中程式语的使用及其搭配上，大量存在与目的语使用习惯不符的情况。如程式语二"in accordance with"及程式语四"according to"均用以表达"根据"意义。在 SLC 中，"in accordance with"承接"（the）law"表示"依法"意义，占所有表达的 76%；而在 BNC Law 中，此种搭配只占所有搭配的 4%，其余高频搭配均为表示具体法规"条""款""项"的英文相关表达形式，即"paragraph""regulation""term"。这样的差别与我国实际立法习惯有关，即宏观规范的法规比较普遍。与"in accordance with"具有同样语义内涵的"according to"在 SLC 中搭配"the terms of"（……条款）的情况占全部搭配的 64%，而 BNC 中仅出现一次，其余搭配均比较随意且日常词汇较多。可见相比原文而言，"according to"在翻译文本中的使用更加正规，搭配集中在"law""article""regulation"等术语，相对差异较大。

程式语五"be sentenced to"译为"被判处"，在 BNC Law 中仅出现 1 次，为"imprisonment for a term of 5 year"（被判处 5 年监禁）；在 SLC 中出现 761 次，包括多种搭配形式，均以正规词汇用法为主，主要包括"fix-term imprisonment of..."" confiscation, compensation""depravation"等等。其中，"fix-term imprisonment of..."（有期徒刑……）占全部搭配的 45%。该程式语使用差异较大的主要原因与我国立法逻辑结构相关：假定、处理和制裁是我国法律规范的三要素，其中制裁作为立法的必要组成部分不可或缺；而英美法系中，制裁部分并非必要组成要素，故两者在使用频率上差异较大。同时，两种语言使用习惯存在区别，翻译文本中的"fix-term imprisonment of"表示"有期徒刑"，而"of"后往往会搭配具体惩罚年限，与前面"fix-term"语义重叠。因此 BNC Law 中的表达型式更为准确。

程式语七"in violation of"一般译为"触犯""违反""侵犯",在 BNC Law 中仅出现 3 次,分别是:(1)"…right"(侵犯权利);(2)"…the plaintiff's actual rights"(侵犯原告实际权利);(3)"…the terms of Article 6"(触犯第六条款)。在 SLC 中,其搭配集中在对"law""provision""article""regulation"等正规法律条款的表达,未见后接"right"(权利)的型式出现。可见翻译文本中该程式语的使用相比原语言存在较大差异,翻译文本中的使用更加正式。

程式语八"approval of"一般译为"批准""许可",在 SLC 及 BNC 中均包含较高使用频率的"the approval of"型式,真正的施为名词结构出现在"of"后面,如"the approval of arrest"(批准逮捕),"the approval of the court"(法院批准),"the approval of the legislature"(立法机关批准),可见右侧搭配未见异常。但在左侧搭配中发现,在 SLC 重复出现的"advance approval of"在 BNC Law 未见,而"prior approval of"却反复出现其中。根据两者出现的语言环境,在语义内涵上并无差别,均表示"预先批准"。可见,在翻译文本中该程式语的使用与原语言使用存在差异。

程式语九"have the right to"一般译为"有权",右侧搭配集中在"request""refuse""apply""acquire"此类包含"主动""意愿"意义的词汇,具有赋予法律主体相应法律权利的语义内涵,即赋予法律主体一定的法律权利可以发生某种行为或不发生某种行为。[①] 该程式语在 SLC 及 BNC Law 中的使用未见显著差异。而在左侧搭配中发现,在 SLC 中"shall have the right to"(应有权)出现 201 次,占全部搭配的 78%;在

---

① 封鹏程:《现代汉语法律语料库的建立及其词汇计量研究》,南京师范大学 2005 年硕士学位论文,第 40 页。

BNC Law 中则使用比较灵活，包括"parties""barristers""judges"
"police""shall""should""will"等等，其中情态词出现三种类型，仅占全
部搭配的29%。可见，翻译文本中存在过度使用情态词"shall"的情
况，与原文使用存在差异。

　　综上所述，由于法律文本翻译力求精确、对等及法律效力的开展，
在翻译过程中尽量采用常规化和通顺的翻译策略。但由于本族语使用
习惯的影响，在翻译成目的语的过程中难免出现异常化的现象。在对
9个高频程式语进行考察后发现，67%的搭配在翻译文本和原语言使
用中存在差异。可以判断，相对法律实践原文，翻译文本中的搭配模式
存在异常化现象。

四、研究结论和启示

　　本部分运用对比语料库语言学的方法，针对我国法律汉译英翻译
文本中程式语搭配特征进行全面研究。找出程式语型式的同时，观察
其搭配的整体特征，发现与其他语类翻译（尤其以文学语类为例）不同
的是，法律文本中程式语翻译并不呈现简化特征，甚至出现复杂化现
象。而常规化及异常化翻译特征并存于我国法律翻译文本中，这种现
象的出现与我国目前法律翻译规范性仍然未完善相关。这些发现为法
律翻译规范化研究奠定了扎实基础。

　　搭配作为重要的语言组织原则是翻译研究中的一个具体问题。针
对搭配的研究可以发现翻译与原语使用中存在的根本性区别，包含简
化、常规化及异常化特征等等。本章是对立法文本中程式语搭配的整
体研究，拓宽了程式语的研究范围，由型式功能的研究扩展至与之搭配

词汇结构的研究。这样可以更好地说明在法律文本中程式语的使用特征及其搭配特性,为进一步建立法律程式语研究的理论体系奠定基础。本章的研究同时拓宽了法律程式语的研究范围,由自身型式功能研究扩展至搭配词汇的特征探讨。同时,研究方法主要运用 SLC 与 BNC Law 参照库考察翻译文本中程式语使用与原语言的差别,其中数据分析及卡方检验方法能够更加有效地进行对比分析,对今后语料库法律翻译研究有所启发。

第三章
法律翻译数据库平台建设

第一节　汉外法律翻译数据平台的创设背景

　　汉外法律翻译数据平台建设是以"新文科"为理念引导,基于国家与地方重点现实需求,旨在从法律翻译语料切入,通过部署网络数据平台来完成教学、实践和科研项目,以服务翻译学、法学学科建设和远景发展。通过对接社会服务(包括法院翻译、律所翻译、出版业翻译、语言服务企业),法律翻译数据平台现已形成的内部语言资产包括汉英、英汉(双语平行)翻译语料库,库容千万词频以上,涵摄当代中国的主要法律辞书、词典,如《汉英法律词典》《新编法律大词典》《法律行业术语》及《英汉法律用语大辞典》等。数据平台对以上辞书进行电子化编撰以便检索和进行法律翻译、法律史等交叉学科的相关爬梳。同时,平台整合形成了 20 余万句对、共计千万词频的高质量英汉双语法律语料,吸收了"一带一路"沿线国家主要立法及多语对照文本、2018—2020 年《世界营商环境报告》(双语)、2018 和 2020 年度(上海)金融审判白皮书及十大案例等相关数据,同时包括现行的十大部门法(宪法、行政法、民法、商法、经济法、社会和劳动保障法、环境法、刑法、诉讼程序法、军事法,又或宪法、行政法、民法、经济法、劳动法、科教文卫法、资源环境保护法、刑法、诉讼法、军事法）及相关行政法规（包括其英译），共计约 900 件法律法规。依托平台，译者们可进行法律翻译实践与法律翻译研究等活动。同时，依据不断动态更新的语料库数据，平台可为国家语言战略与政策制定贡献智识支持。

在平台建设过程中的关键问题是如何革新双语自动对齐、在线对齐技术，从而实现以句子为单位进行高效匹配。因此，对齐技术的开发及对齐方案的确定便是平台建设中的核心问题。平台数据的主要构成和建设原理，主要有以下三点：

一是通过整合目前的双语（汉英）法律文本数据，基于真实法律翻译项目，搭建法律特色语料库。汉外法律翻译数据库的建设历经三年、前后三期语料库的收集及录入。这是一个囊括我国现行权威法律法规翻译文本、重点领域司法翻译数据的法律垂直领域大型数据库平台。一期建设包括形成汉英、英汉（双语平行）翻译语料库，包括十大部门法及相关行政法规共计约 900 件法律法规，总库容约为 400 万词频。重点将《中华人民共和国民法典》原文及权威英译、《2020 年世界营商环境报告》原文及英译、《2020 年上海市城市法典》原文及英译，以及 2017—2019 上海市高院商事审判白皮书、案例原文及英译等具有时代性、旗帜性的双语文本进行结构编撰并录入平台。二期项目建设中，重点将各类主流的法律辞书进行结构化处理并入库，包括英美法词典、法律行业术语、新编法律大词典，以创建法律双语术语库，形成代表性术语库资源，录入词条达 2 万余对。三期项目建设中，基于 Spring Boot 微服务，使用 Java 1.8 开发，完成了翻译实践及教学平台的搭建。

二是完成翻译教学体系建设。通过语料库资源的 API 设置及调用，利用已有的 SDL-Trados 及 Transmate 软件进行计算机辅助翻译（CAT）、法律翻译等教学。基于平台建设的专门术语库服务于法律翻译,对重要法律辞书的电子数据进行整理和入库,以为法律翻译、翻译史学习、法律专业学习同时提供数据资源和检索途径。

三是推进科学研究。基于语料库平台进行法律翻译、法律语言学、法律史等相关学科的研究。在对法工委、法制办出版的(双语)法律法规及行政规章语料库进行处理的基础上,形成双语语料库。结合语料资源的数据统计,通过标注进行语言态度计算,进而实现情感分析、自然语言处理及话语分析,从而形成高水平论文及相关论著。在法律辞书电子化及汉化后,拟实现词条对应具体辞书及页码的精细化信息检索,可以推进法律、翻译、历史等相关研究的数字化、电子化进程,形成的一系列专门研究亦可以成就专业学科的数字人文作品。

第二节　语料对齐概述

双语语料的对齐(align)是自然语言处理(natural language process)的一个重要课题。平行语料的出现不仅为翻译研究注入了活力,对语言服务行业的意义更加重要。概因平行语料接入 CAT 软件后,通过 CAT 软件的预翻译和语言片段检索功能,不仅可以为语言服务企业节约大量成本,还可以有效降低翻译难度,提高译者的翻译速度和翻译水平等。而制作平行语料的一大关键技术就是语料对齐技术。为此,本节在回顾现有语料对齐技术的基础上,对最新的在线语料对齐方案进行介绍和探讨。

一、语料对齐的定义

从语料对齐的本质来看，通常是指双语文本平行语料库中对应句段之间的关联。其定义涉及三个维度，换言之，可以从三个方面对对齐定义进行分析，分别是：切分单位、对齐工具、对齐方法。其中，切分单位是对齐定义的基石，能够说明对齐的基本原理；对齐工具是从手段方面对其进行定义；对齐方法则是从方法论的角度定义对齐。从切分单位来看，对齐是通过切分两个（或多个文本）为 n 个单位，并确保原文文本的第 n 个切分单位与译文文本的第 n 个单位相关联。从对齐工具来看，对齐是指能够将原文文本和译文文本切分与关联的软件，此类软件多为半自动化工具，对齐过程中需要不同程度的人工介入。目前商业领域运用的对齐工具主要有国外的 SDL Trados 的 WinAlign 和 Wordfast 自带的对齐组件等，以及国内的 Transmate 对齐组件等。从对齐的方法来看，对齐是指通过不同的思路，找到原文和译文中对应语言片段、句子、段落的关联性，从而实现最大程度的对齐自动化。以上对定义的梳理为后文确定对齐方案提供了概念依据。

二、语料对齐的方法

语料对齐方法的提出是基于语料对齐的需求，而语料对齐的基本需求以语言片段和句子层面进行语义或翻译单位的对齐为主。此处所指的语言片段,即原文和译文中的名词性标题等语料,句子片段是指以句子为切分单位的语料。在平行语料对齐中,绝大多数是以句子为单位的语料,而原文和译文在很多时候并非一一对应的,概因原文(或译文)中的一个或多个句子极可能被"断裂"翻译为两句或两句以上的译文(或原文)(简称"一对多""多对一"或"多对多")。能否自动识别原文中一个句子和译文中多个句子的关联性,便成为判断对齐方法优劣的核心所在。目前,从理论研究和实际应用领域来看,语料对齐的方法可分为四类:

(一)基于规则的方法

在语言服务领域中,语料对齐的切分单位往往是以换行符为切分符号的语言片段和以句子终止符为切分符号的句子。切分符号是指对齐工具在关联原文和译文的对应语言片段前,先进行原文和译文文本解析、切分的依据性符号,例如换行符(硬回车、软回车)、句号、问号、感叹号等。基于规则的对齐方法,就是先按照切分符号对原文和译文进行切分,然后再机械地进行一对一的关联。实际应用领域的绝大多数软件均属此类,如 SDL Trados 的 WinAlign、Wordfast 的对齐工具等。该方法的优点是逻辑简单、易于实现;缺点是无法自动识别"一对多""多对一"或"多对多"的语料。

(二)基于词汇锚定的方法

基于词汇锚定的方法,就是通过利用双语词典(垂直领域需调用专门领域词典,如法律词典等)或词汇信息映射原文和译文句子中的词汇,找到关联性,从而实现对齐。凯(M. Kay)、罗斯切森(M. Röescheisen)和斯坦利·F. 陈(S. F. Chen)等人就是基于词汇锚定的方法进行了英德和英法平行语料的对齐。① 该方法的优点是在一定程度上可实现自动识别"一对多""多对一"或"多对多"的语料;缺点是需要大量的双语词典或词汇信息作为锚定基础,这给实际操作带来了巨大困难。

(三) 基于句长统计的方法

基于句长统计的方法是根据两种语言句子的长度及长度分布信息构建模型,从而以长度关系为基础,构建平行语料的长度关系并进行对齐。该方法最早由盖尔(W. A. Gale)、丘奇(K. W. Church)及布朗(P. F. Brown)等人提出②。此种方法可较好地处理形式化强的欧洲语言大类,但对汉语(意合语言、孤立语)的处理效果欠佳。

(四) 基于词汇锚定和句长统计的综合方法

基于词汇锚定和句长统计的综合方法又被称为混合法。基于句长统计的方法模型的优越之处在于结构简单,仅依赖于统计,不依赖任何语言知识,但也因此其对齐效果不佳。而基于词汇锚定的方法虽然精确度较高,但是计算又相对复杂。因此本节尝试将以上两种方法结合起来进行对齐实验。研究同时借鉴香港大学的吴德恺通过建立词汇表对基于句长统计的方法加以改进,③进行了对齐试验,效果较好。

① M. Kay, M. Röescheisen, "Text-Translation Alignment", *Computational Linguistics*, Vol. 19, No. 1, 1993, pp. 121-142; S. F. Chen, "Aligning Sentences in Bilingual Corpora Using Lexical Information", in *Proceedings of the 31st Annual Meeting of the ACL*, 1993, pp. 9-16.

② P. F. Brown, J. C. Lai & R. L. Mercer, "Aligning Sentences in Parallel Corpora", in *Proceedings of the 29th Annual Meeting of the ACL*, 1991, pp. 169-176; Gale, Church, "A Program for Aligning Sentences in Bilingual Corpora", *Computational Linguisties*, Vol. 19, No. 1, 1991, pp. 75-102.

③ See Wu Dekai, "Aligning a Parallel English-Chinese Corpus Statistically with Lexical Criteria", in *Proceedings of the 32nd Annual Meeting of the ACL*, 1994, pp. 80-87.

三、在线对齐语料技术

自 CAT 技术逐步在语言服务领域大规模应用以来,语料对齐的应用就变得越来越多,虽然对其理论方法已进行了较多的探讨,但在实践应用中,大部分对齐工具仍未实现理想的对齐效果。尤其是已商业化的对齐软件,大多数使用基于规则的方法,导致自动对齐后仍需要大量的人工干预——主要是"一对多""多对一"或"多对多"情况下的多个句子需要人工合并为一个句子,从而耗费了大量的人力物力。有鉴于此,本项目组对在线对齐技术进行了深入研究,并开发了相应的工具①。该项对齐技术以在线形式呈现,用户无须安装,界面友好,操作简单,对齐效果佳。该项技术被运用到汉外法律翻译平台建设中,实现了较好的记忆库调用,实际服务了实践需求。

(一) 支持多种文本格式

支持 Txt、Word(＊.doc、＊.docx)、Excel、PPT(＊.ppt、＊.pptx)以及可编辑的 PDF 文件。在线上传这些文本格式的原文和译文后,文件解析过滤器对文件进行解析,将上传的文件解析为纯文本,然后由过滤器对相应文本进行过滤,最后按段落信息展示给用户,其流程如图3－1所示:

---

① 此处是指与 Tmxmall 合作开发的 Tmxmall aligner 对齐工具,https://www.tmxmall.com/aligner。

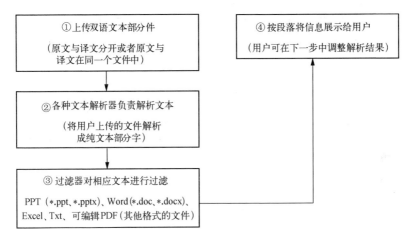

①上传双语文本部分件

（原文与译文分开或者原文与译文在同一个文件中）

②各种文本解析器负责解析文本

（将用户上传的文件解析成纯文本部分字）

③过滤器对相应文本进行过滤

PPT（*.ppt、*.pptx）、Word（*.doc、*.docx）、Excel、Txt、可编辑PDF（其他格式的文件）

④按段落将信息展示给用户

（用户可在下一步中调整解析结果）

图3-1 文件解析过滤器工作流程

（二）支持段落调整

为了解决"一对多""多对一""多对多"的自动识别难题,本项在线对齐技术创新性地开发了新的对齐算法,该算法以段落对齐为基础,自动实现了句子层面的对齐,从而将人工干预从句子层面调整到段落层面,极大地降低了人工参与度及工作量。段落对齐的目的就是使译文和原文实现段与段之间的对照,在实际的翻译过程中,绝大多数文件都是在原文的分段格式上进行翻译的,只有极少数文件由于种种原因,对译文的分段进行了重新调整。可见,实际上需要进行段落调整的人工参与工作很少,甚至没有。为了实现原文和译文的段段对照,本研究中的在线对齐技术支持段落调整,具有句段合并、拆分、插入、删除、上移和下移功能。

1. 合并

合并是指将多句原文或译文合并到一个段落中。有时需要同时将多句原文或译文分别合并到单独的一个句段中,有时则仅需将多句原文或多句译文之一单独合并到一个句段中。对于这两种情况的句段合并,该在线对齐技术均予支持。

2. 拆分

原文中的两个句段在译文中被放在了同一个句段中,或者译文中的两个句段在原文中对应的句段只有一个,此时,就需要将一个句段进行切分。

3. 插入

由于种种原因,原文或译文中存在一个句子或多个句子的缺失,为了保证译文的完整性,这时就需要对其进行补全,而补全就需要插入一个或多个空行。为此,本在线对齐技术在句段调整层面支持空行插入功能。

4. 删除

在对齐过程中,存在译文和原文均有错误的情况,也存在仅有原文或译文的情况。为了保证整体语料的质量并节约时间,有时需直接将整行的对照原文和译文删除,有时也需直接将缺乏对应原文或译文的译文或原文句段删除。对于这两种情况,本在线对齐技术均予支持。

5. 上移、下移

在对齐过程的第二步即解析原文和译文的过程中,有时由于原文和译文格式的差别,解析后的原文或译文句段会发生错行的情况。此时就需要通过上移或下移某个或多个句段。针对语料对齐的此类需求,本在线对齐技术对句段的上移和下移功能均予支持。

(三)采用创新性的对齐算法

本在线对齐技术创新性地采用了句子排列组合算法和基于机器翻

译的相似度计算,以段落为单位进行对齐计算,将中文和英文通过断句规则进行断句。断句后可以得到中文和英文的句子个数,比如中文句子数量为 m,英文句子数量为 n。而后计算中文句子的排列组合情况 Perm(m)的集合,根据中文句子的每种排列,使用插空法求解每种排列对应的英文句子排列组合。再计算每种中英文排列组合的对应句子相似度,从而挑选出相似度最大的中文和英文的排列组合,即为最终的对齐结果。

1. 句对排列计算

假设 m 个中文句子中最多有 2 个可以合并到一起,则 m 个句子的组合情况总数为斐波那契按数列①,即 $F(m) = F(m-1) + F(m-2)$,再辅以递归算法求解每种排列情况。如假设中文段落分句以后句子数量 m=4,排列组合情况如表 3-1 所示:

表 3-1　句子排列组合情况

序号	中文组合情况	情况说明
1	[1][2][3][4]	①段落被分割为四句
2	[1-2][3][4]	
3	[1][2-3][4]	②段落被分割为三句
4	[1][2][3-4]	
5	[1-2][3-4]	③段落被分割为两句
6	[1-2-3-4]	④段落被分割为一句

①　斐波那契数列(Fibonacci sequence),又称黄金分割数列,因数学家莱昂纳多·斐波那契(Leonardoda Fibonacci)以兔子繁殖为例子而提出,故又称为"兔子数列",指的是这样一个后一数字为前两个数字之和的数列:0、1、1、2、3、5、8、13、21、34……在数学上,斐波那契数列被以如下递推的方法定义:$F(0) = 0, F(1) = 1, F(n) = F(n-1) + F(n-2) (n \geq 2, n \in N^*)$。

对于每种中文句子排列,可通过插空法求解英文对应的排列情况,要求是英文句子中最多有 3 个句子可合并成一句。如英文句子个数为 n=6,针对情况①,根据插空法计算出可能的英文句子组合如表 3-2 所示:

表 3-2 句子组合情况

序号	中文组合情况
1	[1-2][3-4][5][6]
2	[1-2][3][4-5][6]
3	[1][2-3][4][5-6]
……	[1][2-3][4-5][6]
10	[1][2][3][4-5-6]

其他情况下的英文句子计算方式以此类推。m 个中文句子最多可以有 2 个句子合并,在插空法求解英文句子对应的排列组合时,英文句子最多可以有 3 个句子合并,这样就可以自动识别对齐结果中“一对多”“多对一”以及“多对多”的情况。

2. 相似度计算

对于每种中英对应的排列组合情况,先将中文句子通过机器翻译成英文,再使用 BLEU 算法计算机器翻译的英文结果与原始的英文译文当下排列的句子相似度之和,最终求解得到最大相似度的排列组合所对应的中英文排列结果,即为该中英文段落句子对齐的最优解。

仍以上述中文组合{[1][2][3][4]}为例计算与英文各种组合情况相似度的总值。例如,要计算上述示例中中文组合{[1][2][3][4]}与英文组合{[1-2][3-4][5][6]}之间的相似度,则需要分别计

算:｛中文[1]<->英文[1-2]｝、｛中文[2]<->英文[3-4]｝、｛中文[3]
<->英文[5]｝、｛中文[4]<->英文[6]｝的相似度。将计算结果累加得
到该种组合的整体相似度。例如,｛中文[1]<->英文[1-2]｝相似度计
算方法是:先将英文的 1、2 句通过机器翻译成中文,然后再用 BLEU 算
法计算中文[1]和翻译后的结果[1-2]的相似度,其结果即为｛中文
[1]<->英文[1-2]｝的相似度。

第三节　语料对齐应用检验

为了进一步优化上述在线对齐技术的实践应用效果,本节特选
取五份中英单语双文档(法律类、文学类、工程类、机械类、经济类)
作为实验对象,分别用 Tmxmall Aligner、Abbyy Aligner、Transmate
Aligner、SDL Winalign 这四种目前应用较为广泛的语料对齐工具
进行对齐,并从文本导入时间、人工调整句占总句对数量百分比、
调整时间、不同领域对齐所需总时间这四个维度采集实验数据,
以对比分析不同对齐工具自动对齐的效果,作为参考。

一、试验步骤

第一步:将法律类文本(中文字数 9919、英文词数 6725)分别导入
Tmxmall Aligner、Abbyy Aligner、Transmate Aligner、SDL Winalign,对相关
实验数据记录如下表所示。

表3-3　法律类文本试验结果对比情况

	Tmxmall Aligner	Abbyy Aligner	Transmate Aligner	SDL Winalign
导入时间(秒)	5	7	5	12
总句段(个)	293	402	513	408
调整句段(个)	19	57	114	348
调整总时间(秒)	425	1167	2094	3132

　　第二步:将文学文本(中文字数12071、英文词数6642)分别导入Tmxmall Aligner、Abbyy Aligner、Transmate Aligner、SDL Winalign,对相关实验数据记录如下表所示。

表3-4　文学类文本试验结果对比情况

	Tmxmall Aligner	Abbyy Aligner	Transmate Aligner	SDL Winalign
导入时间(秒)	7	8	6	9
总句段(个)	199	241	458	285
调整句段(个)	18	24	134	271
调整总时间(秒)	385	496	1358	2363

　　第三步:将工程文本(中文字数13090、英文词数8233)分别导入Tmxmall Aligner、Abbyy Aligner、Transmate Aligner、SDL Winalign,对相关实验数据记录如下表所示。

表3-5　工程类文本试验结果对比情况

	Tmxmall Aligner	Abbyy Aligner	Transmate Aligner	SDL Winalign
导入时间(秒)	6	9	8	11
总句段(个)	626	1004	662	592

	Tmxmall Aligner	Abbyy Aligner	Transmate Aligner	SDL Winalign
调整句段(个)	60	112	173	477
调整总时间(秒)	1146	1325	1997	4267

第四步:将机械类文本(中文字数 7551、英文词数 6150)分别导入 Tmxmall Aligner、Abbyy Aligner、Transmate Aligner、SDL Winalign,对相关实验数据记录如下表所示。

表 3－6　机械类文本试验结果对比情况

	Tmxmall Aligner	Abbyy Aligner	Transmate Aligner	SDL Winalign
导入时间(秒)	7	6	6	14
总句段(个)	479	1653	657	563
调整句段(个)	91	427	295	546
调整总时间(秒)	1326	2552	3645	4795

第五步:将经济类文本(中文字数 8640、英文词数 4550)分别导入 Tmxmall Aligner、Abbyy Aligner、Transmate Aligner、SDL Winalign,对相关实验数据记录如下表所示。

表 3－7　经济类文本试验结果对比情况

	Tmxmall Aligner	Abbyy Aligner	Transmate Aligner	SDL Winalign
导入时间(秒)	5	6	5	9
总句段(个)	244	258	324	270
调整句段(个)	14	28	110	194
调整总时间(秒)	311	594	1107	1811

二、对比分析

（一）文本导入时间

Tmxmall Aligner 和 Transmate Aligner 的整体导入速度并列四类对齐工具之首（30 秒），其次为 Abbyy Aligner（36 秒），最后为 SDL Winalign（55 秒）。实验同时发现 Abbyy Aligner、SDL Winalign 的导入速度极不稳定，这可能是因为需要加载的程序过大，影响了整体的速度。

（二）人工调整句/总句对数量百分比

Tmxmall Aligner 在对齐五类文本时，需要人工调整句段占总句对数量的百分比均为最低（23%），其次为 Abbyy Aligner（37%）、Transmate Aligner（43%）、SDL Winalign（56%）。其中，Tmxmall Aligner 与 Abbyy Aligner 自动对齐匹配准确率相对较高，SDL Winalign 自动对齐效果则比较差。

（三）调整时间

据图 3-2，Tmxmall Aligner 在对齐五类文本时，需要人工调整的时间均为最低，即需要人工参与的工作量最小，其次为 Abbyy Aligner、Transmate Aligner、SDL Winalign。

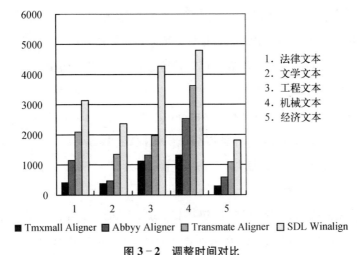

图 3－2　调整时间对比

（四）不同领域对齐所需总时间

经过试验，Tmxmall Aligner 用于对齐五类文本花费的总时间最少（3593 秒），其次为 Abbyy Aligner（6134 秒）、Transmate Aligner（10201秒）、SDL Winalign（16368 秒）。其中，Tmxmall Aligner 和 Abbyy Aligner较为接近，对齐所用总时间均较少；Transmate Aligner、SDL Winalign 较为接近，对齐所用总时间均较多。

本次实验中，影响对齐质量和速度的因素有三个：（1）程序运行速度；（2）自动对齐匹配准确率；（3）编辑功能的便捷程度。关于程序运行速度，Tmxmall Aligner 作为在线对齐工具，极大减轻了电脑运载程序的负荷；而 Abbyy Aligner、Transmate Aligner、SDL Winalign均属于单机版对齐工具，速度相应会受到一定影响。关于自动对齐匹配准确率，Tmxmall Aligner 采用了句子排列组合算法和基于机器翻译的相似度计算，解决了"一对多""多对一"和"多对多"的自动识别难题,极大提高了自动对齐的准确率;而 Abbyy Aligner、Transmate Aligner、SDL Winalign 基于的对齐算法对"一对多""多对一"和"多对多"的处理结果相对较差,自动对齐匹配准确率也相应低些。

关于编辑功能,Tmxmall Aligner 提供了合并、拆分、插入、删除、上移和下移六种手段,并辅以相应的快捷键;Transmate Aligner 提供了合并、拆分、插入、删除、上移、下移、原译文对换七种手段,但没有相应的快捷键;Abbyy Aligner 提供了合并、拆分、删除、上移和下移五种手段,但没有相应的快捷键;SDL Winalign 虽也有合并、拆分、插入等编辑功能,但其中匹配的翻译单元均以虚线连接,连线不对处需要先断开连线再进行对齐编辑。可见,使用 Tmxmall Aligner、Abbyy Aligner、Transmate Aligner 进行对齐编辑时,操作简便,效率较高;SDL Winalign 则显得较为繁复,不易操作。综上,Tmxmall Aligner 的对齐效果以及对齐速度均为最佳,其次为 Abbyy Aligner、Transmate Aligner、SDL Winalign。

在语料对齐技术开发过程中,针对"一对多""多对一"和"多对多"的对齐难点,本节尝试引入了断句后的组合排列算法,并结合机器翻译的相似度算法进行实现。这种句子组合方法以排列组合为基本思路,结合机器翻译后译文的相似度对比作为核心算法。该方法相较于以往基于规则和词典的方法,能够获取的对应锚点更多,可彻底解决对齐中以往方法无法解决的"一对多""多对一"和"多对多"的难题。通过与多种对齐软件的对比,该方法确实能够在很大程度上降低人工参与度和工作量,同时核心算法对对齐难题的解决,使对齐效率较其他软件有大幅度的提高。

第四节　在线法律翻译及教学功能应用

在依托上述数据库和智能语言技术的基础上,项目进行中开发了定制化部署的教学模块（网址：https://ecupl. yicat. vip/yicat/workspace/tasks）,可作为本科生和研究生课程教学的延伸。利用该平台,教师可布置和批改作业、教授课程,学生可完成和提交作业。该平台可通过五步骤的具体操作实现在线教学模式:(1)创建内部账号/平台邀请。(2)激活项目成员,按班级或团队查看成员。(3)开启作业模式,批量分配作业。(4)实时查看进度。(5)批改后查看报告。具体操作步骤如图3-3至图3-7所示。

不难看出,平台的搭建为一线教师提供了更多教学案例,有利于其摆脱以前基于经验的教学模式,形成一套新的翻译教学方法。利用在线辅助翻译工具、术语提取和语料私有云,教师可教授学生掌握预翻译、项目术语准备、术语统一、语料信息检索、协同翻译等当下翻译流程的关键环节,使学生所学与将来工作无缝对接,提高学生的竞争力。

图 3-3 创建内部账号/平台邀请

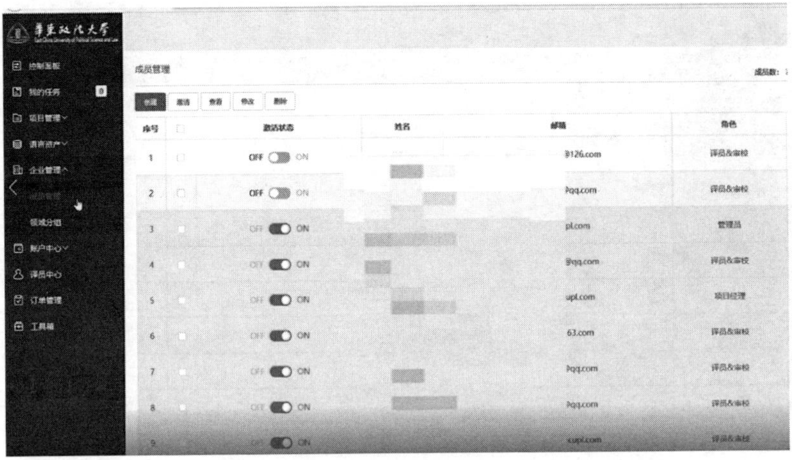

图 3 - 4　激活项目成员,按班级或团队查看成员

同时,先进的云端平行语料检索技术也为学校在大规模平行语料的研究上提供了针对性的检索及分析技术;基于语料库开展各项研究,为学校在翻译学教学与研究方面提供更丰富的研究素材和工具;通过使用该语料库管理系统,研究人员可以获取丰富的双语句对表达,并通过对比进一步发现语言内部信息。

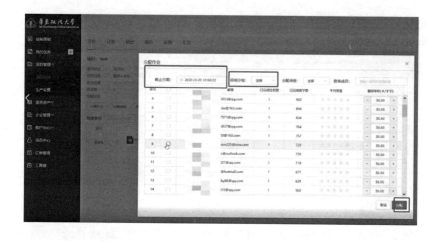

图 3 - 5　开启作业模式,批量分配作业

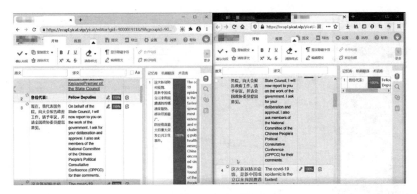

图3-6　实时查看进度

在此基础上,将高校的语言资源及需求同先进的技术及平台优势相结合,建设特色专业语料库,不仅可以辅助授课教师基于特色语料库开展教学、科研、学科建设,还能够建设面向企业和社会的特色语料库开放平台,实现科研的成果转化。特别对于后者,该平台与知识类互联网产品(例如谷歌知识图谱、搜狗知立方)合作,获得相应的收益,并基于语料库开发面向文化、教育、出版市场的软件或互联网产品。

可见,法律垂直领域语料数据库作为外语教学、语言学、翻译学和其他学科交叉发展的平台,为探索法政领域翻译提供了研究创新平台。

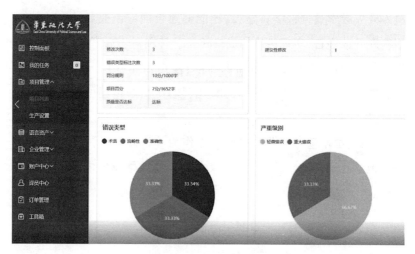

图 3-7 批改后查看报告

第四章
从法律意义单位到法律翻译单位

第一节 基于语料库短语学的意义单位考察

语料库短语学是以单语或双语中短语意义单位为基元,采用基于语料库的(或是语料库驱动的)研究范式进行语言学的相关研究。在人工智能时代,语料库也从机读文本小规模集合发展为语言资源类的大数据集合,语料库短语学的观察对象由此变得更为丰富,挖掘也变得更有深度。从语料库短语学的时代走向、逻辑走向及实践走向三个方面进行梳理,可以发现:一、语料库短语学更符合时代要求,研究范式已经突破语言学本身,广泛地与信息科学理论相结合。二、语料库研究的发展已使对比短语学确立为一门独立学科,应用在大数据时代的翻译研究中,发展了语言本体研究。三、语料库短语学在自然语言处理与机器翻译中的应用及其发展趋势更加明显。

单词一直是语言学传统理念中最普遍的意义单位,但随着信息技术的不断发展,意义承载单位的边界在不断地扩展,语言学家辛克莱在20世纪60年代就提出,文本中承载意义的最重要单位是词语搭配,而非单词。① 经过约 50 年的发展演变之后，短语学被确立为语言学的一个专门学科领域②，并应用于语言习得、教学、自然语言处理等领域。尤其在人工智能技术辅助下（如自然语言处理、机器翻译）的短语学发展已经引起了语言学、翻译学、信息科学等交叉学科的共同关注，其重要性逐渐凸显。但学界对短语学的研究单位一直存在争议，这使得其在发展速度、深度和广度方面受限。基于此，厘清短语学的概念内涵和外延是开展进一步研究的基础。

一、短语学发展的时代转向

（一）传统语言学理论中的短语学

本部分所指短语学是基于词项共现频率，以计算机技术和定量分析为重要支撑的语料库（驱动）短语学，主要研究对象分为以下两种类型：（1）具有固定或半固定形式的多词结构，如"strong tea""a felling of""want to"等等。（2）语法化短语（非语法关系），如特定的词项常以特定的语法结构出现（如动词 hem 一般用于被动态），这里还要注意一种情况——非连续式多词结构，即词项成分之间存在一定距离（也称为 n-gram）的情况。格里斯（S. Geries）所强调的短语单位，是指在语义层面上，考虑到语义整体的问题，也就是具有单独词元或词汇意义的词

---

① J. Sinclair, et al. , *English Collocation Studies：The OSTI Report*, London：Continuum, 2004.

② S. Granger, M. Paquot, "Dissentangling the Phraseological Web", in S. Granger, F. Meunier (eds.), *Phraseology: An Interdisciplinary Perspective*, Amsterdam/Philadelphia：John Benjamins, 2008, p. 27.

素组成的语义统一体。① 在不同的语言学派,短语学的地位也存在很大差异。如生成语言学派(Generative Linguistics)对短语学的关注不多,直至20世纪末,短语学才被重视起来,库里卡弗(P. W. Culicover)论述了不同的短语型式,指出这是对转换生成语法的极大冲击。② 根据格里斯的观点,短语学颠覆了转换生成学派的以词为基本单元去分析生成机制,把单位扩大到模块化组织,这与自然语言处理中"算式语法及词法"(algorithmic grammar and a lexicon)的核心概念非常相近。③ 而这种研究的发展对认知语言学(尤其是构式语法)以及语料库语言学的影响更大。同时,认知语言学(构式语法)对短语的认识更接近经典短语学。兰艾克(R. W. Langacker)就曾论述过这样的观点,即多词结构是母语使用者天然的、无须集中注意力就能使用的语言单位。④ 这样的符号单位(多词结构)也是型式与意义的组合,符号单位越稳固地进入语言使用者的语言系统,就越被广泛地使用,反之亦然。也就是说,母语者是机械地整体调动多词结构,而非分析生成;而短语学真正的发展与语料库语言学的发展休戚相关,毫无疑问,语料库是观察短语共现率和复现率的最佳载体。

(二) 多词单位的语料库分析

目前,语料库语言学主要研究机器可读自然语言文本的采集、存储、

① S. Geries, "Corpus Linguistics and Theoretical Linguistics: A Love-hate realtionshi? Not necessarily", *International Journal of Corpus Linguistics*, Vol. 15, No. 3, 2010, p. 327.

② P. W. Culicover, *Simpler Syntax*, Oxford: Oxford University Press, 1999.

③ S. Granger, M. Paquot, "Dissentangling the Phraseological Web", in S. Granger, F. Meunier (eds.), *Phraseology: An Interdisciplinary Perspective*, Amsterdam/Philadelphia: John Benjamins, 2008, p. 27.

④ R. W. Langacker, *The Foundations of Cognitive Grammar: Theoretical Prerequisites* Vol. 1, Redwood City: Stanford University Press, 1987.

检索、统计、语法标注、句法语义分析等,以及具有上述功能的语料库在语言教学、定量分析、词汇研究、词语搭配研究、词典编撰、语法研究、语言文化研究、法律语言研究、作品风格分析、自然语理解和机器翻译等领域中的应用。语料库语言学是自然语言计算机处理的一个重要内容[1],由于强调的重心不同,不同的学者倾向用不同表达式来指称多词结构(短语),如刘易斯(M. Lewis)选用"lexical chunks"(词汇组块)[2],纳丁格(J. Nattinger)和德卡里科(J. Decarrico)选用"lexical phrases"(词汇短语)[3],考伊选用"ready-made complex units"(预制复合单位)[4],波利(A. Pawley)和西德尔(F. H. Syder)则选用"lexicalized sentence stems"(词汇化句干)[5]。除此之外还有"chunk"(语块)、"semi-fixed patterns"(半固定式短语)、"speech formulate"(言语程式)等等。

语料库语言学中的短语单位研究一般采用语料库驱动的研究方法,即概念界定→建库→工作方法确认→多词结构提取→从语言学层面分析(语法层面、语义层面、语用层面)→功能聚类(概念功能、谋篇功能、人际功能)。随着自然语言处理技术的不断成熟,可以发现语料库驱动的短语单位研究已经突破单纯的语言研究领域。以"语料库"及"短语学"为关键词,通过中国知网(CNKI)进行检索,调整阈值为6后进行共现分析,可以得到图4-1:

---

① 冯志伟:《自然语言处理简明教程》,上海外语教育出版社 2012 年版,第 605 页。

② M. Lewis, *The Lexical Approach: The State of ELT and a Way Forward*, London: Language Teaching Publications, 1993.

③ J. Nattinger, J. DeCarrico, *Lexical Phrases and Language Teaching*, Shanghai: Shanghai Foreign Language education Press, 1992.

④ A. P. Cowie, *Phraseology: Theory, Analysis, and Application*, Oxford: Clarendo Press, 1998.

⑤ A. Pawley, F. H. Syder, "Two Puzzles for Linguistic Theory: Nativelike Selection and Nativelike Fluency", in J. C. Richards, R. W. Schmidt (eds.), *Language and Communication*, New York: Lonyman, 1983, pp. 191-226.

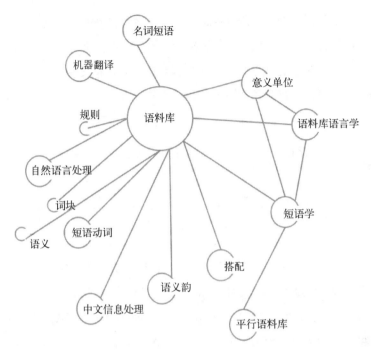

图 4-1　语料库短语学共现网络

　　图中的圆圈大小代表文献数量,不难看出,语料库短语学研究目前活跃的领域已经延伸至自然语言处理、机器翻译及中文信息处理范畴,这是对经典短语学的发展,也是对语料库语言研究的发展。语料库短语研究对优化自然语言处理领域中双语对齐算法的鲁棒性(Robustness)和稳定性提供了数据支持。传统双语文本对齐采用"分析—分析—匹配"的方法,首先对某种语言文本的句子进行句法分析或多层句法分析,并通过启发式过程对两种语言的每一对句子、短语进行对齐,从而得到短语对齐的双语系统。利用语料库方法进行对齐、机器翻译训练,则采用共现频率的统计信息来进行短语对齐,也就是通过短语在整个库中的共现情况来发掘对应信息。

关于翻译短语对的研究不但是机器翻译课题中的一个重要环节,而且也是自然语言处理中亟待解决的问题。多年来研究者一直致力于在句子对齐和词汇对齐的基础上进行双语语料库的短语对齐加工,其目的也就是为了获取翻译短语对。但是现行的短语对齐方法在处理像汉-英这样具有异构语法体系的语言对来说,会遇到很多问题,比如:

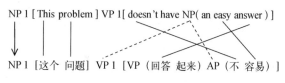

图 4-2　短语对齐实例

在图 4-2 中的汉-英双语句对中,用方括号标出了两个句子的短语型句法分析结构,其中的词汇对应关系用细实线进行表示。使用一般的"分析—分析—匹配"对齐策略,可以得到短语翻译对 NP1[This problem]<=>NP1[这个 问题]。但是 AP[不 容易]这个短语就很难在英语句子中找到与之对应的译文,其原因是汉语单词"不"与英语句子 VP1 中的"doesn't"相对齐,而"容易"与英语句子中 NP 中的"easy"相对齐。很明显,在英语句子中很难找到 AP[不 容易]的准确对应译文。在"分析—分析—匹配"策略中,整个对齐过程受单语句法分析精度、词对齐结果及双语语法体系不一致性的制约,因而效果较差。

在当前自然语言处理(NLP)领域(包括机器翻译),对于短语对齐效果普遍认可的方式当属基于译文等价树的汉-英短语对齐,其主要工作流程是:第一步,对源语言句子进行词性标注,对目标语句子进行词性标注;第二步,使用词对齐工具对双语句对进行词对齐;第三步,使用句法分析器对源语言句子进行句法分析;第四步,以源语言句法树、目

标语句子和词对齐结果为基础,建立译文等价树;第五步,从译文等价
树中抽取短语翻译对。整个过程如图4-3所示:

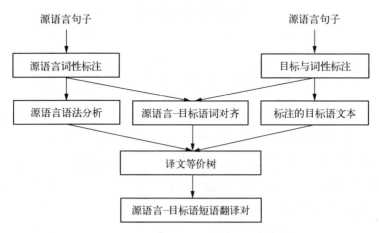

图4-3　基于译文等价树的短语翻译对抽取

短语对齐的机器翻译系统训练在译文准确性上明显高于词对应的
机器翻译训练,同时基于译文等价树的抽取方法去获取短语翻译对时,
其效果要好于"分析—分析—匹配"策略。其原因是:在"分析—分
析—匹配"策略中,整个对齐过程要受到目标语句法分析精度和双语
语法体不一致性的制约,所获取短语对的质量较低;而在基于译文等价
树的方法中,对齐结果不受目标语句法分析精度和双语语法体系不一
致性的制约,因而效果较好,实验证明对齐精确度可以达到80.97%。
这也是短语学应用于 NLP 实践领域的重要意义所在。语料库短语学
汲取了大量 NLP 领域的原理和运算以拓展它的理论疆界和开发更符
合短语学的操作方式,在这样的背景下同时伴随着语料库语言学研究
的不断成熟,对比短语学应运而生,也是对比语言学与短语学在新的学
术语境和技术环境下的发展与延伸。

二、短语学的逻辑走向

（一）对比短语学的要旨和方法

对比短语学是以探索跨语言对应意义单位（corresponding units of meaning）为要旨，依赖双语语料库资源，基于双语语料库的真实语言，使用证据进行跨语言意义单位的对应研究。意义单位即是辛克莱等人所提的"词项"（lexical item）①，国内学者卫乃兴②、李文中③、濮建忠④所提的意义单位也是这一意义。其研究范式打破了以单个词为核心的基本结构，而是由语用（交际目的）决定的多词单位。对比短语学基于可比语料库或平行语料库，从单语中发掘意义单位［后来托伯特（W. Teubert）等人也称其为翻译单位（translational unit）⑤］。对比短语学是语料库语言学由单语语料库（monolingual corpora）研究向双语和多语语料库（multilingual corpora）研究发展而催生的研究方向，是传统的对比语言学与短语学在新的学术语境下的必然发展。对比短语学旨在发现和描述对应或对等的跨语言意义单位，通过观察、比对双语词语的组

---

① J. Sinclair, et al., *English Collocation Studies：The OSTI Report*, London：Continuum, 2004.

② 卫乃兴：《再探经典短语学的要旨和方法：模型、概念与问题》，《外语与外语教学》2011 年第 3 期。卫乃兴、陆军等：《对比短语学探索——来自语料库的证据》，外语教学与研究出版社 2014 年版。

③ 李文中：《平行语料库设计及对应单位识别》，《当代外语研究》2010 年第 9 期。

④ 濮建忠：《语料库驱动的翻译研究：意义单位、翻译单位和对应单位》，《解放军外国语学院学报》2014 年第 1 期。

⑤ W. Teubert, "Directions in Corpus Linguistics", in M. Halliday, W. Teubert, C. Yalop & A. Germakova（eds.）, *Lexicology & Corpus Linguistics*, London & New York：Continuum, 2004.

合行为异同,尤其是比对词语的形式、意义和功能特征异同,确立跨语言交际中使用的多词意义单位。它与翻译研究、对比语言研究、计算机辅助翻译研究和语言教学研究关系密切,有望为这些领域提供有价值的理论启示与方法参照。其主要的学术理念与方法都根植于辛克莱的意义单位理论与语料库驱动的方法论思想。

　　研究中所使用的语料库涉及两类:一类是可比语料库,另一类是平行语料库。用于对比研究时,可比语料库与平行语料库优势互补,两者缺一不可。可比语料库的优势在于其真实的语言特征,但双语文本间未建立起连接,缺乏直接、可观察的形式对应,研究者需要借助别的手段(如双语词典或个人经验)确定合适和可行的被比对象;而平行语料库的译语文本和原语文本已经建立连接,双语形式的对应直观易见,便于确定被比对象并进行量化信息处理,因此在研究时应将两种语料库结合使用。语言交际过程中的共选是对比语言学的重要理论支撑,扩展意义单位是其主要的工作模型。共选(co-selection)是辛克莱根据单语语料库研究提出的,是指形式与形式、形式与意义、形式与功能之间的内在关系。① 扩展意义单位是语料库驱动的短语学的工作模型。如前所述,根据辛克莱的观点,扩展意义单位共有节点词、语义韵、搭配、语义趋向和类联接5个构成成分。其中,类联接是节点词语法关系的抽象,是其共现于的语法或结构类,而语义趋向是对搭配词语义特征的抽象,在分析比较研究对象及其英文对应语时应考虑到这两个因素。② 在一般翻译单位对应研究中主要利用 B. 阿尔滕贝格提出的相互对应

---

① J. Sinclair, "Corpus, Concordance, Collocation", *Modern Language Journa*, Vol. 78, No. 3, 1991, p. 407.

② 陆军、卫乃兴:《扩展意义单位模型下的英汉翻译对等型式构成研究》,《外语教学与研究》2012年第3期。

率计算两个词语的互译概率,探讨对应关系。① 具体方法包括:(1) 语言 A 译为语言 B 过程中,词汇 X 产生的翻译对等 Y 及其概率;(2) 考虑 Y 在语言 B 译为语言 A 过程中产生的翻译对等 X 及其概率;(3) 利用相互对应率公式计算 X 与 Y 的对应程度,考察并确定对应关系。② 为了说明该工作方法的可操作性,项目组采用一个自建的(汉英)政治文本平行语料库(Political Texts Parallel Corpus,以下简称 PTPC),其中包括自 2009 年至 2016 年历年政府工作报告全文,以及 2009 年至 2017 年发布的中国政府白皮书(总库容 207 万形符)。同时采用一个在线可比语料库——库容 4 亿形符的美国当代国家语料库(Corpus of Contemporary American English,以下简称 COCA),该语料库也被认定为全球最大的英文可比语料库。按照以上工作步骤,我们将分析几个高频多词单位的汉英双语对应情况,包括"社会主义现代化建设""忧患意识""全面深化改革"。

(二) 多词单位的双语对应率研究

上述三个多词单位是具有典型社会主义话语体系特征的语词,在 PTPC 中检索亦属于高频出现的多词单位,其中"社会主义现代化建设"20 次、"忧患意识"16 次、"全面深化改革"15 次。值得注意的是,三个单位具有不同的组成结构:"社会主义现代化建设"属于术语结构,即固化表达;"忧患意识"是偏正结构的短语,属于常见单位;"全面深化改革"属于一般祈使结构单位。这导致在机器分词时就极易出现错误,比如分词效果 1 为"社会/主义/现代化/建设",或分词效果 2 为"社会主义/现代化建设",这些都会给机器学习和机器翻译带来歧义。这就需要

---

① B. Altenberg, "Adverbial Connectors in English and Swedish: Semantic and Lexical Correspondences", in H. Hasselgard, S. Oksefjell (eds.), *Out of Corpora: Studies in Honour of Stig Johansson*, New York: Rodopi, 1999.

② 卫乃兴、陆军等:《对比短语学探索——来自语料库的证据》,外语教学与研究出版社 2014 年版。

从人工角度进行算法和平行训练数据,也就是基于平行语料库进行精确的对应单位确认。此项研究主要考察:(1)汉译英翻译复现对等情况;(2)英译汉翻译复现对等情况;(3)英汉、汉英相互对应率。

以上述三个多词结构为例,首先需要考察的是汉译英过程中产生的复现翻译对等。"社会主义现代化建设"在 PTPC 中出现了 20 次,全部翻译为"Socialist Modernization",类符数为 1;复现翻译对等共使用 20 次,为形符数,占全部翻译对等形符数的 100%(20/20)。由此可以认定"社会主义现代化建设"与"Socialist Modernization"在结构层级上呈现短语对短语的结构对等,词语层级上呈现一对一的简单对应关系。数据轮廓及其对应关系说明:"社会主义现代化建设"类型的术语固化结构在汉译英过程中译为短语的倾向性极强。

"忧患意识"则不同,在 PTPC 中出现了 16 次,10 次被译为"be mindful of potential perils and crises/dangers/adversity"(62.5%),4 次译为"awareness of potential dangers/latent problems"(25%),2 次译为"awareness of potential dangers"(12.5%),类符数为 3。根据数据轮廓和对应关系可以看出,在译文中"be mindful of +(potential dangers/latent problems/adversity/crises)"是与"忧患意识"具有较强对应度的结构,其中"be mindful of"是固定部分,也恰对应"忧患意识"这个偏正结构中的核心词"……意识",而"忧患"则并未固定,具有多个对应表达形式。

"全面深化改革"在 PTPC 中出现 15 次,7 次译为"comprehensively deepen reform and opening up"(46.7%),5 次译为"build a moderately prosperous society in all respects and deepening reform and opening up"(33.3%),2 次译为"intensify reform in all respects"(13.3%),1 次译为"deepen reform across the board"(6%),共 4 个类符。根据数据轮廓及对应关系看,"全面深化改革"英文对应单位均为短语结构,但最高频率对应型式仍未超过 50%,因而需进一步考察其英译汉过程中产生的复现翻译对等,如下表:

表4-1　"全面深化改革"多词单位英汉、汉英对应数据表

汉语原文	汉译英翻译对等数据（PTPC）		英译汉翻译对等数据（COCA）		
	英译文	频数	英语原文	汉译文（及频数）	频数
全面深化改革	comprehensively deepen reform and opening up	7	comprehensively deepen reform and opening up	全面深化改革(3)；全面改革开放(1)	4
	build a moderately prosperous society in all respects and deepening reform and opening up	5	build a moderately prosperous society in all respects and deepening reform and opening up	全面建设富强社会，深化改革开放(1)；建设富强国家，加深改革开放(1)	2
	intensify reform in all respects	2	intensify reform in all respects	全方位加强改革(1)；全面深化改革(1)	2
	deepen reform across the board	1	deepen reform across the board	深度加强国内改革(1)	1

为了进一步测量和评估双语多次单位的对应程度,需要引入前述阿尔滕贝格提出的相互对应率概念及算法来处理出数据。根据该公式,可以计算出"全面深化改革"与各个译文对应单位的相互对应率。相互对应率越高,越有可能是跨语言的对应单位。

表4-2　"全面深化改革"与其译文的相互对应率数据

对应单位		汉英对应率	英汉对应率	相互对应率
全面深化改革	comprehensively deepen reform and opening up	46.7%	75%	91%
	build a moderately prosperous society in all respects and deepening reform and opening up	33.3%	0%	16.6%
	intensify reform in all respects	13.3%	50%	33.3%
	deepen reform across the board	6%	0%	1.25%

由上可见,"全面深化改革"与"comprehensively deepen reform and opening up"相互对应率为91%,呈现强对应;最弱的对应型式是"deepen reform across the board"。可以发现:"全面/adv.""深化/v.""改革/n."与"comprehensively/adv.""deepen/v.""reform and opening up/nn."[①]在结构上完全对应,这也缘于中国特色社会主义话语体系中的半固化表达多采用归化翻译对应型式的习惯。值得注意的是,这种固化程度高的语言表达为机器学习和机器翻译的训练提供了有力保障,但若探讨对应型式的准确性,则需要从关键词搭配及扩展意义单位两个方面进行考虑。

---

① 　此处为词性符码后结构,adv. =副词,v. =动词,n. =名词,nn. =多个名词。

（三）多词单位的最佳翻译对应单位考察

为了进一步说明确认对应单位的步骤,可以选取政治文本中经常出现的具有人际功能的偏正结构短语"认真落实"为例进行说明。根据 PTPC 检索,"认真落实"后所跟随的搭配词为政策、措施及各类正式文件,又由于政治文本中多无主分句的特点,"认真落实"左边一般无搭配词,以下为随机抽取的检索行:

表4-3　"认真落实"随机检索行

认真落实和完善支持小型微型企业和个体工商户发展的各项税收优惠政策(2012)
认真落实对农产品批发市场、集贸市场、社区平价菜店等的扶持政策(2013)
认真落实西部大开发新十年的政策措施(2011)
认真落实中央支持少数民族和民族地区发展的政策措施(2010)
认真落实国务院关于鼓励引导民间投资新36条(2014)

按照前文提到的初似对等单位的确认步骤,可以得到频数大于2的5个初似对等单位,如表4-4所示:

表4-4　"认真落实"初似对等单位(>2)

汉语原词	初似对等单位	频数
认真落实	conscientiously implement	15
	fully implement	4
	diligently implement	3
	implement in earnest	2
	carry out in earnest	2

在机器进行自动匹配时,很容易依频数比例将"conscientiously implement"标记为最佳翻译对应单位。为了确定该表达是否可靠,需要利用可比语料库进行验证。在 COCA 中对"conscientiously implement"进行检索,观察其搭配和类联接,发现其频数为0,表明母语表达者中无人使用。而频数第二高的初似对等单位"fully implement"检索显示98条结果。同时,以"implement"为关键词的副词搭配检索得到,常见搭配按照频数大小依次为"fully"(98)、"effectively"(97)、"successfully"(80)、"actually"(46)、"quickly"(31)、"immediately"(20)、"properly"(13)、"carefully"(10)、"consistently"(9)、"efficiently"(9)、"faithfully"(9)。在提取随机行后进行比较,发现"fully implement"通常用于 VN 类联接中,左侧都出现了主语成分,均为"fully implement"的施事主语。值得注意的是,"fully implement"与"认真落实"搭配词语义近似程度高,如其常用搭配"agreement""law""initiative""specifications"均表示正式的规定、政策、措施或法律文件,与"认真落实"的语义趋向高度相似。根据标准的语料库语言学检验步骤,对比关键词的搭配、类联接、语义趋势可以确定,"fully implement"是"认真落实"的最佳对应单位。

三、短语学的实践走向

(一) 自然语言处理(NLP)

自然语言处理一直被认为是人工智能的重要分支,旨在建立一种理解、生成语言的自动系统。当前的 NLP 研究提倡建立语料库,使用机器学习的方法,让计算机自动地从浩如烟海的语料库中获取准确的语言知识。① 这也是 NLP 的优点之一:只要具备精度高的大规模训练语料库,即便研究者不懂有关语言,仍可以使用自动分析软件得出不错的分析结果。这与短语学发展对语料库基础的依赖不谋而合。同时,一般认为 NLP 主要分为两个组成部分:自然语言理解(NLU)及自然语言生成(NLG)。从结构上讲,NLU 主要解决的是词法歧义、句法歧义、语义歧义以及回指歧义②,它被认定与人类语言理解的方式相吻合。而随着短语学的不断发展,语言学家们发现多词单位(也称作"语块"等)是整体储存在母语者大脑中的语言结构,在使用时会被整体调用。这种短语倾向的语言学研究也影响到自然语言处理:自然语言中充满了歧义,这个问题不仅与概率和结构有关,还与短语特性有关。正如 A. 雷说过的那样,"语块是一串预制的连贯或不连贯的词或其他意义单位,它整体存储在记忆中,使用时直接提取,其形式可以原封不动或是稍作改变"③。词法歧义性一直是 NLP 处理的一个难点,从短语学角度分析,单词都不具备独立含义,只有在考察其搭配、类联接选择、语义趋向和语义韵之后,才可以确定其含义和使用方式,也就是理解语义的最普遍单位实则并非单词,而是多词。词法消歧又会影响到句法消歧和语义消歧,基于此,对多词单位的准确理解就直接影响自然语言处理的效果和准确性,并主要体现在 NLP 中词义消歧方法的自立方法(stand-alone approach)上。

　　与语料库短语学联系紧密之处在于,这种方法不需要制定规则,而是通过词类标注来开展工作,从而最大限度地降低提供的信息量,做到

---

① 　冯志伟:《自然语言处理简明教程》,上海外语教育出版社 2012 年版,第 10 页。

② 　回指歧义主要是指上文提到的短语或单词在后面句子中有不同的含义。

③ 　A. Wray, *Formulaic Language: Pushing the Boundaries*, Oxford: Oxford University Press, 2008, p. 9.

"自立"(stand-alone)。这是一种对系统进行训练,使其具备自行消歧功能的方法。进行词义消歧的称为目标词(target word),与之形成上下文关系的语言学特征包括搭配特征和共现特征。基于语料库短语学的训练流程是以多词为中心代替以单词为中心对其上下文进行编码,例如"我们要准确判断形势,保持清醒头脑,增强忧患意识,做好应对风险的准备"一句,这里取"忧患意识"左右两个词及词性标记为特征向量,搭配特征标注如下:

[增强,VVB,忧患意识,NN1,做好,VVB]

这样的标注需要与共现特征结合起来[1],特征的值即是出现在中心短语周围的次数。如果使用垂直领域语料库,训练效果会更好,如本部分提到的 PTPC 结合 BCC[2]。通过随机检索行的观察,在政治语体中与"忧患意识"同时出现的 9 个共现(多)词是:"强烈的""(没)有""危机意识""责任意识""强化""加强"居安思危的"民族""国民"。我们以这 9 个词为窗口(window),在上述例子"……保持\清醒头脑,增强\忧患意识,做好\应对\风险的\准备……"中,这 9 个共现词的特征向量为(增强出现 1 次,其余为 0 次):

[0,0,1,0,0,0,0,0,0]

根据这样的向量,完全可以确定"忧患意识"的具体含义,还可以确认其出现的具体语境。

---

① 这里还涉及句法依存关系,属于文本数据挖掘(Text Data Mining)范畴,考虑到本节只是指出短语学与 NLP 之间的结合以及发展趋势,关于文本挖掘部分,在此不赘述。

② 北京语言大学语料库中心(BLCU Corpus Center,简称 BCC)是以汉语为主、兼有英语和法语的在线语料库,是服务语言本体研究和语言应用研究的在线大数据系统。BCC 语料库总字数约 150 亿字,包括报刊(20 亿)、文学(30 亿)、微博(30 亿)、科技(30 亿)、综合(10 亿)和古汉语(20 亿)等多领域语料,是可以全面反映当今社会语言生活的大规模语料库。BCC 语料库具有数据量大、领域广和检索便捷等优点。

（二）机器翻译

　　语料库短语学影响的另一个实践领域就是狭义的机器翻译训练。机器翻译系统的训练有很多种方式，随着计算机技术不断成熟和语料库语言学的不断发展，基于语料库的机器翻译训练方法已经得到广泛应用。基于语料库的机器翻译训练下分两种方式：一种是基于统计的机器翻译，一种是基于实例的机器翻译。

　　值得注意的是两者的区别：在基于统计的机器翻译方法中，知识的表示仅是统计数据，而不是语料库本身；翻译知识的获取是在翻译之前完成的，在翻译的过程中一般不再使用语料库。在基于实例的机器翻译方法中，双语语料库本身就是翻译知识的一种（不一定是唯一的）表现形式，翻译知识的获取在翻译之前没有全部完成，在翻译的过程中还要查询并利用语料库。[①] 同时也存在基于语料库的方法和基于规则的方法同时采用的机器翻译系统训练方法。不论何种方式，只要是基于语料库的机器翻译训练，势必与语言模型训练数据的规模和精确度相关，也就是说，训练的语料库规模越大，机器翻译的精度越高。日本机器翻译专家长尾真（Nagao Makoto）曾指出，人类并不通过做深层的语言学分析来进行翻译，人类的翻译过程是：首先把输入的句子正确地分解为一些短语碎片，接着把这些短语碎片翻译成其他语言的短语碎片，最后再将这些短语碎片构成完整的句子。每个短语碎片的翻译都是通过类比的原则来实现的，也就是"通过类比来进行翻译"（translation by analogy），这是基于实例的机器翻译训练的原理，也恰恰是对短语学原

---

　　① 　冯志伟：《自然语言处理简明教程》，上海外语教育出版社2012年版，第649页。

理的进一步印证和实践。①

基于实例的机器翻译过程一般可分为三个阶段:匹配(matching)、对齐(alignment)、重新组合(recombination)。首先,正确地进行双语自动对齐:实例库中提供的一般是句级对齐,根据短语学理论和机器翻译的需要,短语级的对齐更具有效度。其次,建立有效的实例匹配检索机制:很多研究者认为,基于实例的机器翻译的潜力在于充分利用短语一级的实例碎片,也就是在短语一级进行对齐;但是,利用的实例碎片越小,碎片的边界越难于确定,歧义情况也就越多,从而导致翻译质量的下降,为此要建立一套相似度准则(similarity metric),以便确定两个句子或者短语碎片是否相似。最后,根据检索到的实例,生成与源语言句子相对应的目标语言译文:由于基于实例的机器翻译对源语言的分析比较粗,生成译文时往往缺乏必要的信息,为了提高译文生成的质量,可以考虑把基于实例的机器翻译与传统的基于规则的机器翻译方法结合起来,对源语言也进行一定深度的分析。②

语料库研究的电子属性决定了它在人工智能时代的蓬勃发展,由语料库催生出的短语学及对比短语学则结合了信息科学原理和标准语料库语言学的标注、统计、描述体系,是对传统语言学理论、自然语言处理及机器翻译实践的延伸和丰富。本节对其进行理论梳理,对研究步骤和应用领域进行说明,旨在指出语料库语言学的演进过程和发展趋向。值得一提的是,这一学科方向与自然语言处理的主要差别在于并

---

① Nagao Makoto, "A Framework of a Mechanical Translation between Japanese and English by Analogy Principle", in Sergei Nirenburg, Harold L. Somers, Yorick A. Wilks (eds.), *Readings in Machine Translation*, Cambridge, MA: The MIT Press, 2003, pp. 173-180.

② 刘群:《汉英机器翻译若干关键技术研究》,清华大学出版社2008年版,第101页。

非追求纯粹的机器自动化,而是寻求在人工智能大时代下人机结合的最佳耦合点。

第二节 《中华人民共和国民法典》的用词差异性及翻译启示

2020 年 5 月 28 日,十三届全国人大三次会议表决通过了《中华人民共和国民法典》,并确定《民法典》自 2021 年 1 月 1 日起施行。《民法典》被认为是我国民法的集大成之作,承前启后、树立典范,是国家治理体系现代化的制度保障。[①] 作为"市民生活的百科全书""公民权利的法律宝典",它不仅承担了为作为平等主体的公民、法人或者非法人组织从事民事活动提供法律依据的作用,更是我国普法推广的重要工具。在内容上,《民法典》对相关法律有继承、修改,更有创新,在形式上亦是如此。语言是法律的载体,其变化绝非简单的"文字游戏"。《民法典》的功能要得到全面充分的发挥,其体系构建和表达方式都值得关注。若要提升法律编纂的科学性,对法条表述技术和规则的研究必不可少。[②] 本节通过结合语言学、法学、翻译学知识,利用语料库工具,探讨《民法典》与先前的《民法通则》及七部单行法在语言上的差异、变化,解释其变化的原因。在此基础上,探讨产生变化的词语的英译并提出一些建议。

---

① 王利明:《民法典:国家治理体系现代化的保障》,《中外法学》2020 年第 4 期。
② 黄文煌:《民法典编纂中的法条表达技术——对〈中华人民共和国民法典(草案)〉条文的梳理》,《暨南学报(哲学社会科学版)》2020 年第 1 期。

一、《民法典》中的用词差异性

《民法典》的形式之变体现在其语言表达、结构安排方面。本部分将聚焦于前者,通过语料库观察《民法典》和已经失效的八部法律的索引行,建立词表,主要关注其中用词的变化。下文将对《民法典》语言偏差实验过程做简单陈述,并展示相关结果。

本研究所用语料为《中华人民共和国民法典》《中华人民共和国民法通则》《中华人民共和国婚姻法》《中华人民共和国继承法》《中华人民共和国收养法》《中华人民共和国担保法》《中华人民共和国合同法》《中华人民共和国物权法》和《中华人民共和国侵权责任法》共九部民法文本,总计 20.4 万字。由于《中华人民共和国民法总则》与《民法典·总则编》表达的重合度较高,因此《民法总则》并未列入目标语料范围,仅用作参考文本。以上所有语料均来自北大法宝法律数据库,冗余信息较少,但仍需做进一步清噪和标注。整理清噪方面,作者使用了文本整理器软件,以方便对多个文本进行批量整理,去除多余空格、段间空行和跳格等。然后使用 PowerGREP 进行重新编码,采用 Windows 936 格式,方便之后运用语料库进行汉语文本的检索。对以上民法纯文本进行分词处理使用的软件是 Yacsi0.96 汉语分词工具,在分词的同时,软件还可以对词类进行标注,为之后观察分析语料打下了基础。

分词完成后,语料总规模为 105375 词。将《民法典》和另外八部民法文本录入 AntConc,并分别生成词表,使用停止词表工具去除如法条

序号等干扰词,得到《民法典》词表共 2540 项,其他民法词表共 2423
项。在此基础上,笔者选用卡方检验的方法,以其他民法词表为参照,
检验《民法典》的用词差异。本部分所选用的卡方检验工具由北京外
国语大学梁茂成教授开发,是检验词项跨库差异显著性的常用工具。①
图 4-4 是《民法典》词表录入工具后的部分结果展示,梁教授在卡方工
具中给出了卡方值对应的显著性水平的 P 值(分别为 0.05、0.01 和
0.001),并标注了区间星号(对应 *、** 和 ***),便于使用者观察。
因此,我们可以通过 significance(显著性)一栏可以清楚地看出《民法
典》中各词项与之前的民法文本相比是否存在显著差异,并从后方的
"+"或"-"辨别某词项在《民法典》中是过多使用(overuse)还是使用不
足(underused)。

Chi-Square Calculator

	Corpus 1	Corpus 2	
Corpus Size:	52,087	49,072	

Word	Freq in Corpus 1	Freq in Corpus 2	Chi-Square	Significance	
的	4053	4113	12.2720	0.0004597977 ***	-
或者	1027	819	12.9249	0.0003242441 ***	+
不	599	498	4.3034	0.0380362084 *	+
有	586	477	5.6885	0.0170763019 *	+
合同	557	692	24.0667	0.0000009306 ***	-
权	544	675	23.2704	0.0000014075 ***	-
物	406	501	16.5822	0.0000465855 ***	-
责任	379	446	10.2606	0.0013590135 **	-
民事	268	186	10.3817	0.0012727105 **	+
其	258	144	26.0164	0.0000003385 ***	+
行为	248	181	6.8864	0.0086852102 **	+
财产	233	295	11.5154	0.0006902278 ***	-
被	230	156	10.1661	0.0014304427 **	+
请求	229	93	49.8229	0.0000000000 ***	+
期限	223	121	24.5750	0.0000007147 ***	+
但是	221	3	199.9850	0.0000000000 ***	+
法人	183	90	26.4751	0.0000002670 ***	+

图 4-4　卡方检验部分结果

---

　　①　梁茂成、李文中、许家金:《语料库应用教程》,外语教学与研究出版社 2010 年版,
第 92 页。

卡方检验的结果显示,《民法典》词表中共有 195 项存在显著偏差,占总数的 7.6%。其中有 95 项为过多使用的词,100 项使用不足。在 95 项过多使用的词项中,有 29 项差异极大($p<0.001$),30 项差异很大($0.001<p<0.01$),36 项差异大($0.01<p<0.05$);相应地,在使用不足的词项中,差异极大的有 28 项,差异很大的有 23 项,差异大的有 49 项。由此可见,《民法典》在语言表达上与其前身存在一定差异性,在用词方面差异较小。即使在存在显著差异的用词当中,也是差异大的一类数量最多,差异极大和很大的数量较少。另外,使用过多和使用不足的词数量相当,其中差异极大的词数量尤为相近,有可能构成相应的增减关系。

二、从"要求"到"请求"的差异分析

在以上数据基础上,笔者对于《民法典》中差异性显著的用词进行了更细致的观察和比较,并参考王轶教授对《民法典》之"变"的相关分类[①],将《民法典》语言的差异表达分为两类:第一类属于解释选择的结果,第二类则属于立法技术引发的差异。前者是为了使用有限的民法条文来表达尽可能多的生活概念,比如确定某一生活概念是否应该入法,或者明确某个民法概念的行文,即其并不涉及事实判断或者价值判断;而后者则涉及诸多价值判断结果的共存问题,比如法典的体例编排和一些下位概念的区分问题。[②] 本部分将聚焦于第一类由解释选择问题引发的差异化表达,此类修改虽然形式有变,但词义内涵改变幅度较

---

① 王轶:《民法典之"变"》,《东方法学》2020 年第 4 期。
② 王轶:《民法典编纂争议问题的类型区分》,《清华法学》2020 年第 3 期。

小。因此，如何在翻译中使其内涵和形式做到统一，是《民法典》英译的关键之一。根据卡方检验结果，笔者选择了其中较有代表性的一组用词改变，即从"要求"到"请求"，以探讨其背后的原因，并据此对相关词语的翻译提出一点自己的建议。

《民法典》中，"要求"和"请求"两词存在相应减少和增加的现象，属于有显著性差异的词，且差异极大。根据语料库检索数据，在前八部法律文本中，共有141处"要求"，其中107处为动词。而在《民法典》中，"要求"一词的频数骤减至57处，且仅有22处用作动词，属于典型的使用不足词。经过对相关索引行的对比可以发现，《民法典》中其他涉及"要求"用作动词的表达均被修改为"请求"。

笔者认为，这一修改不仅对具有细微差异的汉语词做出了更精细的区分，更体现了《民法典》对于请求权的明确：一直以来，请求权都是民法权利义务体系的构成枢纽。此概念贯穿《德国民法典》全文，据其总则部分一百九十四条第一款规定，请求权（anspruch）是一种"向他人请求作为或不作为的权利"[1]（the right to demand an act or forbearance from another[2]）。即请求权至少涉及两个对象，一为权利人，二为义务人。但请求权的客体并非义务人，而是义务人的行为，需要义务人的配合，权利人无权强制义务人作为或不作为。[3]

在本部分涉及的前八部法律文本以及 2017 年颁布的《民法总则》中，具体描述权利人行使请求权的条文均使用"要求"一词。如《合同法》第九十七条规定："合同解除后，尚未履行的，终止履行；已经履行的，根据履行情况和合同性质，当事人可以要求恢复原状、采取其他补

---

[1] 《德国民法典》（第 4 版），陈卫佐译注，法律出版社 2015 年版，第 66 页。

[2] Wang Chonghui, *The German Civil Code Translated and Annotated with An Historical Introduction and Appendices*, London：Stevens and Sons Limited，1907，p. 43.

[3] 金可可：《德国民法上的请求权概念》，《求索》2007 年第 3 期。

救措施,并有权要求赔偿损失。"结合合同性质和请求权定义,不难发现当事人此处行使的权利为典型的请求权,是合同一方在合同解除后请求中止履行或损害赔偿以减小或弥补自身损失的权利。但合同双方当事人的地位是平等的,权利受到侵害的一方并不会因此拥有类似于形成权的绝对性权利,当事人应仍然以请求的方式提请保护。此条在《民法典·合同编》中,两处"要求"均改为"请求"。① 相比"请求","要求"一词更富强制性,难以体现权利人和请求权作用客体之间的非强制关系。而如《民法典》第二百一十二条(《物权法》第十二条)规定:"申请登记的不动产的有关情况需要进一步证明的,登记机构可以要求申请人补充材料,必要时可以实地查看。"此处的"要求"涉及双方为登记机构和申请人,属行政行为,并非民事权利中的请求权范围,因而保留了原"要求"表达,未做修改。如此一来,"请求"与"请求权"之间的相关性一目了然。这是《民法典》在语言上清晰化、明确化的重要体现。

三、对"请求"一词的翻译探讨

从制定者的意图上来说,"要求"和"请求"在上述语境中应当表达的内涵是相同的,但从词义本身来说,二者存在程度上的差异。因此,其形式上的改变是否需要在译文中有所体现,以及改变译文能否达成《民法典》的明确化意图,是选定其译文的重点。目前,此处可选的译文有四种:在王宠惠先生的《德国民法典》英译本中,他将请求权的动作译为"demand";同时,王宠惠先生的译本中使用"claim"作为"请求权"名词的英译,结合 claim 本身的动词属性,本部分也将其作为译文

---

① 参见《中华人民共和国民法典》第五百六十六条第一款。

候选之一;而在国务院法制办所编制的《合同法》官方译本和北大法宝平台译本中,作为动词的"要求"均译为"require";此外,《民法典》正式颁布之后,秘塔科技和北大法宝的先行译本均采用了"request"作为修改后"请求"的译文。

本部分将从两个角度对相关译文进行选择和验证:首先,从四种备选译文的基础语义入手,从 iWeb 语料库中找出四种译文在现代英语中的常用搭配,从每个词的搭配中选取互信息值最高的 20 项进行语义分析。然后根据《布莱克法律词典》(*Black's Law Dictionary*)①的专业释义验证其是否有法律内涵,并做比较以确定最合适的译文。

(一)基础语义辨析

根据 iWeb 语料库的检索结果,从四种译文各自的显著搭配词来看,三者在基础语义上的侧重点并不相同。表 4 - 5 为"demand"的显著搭配词表,在节点词前后四个词的范围内,共有名词 11 个、动词 1 个、形容词 4 个、副词 4 个,其中表消极语义的词 7 个,积极语义词仅 1 个,中性词 12 个(本部分采用"="表示中性词,"-"表示消极语义词,"+"表示积极意义词)。但中性词中又有 6 项如"reparation"(赔偿)等词,内含重新做某事或补救某事的消极含义。根据词表,可见 demand 常与消极语义的词搭配,如"ouster"(罢免)、"angrily"(愤怒地)、"bossy"(专横的)等。从搭配词的词义来看,demand 语气强硬、直接,且与绑架相关词汇搭配极多,如"ransom"(赎金)、"kidnapper"(绑匪)、"ultimatum"(最后通牒)等,存在一定的"非法性"。

---

① Bryan A. Garner (eds.), *Black's Law Dictionary (10th ed.)*, St. Paul: Thomson Reuters, 2014.

表 4-5　"demand"的显著搭配词表

序号	频数	互信息值	搭配	词类	语义倾向
1	1872	7.14	ransom	n.	-
2	264	7.04	cognitively	adv.	=
3	284	6.48	recount	n.	= -
4	67	6.46	unquestioning	adj.	=
5	152	6.40	ouster	n.	-
6	322	6.34	outstrip	v.	=
7	116	6.26	computationally	adv.	=
8	6659	5.94	physically	adv.	=
9	322	5.86	reparation	n.	= -
10	86	5.82	inelastic	adj.	=
11	206	5.74	retraction	n.	= -
12	151	5.70	kidnapper	n.	-
13	776	5.66	surrender	n.	-
14	251	5.54	angrily	adv.	-
15	1026	5.53	resignation	n.	= -
16	55	5.46	fealty	n.	+
17	63	5.18	recompense	n.	= -
18	169	5.18	fast-paced	adj.	=
19	79	5.14	bossy	adj.	-
20	123	5.14	ultimatum	n.	-

　　表 4-6 展示了"claim"一词的显著搭配项,其搭配中名词最多,共有 10 项;副词其次,共有 7 项;接下来是形容词 2 项、动词 1 项。与 demand 相比,claim 与明显含消极意义的词搭配更多,共有 10 项,其后

为中性词7项、积极含义词2项。根据词义,claim与"判断"这一行为
密切相关,涉及对信任与否、对错、真假的选择,且结果往往为负面的,
有搭配如"falsely"(虚假地)、"credibly"(可信地)和"plausibly"(合理
地)等。

表 4-6　"claim"的显著搭配词表

序号	频数	互信息值	搭配	词类	语义倾向
1	4740	6.96	falsely	adv.	−
2	8672	5.86	deduction	n.	=
3	529	5.61	fraudulently	adv.	−
4	170	5.45	credibly	adv.	+
5	64	5.45	wiretapped	v.	−
6	1172	5.13	adjuster	n.	=
7	67	5.13	sensationally	adv.	−
8	231	5.04	evolutionist	n.	=
9	171	5.04	plausibly	adv.	−
10	785	4.97	tort	n.	=
11	5158	4.94	exemption	n.	= −
12	69	4.90	bragging	adj.	−
13	81	4.84	victimhood	n.	=
14	364	4.82	creationist	n.	=
15	78	4.80	dishonestly	adv.	−
16	52	4.71	overpaid	adj.	−
17	118	4.70	infallibility	n.	+
18	356	4.69	erroneously	adv.	−
19	151	4.60	whiplash	n.	−
20	454	4.58	authorship	n.	=

　　同样地,通过表4-7可以观察到"require"与名词的搭配较多,共15项。不同于前两项译文的是,require 的所有搭配均为中性词,但部分存在消极或积极倾向。如带 re-前缀的"rethinking"(重新考虑)、"re-inspection"(再次检验)等,以及表示绝对多数的"supermajority"。根据"preregistration"(预注册)、"preauthorization"(预授权)、"notarization"(公证)和"statutorily"(法定)等显著搭配词,可见 require 与程序,尤其是法律程序密切相关,语义上有一定权威性,较为正式。另外,相比 demand,require 语气更加和缓,且合法程度高,同时也不带有 claim 所含的判断内涵。

表4-7　"require"的显著搭配词表

序号	频数	互信息值	搭配	词类	语义倾向
1	416	5.99	preregistration	n.	=
2	167	5.44	preauthorization	n.	=
3	315	5.34	supermajority	n.	=
4	286	5.30	soldering	n.	=
5	257	5.19	notarization	n.	=
6	444	5.10	attunement	n.	=
7	202	5.09	self-assembly	n.	=
8	129	4.83	closed-toe	adj.	=
9	671	4.76	forethought	n.	=
10	3372	4.76	hospitalization	n.	=
11	270	4.62	rethinking	n.	= -
12	245	4.59	statutorily	adv.	=
13	100	4.53	phytosanitary	adj.	=
14	129	4.50	recertify	v.	= -
15	1004	4.39	disassembly	adv.	=

序号	频数	互信息值	搭配	词类	语义倾向
16	88	4.36	re-inspection	n.	= –
17	153	4.34	rinsing	n.	=
18	306	4.28	co-signer	n.	=
19	1315	4.26	vigilance	n.	=
20	200	4.24	recalibration	n.	= –

最后,"request"一项与名词的搭配是四项备选译文中最多的(16项),且在互信息值最高的20项中没有与动词的搭配(见表4-8)。通过"respectfully"(恭敬地)和"humbly"(谦逊地)两项副词搭配,可以看出 request 做动词时动作更为和缓,有礼貌之意。语义上,request 与中性词搭配最多,其中也有含消极偏向的词汇,如"unmasking"(暴露)和"recount"(重新计算)等。另有搭配消极意义词 3 项,积极意义词 2 项。根据"rehearing"(重审)、"adjournment"(休庭)等词可以看出,它也和程序密切相关。但与 require 不同的是,request 更强调程序作为客体时,主体对其的动作,如推迟、延期、加快等等,而 require 则强调客体本身。

表4-8　"request"的显著搭配词表

序号	频数	互信息值	搭配	词类	语义倾向
1	501	7.12	interlibrary	adj.	=
2	1102	6.98	reconsideration	n.	= –
3	95	6.80	redetermination	n.	= –
4	58	6.55	preauthorization	n.	=
5	1437	6.25	respectfully	adv.	+

序号	频数	互信息值	搭配	词类	语义倾向
6	51	6.24	unmasking	n.	= -
7	1787	6.17	anonymity	n.	=
8	82	6.05	rehearing	n.	= -
9	383	5.95	deferment	n.	-
10	233	5.69	adjournment	n.	=
11	609	5.68	absentee	n.	
12	7689	5.66	transcript	n.	
13	273	5.58	recount	n.	= -
14	292	5.51	postponement	n.	-
15	628	5.39	expedited	adj.	
16	296	5.36	deferral	n.	-
17	57	5.31	time-off	n.	=
18	369	5.30	extradition	n.	=
19	9398	5.30	refund	n.	= -
20	404	5.13	humbly	adv.	+

　　基础语义的分析体现了 demand、claim、require 和 request 四项备选译文的语义韵倾向。四者虽然都有作为要求和/或请求的释义,但通过搭配,可以发现它们各自强调的重点不同,使用的语气也不同。相较而言,demand 比较强硬,其与 claim 的语义韵为消极,而 require 和 request 更为柔和,且搭配多为中性,较符合"请求"一词在汉语中的定位。

(二) 法律语义辨析

　　在《布莱克法律词典》第十版中,对动词 demand 的释义有两项。

第一项中又有少许区别,分别为:要求、索取应得的东西;与动词 require 同义;寻求救济。第二项则特指传唤,用于"传唤某人到法庭"这一动作。可见 demand 和 require 在法律语义上有重合,都有要求、索取的含义。

另外三项译文 claim、request 和 require 在《布莱克法律词典》中均无用作动词的释义,都以名词形式出现。其中,claim 有三个义项:一为对有待证实的事情的陈述;二是对现有权利的主张,指任何获得款项或衡平法上的救济的权利,且此种权利可以是或有的或暂时的;三是金钱、财产或法律救济的"要求"(原文为"demand"),或是权利人得以主张权利的法律救济。因此,作为法律术语的 claim,其核心意义就在于对权利的主张,这是它特有的法律内涵,在基础语义中并未体现。

request 在《布莱克法律词典》中释义为议会法中的专用术语,解释为议员行使一项权利、寻求行使一项特权的许可或提出问题的动作。此处可见,虽然 request 并无做动词的法律释义,但其仍然是在描述一个动作,且含有"行使权力"的内涵。

而 require 的名词 requirement 是四者中解释最多的词,共有四个义项,分别为:(1)因法律或规则而必须做的事;法律上强加的、要求的东西;强制性命令。(2)某人需求或者要求的东西。(3)被雇主或大学等认定为必要资格的东西。(4)把某物确定为需要或必要的行为;与名词 demand 同义。根据释义,require 与法律密切相关,这与对其基础语义的分析结果相吻合。但 require 的法律释义中,动作有强制、命令、必须之意,这与汉语中"请求"的内涵不符。另外,require 的第四个义项再次证明其与 demand 存在部分语义重合,无论是作为动词使用还是其名词 requirement,require 都可以在特定情况下与 demand 互换。

结合以上两方面的分析,笔者认为《民法典》中"请求"一词选用

"request"最为合适,原因有三:首先,在基础语义上,require 和 request 语气比较和缓,与"请求"相吻合。进一步分析,request 和 require 虽然同样与程序相关,但二者强调的客体并不相同,request 更强调针对程序的动作,符合"请求"这一动作的内涵。其次,在法律内涵上,根据《布莱克法律词典》的释义,require 和 demand 在法律用语中的语义有重合,强调动作的强制性和规定性。而请求权虽有法律基础支撑,受法律保护,但并非强制性权利,在这一点上 require 和 demand 并不合适。claim 和 request 无强制含义,且均表达行使一项权利,更为合适。但是 claim 的基础语义中语义韵消极,常用于判断对错,不及 request 与"请求"契合。最后,经过在中国法律法规汉英平行语料库中的检索,笔者发现 require 和 claim 都曾被用作"要求"一词的译文,因此若在《民法典》译文中将"请求"统一译为"request",能够达到体现其形式变化的目的。事实上,在官方发布的《民法典》英译本中①,由"要求"修改而来的"请求"一词也确实将 request 作为译文,并注意到了与未修改处的"要求"翻译加以区别。

本节结合语言学、法学、翻译学相关知识和方法,对《民法典》中的用词变化及变化后的英译进行了探讨。根据对《民法典》词表进行卡方检验之后的结果,笔者决定对"要求"和"请求"这一对存在显著变化的动词进行分析,并认为此处修改的原因是立法者要将《民法典》中的请求权概念明确化。这一汉语词的改变同时带来了英译词选择的问题。根据现有的翻译,笔者对四个译文候选词 demand、claim、require 和

---

① 该译本 2020 年 12 月于中国人大网首次发布,此后亦经过修改。虽然作为官方发布译本,但其开头部分特别标注"this translation is for reference only",表明其主要具有参考意义。该文本具体内容见 http://en. npc. gov. cn. cdurl. cn/pdf/civilcodeofthepeoplesrepublic ofchina. pdf。

request 进行了语义分析,从其基础语义和法律内涵两方面入手,运用线上语料库和法律专业词典,最终确定最佳译文为 request。作为此语境下与"请求"最为契合的译文,request 不仅能做到在《民法典》译文中体现用词形式上的改变,也能达成《民法典》对请求权明确化的意图。而除"要求"和"请求"这一对有显著变化的词之外,《民法典》中还有由"民事行为"到"民事法律行为"之变、从"社会公共利益""社会公德"到"公序良俗"之变、"损害"和"损失"二词的搭配变化等等文本变更。以上变化均出于使民法概念更加清晰的解释选择问题,相关译文的确定也十分值得探讨。此外,立法技术问题所带来的形式变化同样值得关注。《中华人民共和国民法典》作为我国第一部民法典,必然是中国乃至世界法律学者瞩目的对象,其英译的形式安排、术语推敲不仅能够决定相关法律在实践中发挥的作用,更影响着我国法律甚至国家的对外形象,以及我国在国际上全面构建自身话语体系的努力。在此背景下,以本节的研究为例,希望相关探索能够为《民法典》语言相关研究和翻译提供一定帮助。

第三节　语料库驱动下民法术语变迁及其英译研究(1978—2020)

1978 年 12 月召开的中共十一届三中全会,标志着中国对内改革、对外开放的新时代正式开启。自这场全方位的历史性变革开始,市场化和法治化成为我国发展的主要议题。十一届三中全会提出"有法可依、有法必依、执法必严、违法必究"的"十六字方针";近二十年后,

1997 年的中共十五大又确立了"依法治国"的四字方略；至 2012 年，中共十八大进一步提出了"科学立法、严格执法、公正司法、全民守法"的"新十六字方针"。在这四十多年中，社会主义法律体系建设，尤其是反映市场化改革要求的私法体系建设已经取得了巨大的成就。[①] 2021 年，《中华人民共和国民法典》正式开始施行，这部民法的集大成之作是我国国家治理体系现代化的制度保障，标志着我国民法的法典化运动进入了全新的阶段，其体现的新思想、新内涵都是法学及各交叉领域学者所关注的对象。

但无论我们的法律思想、制度如何变化，表达法律的方式始终不变。"学习法律的第一要务是学习法律的语言，以及与之相关的、使得该语言知识能够在法律实践中得到应用的语言技能。"[②]语言作为法律的载体，是法治精神的具体体现。根据前人研究，可归纳出立法语言存在权威性、准确性、简洁性、模糊性的特征。[③] 在这四十多年的发展历程中，我国民法在术语选择、句法使用、语篇构建等方面都体现了向以上四点靠近的趋势。本节从民法语言的历时变化入手，结合语言学、法学、翻译学知识，采用语料库驱动的研究路径，探讨 1978 年至 2020 年我国主要民法文本在语言上的差异、变化，并解释其变化的原因。回望社会变革和制度变迁，发掘中国法律语言的当代性，有助于我国民事立法语言及其翻译规范的确立。

---

① 柳经纬：《改革开放以来民法学的理论转型——百年中国民法学之考察之二》，《中国政法大学学报》2010 年第 3 期。

② Peter Goodrich, "Law and Languages: An Historical and Critical Introduction", 转引自程朝阳：《法律语言学导论——英美法律语言研究述介》，《中国法学教育研究》2010 年第 1 期。

③ 郭龙生：《浅议立法语言规范》，《语言与法律研究》2020 年第 1 期。

一、1978 年至 2020 年民法文本的差异性

本研究主要采用语料库驱动的研究路径,从我国民法文本的实例中归纳出其在特定阶段的立法语言模式。所使用的语料以《民法典》的七编内容为参考,选取 1978 年至 2020 年间全国人大及其常委会制定的各版本《中华人民共和国民法通则》《中华人民共和国物权法》《中华人民共和国合同法》《中华人民共和国婚姻法》《中华人民共和国继承法》《中华人民共和国收养法》《中华人民共和国侵权责任法》《中华人民共和国担保法》以及《民法典》等共 16 部法律,建成语料库,总计约 25 万字。由于《中华人民共和国民法总则》与《民法典·总则编》表达重合度较高,因此《民法总则》并未列入目标语料范围,仅作为参考文本。

以上所有语料均来自北大法宝法律数据库,冗余信息较少。使用文本整理器软件进行整理和清噪之后,再使用 PowerGREP 将纯文本重新编码为 Windows 936 格式,方便之后运用语料库进行汉语文本的检索。对以上民法纯文本进行分词处理使用的软件是由教育部语言文字应用研究所肖航教授开发的 CorpusWordParser 分词和词性标注工具,软件来源于语料库在线网站。①

分词完成后,语料总规模为 6883 词。为了更准确地进行对比,本部分将目标语料分为三组:第一组为研究阶段内发布且已经失效或已经修订的法律,第二组为该阶段内发布且仍有效的法律,第三组为该阶段内发布但

---

① 肖航:《现代汉语通用平衡语料库建设与应用》,《华文世界》(台湾)2010 年第 106 期;靳光瑾、肖航、富丽、章云帆:《现代汉语语料库建设及深加工》,《语言文字应用》2005 年第 2 期;肖航:《语料库词义标注研究》,云南教育出版社 2016 年版。

尚未生效的法律(即《民法典》)。将所有 16 部法律按上述分组录入 AntConc,并分别生成词表,使用停止词表工具去除如法条序号等干扰词,得到第一组词表共 1818 项,第二组词表共 2485 项,第三组词表共 2580 项。最后使用卡方检验的方法,将三组词表两两对比,检验相邻两组间的用词差异。

卡方检验结果显示,在尚有效组和已失效/已修订组对比中,共有 379 项存在显著偏差,占总数的 15.2%,其中有 135 项为过多使用的词,244 项为使用不足的词。在 135 项过多使用的词项中,有 62 项差异极大(p<0.001),33 项差异很大(0.001<p<0.01),40 项差异大(0.01<p<0.05);相应地,在使用不足的词项中,差异极大的有 97 项,差异很大的有 57 项,差异大的有 90 项。而在未生效组和尚有效组的对比中,共有 180 项存在显著偏差,占总数的 6.9%。其中有 91 项为过多使用的词,89 项为使用不足的词。在 91 项过度使用的词项中,有 31 项差异极大,26 项差异很大,34 项差异大;而在使用不足的词项中,差异极大的有 27 项,差异很大的有 17 项,差异大的有 45 项。

由此可见,1978 年至 2020 年间,民法文本中的术语变化较大,分组之间均存在差异性。相比之下,尚有效组和已失效/已修订组之间的差异性更大,无论是过多使用的词还是使用不足的词,均是差异极大的最多;而未生效组和尚有效组之间从数据来看差异相对小些,即使在存在显著差异的用词当中,也是差异大的一类数量最多,差异极大和很大的数量较少。

二、1978 年至 2020 年民法术语的变迁

基于以上数据,可以对不同组间变化的术语做进一步观察和比较。本节同样参考了王轶教授对民法典之"变"的相关分类,将变化术语分为"解释选择的结果"和"立法技术引发的差异"这两类[1],并聚焦于第

---

[1]　王轶:《民法典编纂争议问题的类型区分》,《清华法学》2020 年第 3 期。

一类变化术语。根据卡方检验结果,本部分选择了其中较有代表性的
两组改变,探讨其背后的原因,并据此对相关术语的翻译提出建议。

（一）公序良俗原则变迁:从"社会公共利益"到"公序良俗"

公序良俗原则是现代民法体系中的基本原则之一,在大陆法系的
民法体系中占据了重要地位。其在民事领域的运用历史可以追溯到古
罗马时期,经过长久的实践与发展,各国对该原则的应用根据实际情况
也有所不同。总的来说,可以将其分为以法国和德国为代表的两种不
同模式:前者对违反公序良俗的法律行为或者法律行为中的某一部分
进行了详细的规定,后者则使用概括式的立法技术。我国对公序良俗
原则的应用有明显的《德国民法典》特征,即直接规定不得违反公序良
俗或违反公序良俗的民事法律行为无效,但并未具体列出构成违反公
序良俗的细节因素。①

但值得注意的是,虽然我国民法在多处对公序良俗原则有所体现,
包括《民法通则》第七条及第五十八条第一款第五项、《合同法》第七条
及第五十二条第四项、《物权法》第七条等等,但"公序良俗"一词在很
长时间内都未在法律文本中直接出现。从 1978 年至 2020 年间,早期
各民事法律文本中多使用"国家利益""公共利益"或者"社会公德"来
规定公序良俗方面的内容。直至 2017 年《民法总则》颁布,其中第八
条首次使用"公序良俗"一词表述该原则,从而明确了其作为我国民法
基本原则的地位。《民法典·总则编》沿用了这一弹性表达(第八条),
并在各分编中规定了公序良俗原则针对特定民事行为的具体应用。

---

① 戴孟勇:《法律行为与公序良俗》,《法学家》2020 第 1 期。

　　根据对研究时段内已失效/已修订、尚有效、未生效的三组语料进行两两对比的结果,"公共利益"和"国家利益"两组术语属于在不同阶段运用差异性极大的词。在第一组已失效/已修订法律和第二组尚有效法律对比中,上述两项术语及"国家计划"的使用显著不足;而在第二组和第三组《民法典》的对比当中,"公共利益""国家利益""社会公德""国家计划"使用率均下降,而"公序良俗"使用率明显提升(见表4-9)。根据该数据对文本进行检索比对可发现,"公序良俗"一词与前三组术语存在替换关系。

表4-9　"公序良俗"相关表达卡方检验对比结果

卡方检验工具(Chi-Square Calculator)						
	尚有效组(Corpus 2)		已失效/已修订组(Corpus 1)			
总词数(Corpus Size)	48036		21500			
词(Word)	尚有效组中词频(Freq in Corpus 2)	已失效/已修订组中词频(Freq in Corpus 1)	卡方值(Chi-Square)	P 值(Significance)		
公共利益	12	22	18. 1801	0. 000	＊＊＊	－
国家利益	3	15	23. 1577	0. 000	＊＊＊	－
社会公德	6	2	0. 1312	0. 717		＋
经济秩序	3	5	3. 7359	0. 053		－
经济计划	0	1	2. 2343	0. 135		－
国家计划	1	4	5. 6395	0. 018	＊	－
公序良俗	0	0	0	/	/	/
	未生效组(Corpus 3)		尚有效组(Corpus 2)			
总词数(Corpus Size)	51158		48036			
词(Word)	未生效组中词频(Freq in Corpus 3)	尚有效组中词频(Freq in Corpus 2)	卡方值(Chi-Square)	P 值(Significance)		
公共利益	11	12	0. 1294	0. 719		－
国家利益	2	3	0. 2682	0. 605		－

词(Word)	未生效组中词频(Freq in Corpus 3)	尚有效组中词频(Freq in Corpus 2)	卡方值 (Chi-Square)	P 值 (Significance)		
社会公德	1	6	3.8972	0.048	*	−
经济秩序	1	3	1.1310	0.288		−
经济计划	0	0	0	/	/	/
国家计划	0	1	1.0650	0.302		−
公序良俗	8	0	7.5124	0.006	**	+

笔者认为,导致此变化的原因可以分为两个方面:从形式上来说,我国对立法语言规范性的重视日益提升,公序良俗作为一种统一表达,起到整合、规范前期大量不同相关表述的作用,体现了我国民法表达越发注重法理与文本的协调性;而在内容上,该表达的变化不仅与我国政治制度和经济制度的发展密切相关,同时也是我国在发展中践行德治与法治相结合的中国特色社会主义法治道路的体现。

具体而言,在形式上,由前两组法律文本的对比可见,早前我国对于公序良俗原则的表达均使用列举的方式。该种表达方式在大陆法系的民法中并不常见。相比《德国民法典》《日本民法典》,我国对"公序良俗"的界定更为细致;但与法国、意大利等国相比,我国又并未详细列出违反公序良俗的行为细节。出于国家政策、立法程序等原因,在各民法文本中,所列举的公序良俗内容各有不同,并无统一规范。因此,将其修改为"公序良俗"不仅可以对之前众多单行法中语义相似但表述不同的相关法规加以统一与整合,更能通过立法的方式明确其地位。同时,四字格也更具书面语的正式属性,符合法律文本的特点。

从内容上讲,一方面,公序良俗原则是我国经济制度的配套法律表述之一。1978 年至 2020 年期间,最早提及公序良俗原则的民法文本为 1981 年制定的《经济合同法》,其中第四条规定:"任何单位和个人不得利用合同进行违法活动,扰乱经济秩序,破坏国家计划,损害国家利益和社会公共利益,牟取非法收入。"随后的 1986 年《民法通则》第七条也有类似表达:"民事活动应当尊重社会公德,不得损害社会公共利益,破坏国家经济计划,扰乱社会经济秩序。"这样的表述与我国当时的国家政策和社会情况息息相关,体现了我国对于该原则的"特殊理解"①:1978 年,中共十一届三中全会召开,邓小平等人提出了"对内改革、对外开放"的理论,中国改革开放正式拉开帷幕。随后从 1979 年至 1986 年,我国分阶段采取了以计划经济为主、市场调节为辅和有计划的商品经济的经济体制。在这种背景下,国家经济计划也成为私法保护的对象之一,在民法文本中,其作为"公序"的具体表达并随之出现。而至 1999 年《合同法》颁布,其中第七条规定:"当事人订立、履行合同,应当遵守法律、行政法规,尊重社会公德,不得扰乱社会经济秩序,损害社会公共利益。"该条去除了关于国家计划或者经济计划的内容,提升了合同自由程度,进一步放开了市场。这也与当时所提出的确立和建设社会主义市场经济体制的政策相吻合。

另一方面,"公序良俗"概念相比于列举型表述更具弹性,它对应的范围较为宽泛,有助于该原则在社会发展与地域变迁的前提下仍保持合理性与适用性。目前法律学界与实务界普遍认为"公序良俗"包括公共秩序与善良风俗。公共秩序包括宪法与法律法规等规定的社会公共秩序,也包括人类社会发展过程中普遍形成的生活秩序;善良风俗

---

① 龙卫球:《我国民法基本原则的内容嬗变与体系化意义——关于〈民法总则〉第一章第 3—9 条的重点解读》,《法治现代化研究》2017 年第 1 期。

包括带有道德约束性的基本社会公德以及处于较高道德层次的良好社会风尚。两者的覆盖范围相比之前的具体规定更加全面。自党的十八届四中全会提出"坚持依法治国和以德治国相结合"以来,如何达到法治与德治的平衡就一直是学界的热点话题。法治与德治相结合要求法律具有良善属性,公序良俗原则简洁而又全面地将基础社会公德与良好社会风尚作为明文法律的补充,以良善道德弥补法律的漏洞,保证了法律的良善属性。同时,公序良俗原则表述的精简有利于向社会公众普及该原则,提升道德治理的规范性与强制性,从而帮助德治更好地融入社会治理体系,实现法治与德治相结合的中国特色社会主义法治建设。

(二) 民事主体变迁:从"其他组织"到"非法人组织"

民事主体一直以来都是民法的重点之一。从 1978 年至今,我国民法中对民事主体的界定和表达也经历了多次修改。根据语料库数据和卡方检验结果可以发现,在民事主体的一系列相关表达中,"非法人组织"与"其他组织"、"自然人"与"公民"两组表达存在对应的增减关系,且在各组对比中均为有差异的表达(见表 4 - 10)。本部分主要聚焦于前者,即"非法人主体"与"其他组织"在研究时段内的变化。由下表可见,在已失效/已修订组和尚有效组中,"其他组织"的使用频率有所增加,而在未生效组中,该表达频率骤降为零;与此相反的是,在前两组中从未出现过的"非法人组织"的使用频率则在第三组中大量上升。经过对文本的进一步检索对照可以确定,"非法人组织"被用于代替所有的"其他组织"表达,并成为《民法典》中固定的术语之一。

表 4-10 民事主体相关表达卡方检验对比结果

卡方检验工具（Chi-Square Calculator）						
	尚有效组（Corpus 2）	已失效/已修订组（Corpus 1）				
总词数（Corpus Size）	48036	21500				
词（Word）	尚有效组中词频（Freq in Corpus 2）	已失效/已修订组中词频（Freq in Corpus 1）	卡方值（Chi-Square）	P 值（Significance）		
其他组织	12	1	3.2841	0.070		+
非法人组织	0	0	/	/	/	/
公民	71	58	11.9308	0.001	＊＊	－
自然人	8	1	1.6535	0.198		+
法人	66	61	17.4432	0.000	＊＊＊	－
个体工商户	10	10	3.4100	0.065		－
农村承包经营户	4	6	3.9599	0.047	＊	－
	未生效组（Corpus 3）	尚有效组（Corpus 2）				
总词数（Corpus Size）	51158	43490				
词（Word）	未生效组中词频（Freq in Corpus 3）	尚有效组中词频（Freq in Corpus 2）	卡方值（Chi-Square）	P 值（Significance）		
其他组织	0	12	12.7815	0.000	＊＊＊	－
非法人组织	29	0	27.2382	0.000	＊＊＊	+
公民	0	71	75.6687	0.000	＊＊＊	－
自然人	65	8	41.0620	0.000	＊＊＊	+
法人	183	66	48.0257	0.000	＊＊＊	+
个体工商户	5	10	1.9985	0.157		
农村承包经营户	3	4	0.2130	0.644		－

　　笔者认为,这一变化直观地体现了改革开放之后我国民事主体的分类随经济活动的增加逐渐明确,相关术语也越发规范化。在我国民法法规制定的过程中,民事主体的"两分"与"三分"一直是学者与立法者争论的焦点。在《民法总则》和《民法典》颁布之前,我国对于民事主体中在"自然人"与"法人"之外是否存在不属于上述两者的第三类主体一直未有明确定论。但在实践中,独立于"自然人"与"法人"的第三类民事主体从1978年至今一直承担着应对越发复杂的经济活动的重要角色。从"其他组织"到"非法人组织"这一术语变化正是明确了该类主体与"自然人"和"法人"并列的独立民事法律地位。

　　我国第一部提出"其他经济组织"概念的法律是于1979年通过的《中外合资经营企业法》(已废止),该法第一条中"其他经济组织"与公司、企业等主体并列存在。之后随着改革开放的不断推进,1981年的《经济合同法》(第五十四条)和1985年的《涉外经济合同法》(第二条)也均承认了该第三类主体的存在。不同之处在于,《经济合同法》中具体列举了"个体经营户、农村承包经营户、农村社员"几项,而《涉外经济合同法》中则将该类主体直接概括为"其他经济组织"。而在1986年通过的《民法通则》则对民法主体的分类持不同观点,尽管其规定了个体工商户、农村承包经营个人合伙、联营等相关制度,但在民事主体的分类上只承认"公民(自然人)和法人"(第二条),即采用"二分"原则;之后的《技术合同法》也沿袭了《民法通则》的相关观点。关于民事主体"二分"和"三分"的观点斗争,在现行的多部单行法中也有所体现。如《著作权法》《民事诉讼法》《担保法》以及1999年颁布的《合同法》中均采"三分"原则,承认"其他组织"作为民事主体的合法地位;而再后来颁布的《物权法》与《侵权责任法》则重新使用二分法。直至《民法总则》和《民法典》最终确定"非法人组织"的表达。正如杨立新教授所说，"法律作为社会经济基础的反映，应当客观地反映经济社会的发展规律，使之适应经济发展的需要"①。在实践中，民事主体三分的法律结构更能适应我国改革开放后经济活动主体逐渐复杂的现状与市场经济不断发展的需求。对于我国改革开放后普遍存在的独资企业、合伙企业、不具有法人资格的专业服务机构及其他组织而言，只有正视该类主体的存在，给予其明确独立的法律地位，才能更好地管理该类民事主体，促使其发挥参与市场经济活动的积极性与活力。

在此背景下，仅使用范围不甚明确的"其他组织"一词，会造成一定的混乱，也无法达到规范立法语言的目的。与"其他组织"或"其他经济组织"相比，"非法人组织"在语义准确性与法律语言的规范性上均更胜一筹："其他组织"由"其他"和"组织"两个词汇结合而成，该组合词汇没有确切的内涵与明确的指向，其具体指代的事物由上下文中与其并列的事项所决定。② 因此，尽管在部分法规中对"其他组织"这一名词进行了释义，如《最高人民法院关于适用〈中华人民共和国民事诉讼法〉的解释》第五十二条规定，"其他组织是指合法成立、有一定的组织机构和财产，但又不具备法人资格的组织"。但该名词本身并非法言法语，不具备法律语言规范准确的属性，且属于常见的日常生活用语。而"非法人组织"这一术语在被创造的同时便已同时被赋予了特定的法律内涵。将"非法人组织"与"法人组织"并列作为民事主体的其中两类后，两者从称谓上便构成了对应关系。此外，根据《民法典》第一百零二条："非法人组织是不具有法人资格，但是能够依法以自己的名义从事民事活动的组织。""非法人组织"在形式上直接点明该类

---

① 杨立新：《〈民法总则〉规定的非法人组织的主体地位与规则》，《求是学刊》2017年第3期。

② 谭启平：《论民事主体意义上"非法人组织"与"其他组织"的同质关系》，《四川大学学报(哲学社会科学版)》2017年第4期。

民事主体不具备法人资格的性质与特征,更符合法律用语的特征。使用该表达"不仅能成就民法典关于民事主体的逻辑性和体系化的需要,有利于更全面地了解法人人格的本质和特征,也能更全面地反映我国社会组织的现实状况和本土环境,具有较强的包容性和开放性"①。

三、对变化术语的翻译探讨

　　本研究主要通过两个步骤来确定上述民法术语的合适译文:首先,通过法律词典和相关法律文本来确定各参考译文的专业语义是否正确,这一步主要借助《布莱克法律词典》《元照英美法词典》以及部分官方英语法律文本来完成。然后,再通过语料库工具验证译文的通用性以确定其接受度。此处所使用的语料库为 iWeb 语料库②。该语料库属于杨百翰大学系列语料库(BYU-Corpus)之一,权威性较高,库容庞大(容量达 140 亿词),语料范围广泛。因此,各表达和搭配在 iWeb 语料库中的频率检索结果能够直观地体现其在现代英语文本中是否常见、通用。

　　上述两组变迁后的术语,均属于对过去及现在较长或不规范表达的统一和精炼,两者翻译在形式上的改变必然要有所体现。对于"公序良俗"一词来说,在保证意义完整正确的情况下还应尽量贴近中文中四字格平行结构。而"非法人组织"则更需要注意表达的简洁性。此外,法律翻译并非单纯的代码转换过程,而是法律本身的迁移。公序

---

　　①　肖海军:《非法人组织在民法典中的主体定位及其实现》,《法商研究》2016 年第 2 期。

　　②　Mark Davies, "The 14 Billion Word iWeb Corpus", https://www.english-corpora.org/iWeb/.

良俗原则和非法人组织在各国法律中都有相关表达和规定,因此参考、分析并最终选用能够为英语读者所接受的标准译法也应当是确定译文的重点之一。对比已经公布的《民法典》英译版本,下文拟对其中个别表达的翻译进行梳理和商榷。

(一)"公序良俗"

目前,该术语可参考的译文共有三种。第一种来自我国台湾地区现行民事规定的英译版本,该文献第十七条规定"自由之限制,以不背于公共秩序或善良风俗者为限",译为"any limitation to liberty shall not be against public policy or morals",因此将对应的"public policy or morals"纳入候选范围。第二种来自国务院法制办所编制的官方英译:2020 年 1 月,中国人大网发布了《民法总则》的英译版本,其中将公序良俗一词译为"public order or moral decency"[1]。第三种是北大法宝和秘塔科技两个平台给出的参考译文,为"public order and good morals"。可见,三种译文均采用了"and/or"平行结构,"公序"在前,"良俗"在后,分别译出。在"公序"部分,区别点在于"policy"和"order"的选择;而在"良俗"部分,"moral"是核心词汇,争议在于使用其名词形式还是形容词形式,以及是否需要另做修饰。

首先,关于 public order 和 public policy 的区分,有学者认为两者并无区别,仅是不同法系国家的不同表达习惯。[2] 但笔者认为并非如此:在《布莱克法律词典》中检索"public order"和"public policy"两种表达可以发现,词典中并未收录前者,而对后者则有较为完整的解释。广义

① *General Provisions of the Civil Law of the People's Republic of China*,中国人大网,2020 年 1 月 3 日,http://www. npc. gov. cn/englishnpc/lawsoftheprc/202001/c983fc8d3782438fa775a9d67d6e82d8. shtml。

② 张潇剑:《国际私法上的公共政策机制之剖析》,《法学评论》2005 年第 4 期。

上的 public policy 是指会影响国民整体或促进公共利益问题的规则、原则或方法。美国法院有时也用该词来支持判决,比如"违反了 public policy 的合同无效";而在狭义上,该词是指"任何人都不允许做任何可能会伤害广大公众的事情"这一原则。① public order 的含义虽然在法律词典中无可参考,但可根据使用该表述的法律文本和法律相关文本进行总结。如直接以此为名的英国法律 Public Order Act 1986 就在前言部分中提到,该法意在对普通法中"暴乱、抢劫、非法集会及聚众斗殴罪行,以及若干与'public order'有关的法定罪行"进行调整。② 在美国和平研究所(United States Institute of Peace,USIP)发布的《稳定与重建指导原则》(Guiding Principles for Stabilization and Reconstruction)中也对"public order"一词进行了解释,认为其代表一种"没有例如绑架、谋杀、暴乱、纵火和对目标群体或个人的恐吓等大量犯罪和政治暴力"的社会状况。③ 由此可见,public order 的语义内涵比 public policy 更具针对性,更多是对一些较严重的破坏社会稳定的犯罪行为的规制,而非广义上的"公共秩序"。欧盟欧洲移民网络发布的文件《关于"public policy"和"public security"概念的特别查询》(Ad-Hoc Query on the Understanding of the Notions of"Public Policy"and"Public Security")明确了上述区分,包括芬兰、意大利、立陶宛等国在内的大陆法系国家均使用"public policy"一词来指代宪法原则上的公共秩序,其范围更广,

---

① Bryan A. Garner (eds.), *Black's Law Dictionary* (*10th ed.*), St. Paul: Thomson Reuters, 2014, p.1426.

② *Public Order Act 1986*, https://www. legislation. gov. uk/ukpga/1986/64.

③ "Public Order", United States Institute of Peace, https://www. usip. org/guiding-principles-stabilization-and-reconstruction-the-web-version/rule-law/public-order #: ~ : text = Public% 20order% 20is% 20a% 20condition, against% 20targeted% 20groups% 20or% 20individuals.

并涵盖了"public order"的内容。①

通过以上分析可以看出,public policy 的内涵与"公序"基本一致,且能够与国际通用表述做到对应。接下来,将两项译文输入 iWeb 语料库,可得到结果:public order(s)共出现 8051 次,public policy(s)则出现了 75222 次。后者使用频率更高,可验证 public policy 的通用性。

而关于"善良风俗"的译法,在《布莱克法律词典》中可找到以下相关词条,分别为"contra bonos mores""good moral character""moral <adj.>"以及"morality"。其中"contra bonos mores"来自王宠惠先生的《德国民法典》英译本,②该法典第一百三十八条规定"违反善良风俗的法律行为无效"③。王宠惠先生直接使用拉丁语固定表达,将"违反善良风俗"译为"contra bonos mores"。根据《布莱克法律词典》的释义,该表述在英语中意为"against good morals"④。词典中其他对于 moral 及其派生词的解释中,均有其为"优良的""好的""正确的""诚实的原则"的表述。可见"moral"一词本身即有积极含义,指向正面的行为,因此修饰词"good"是可以省略的。但考虑到中文中的四字格平行结构,"good morals"或"moral decency"这样的"形容词+名词"搭配会与前项"public policy"更对应,且"good morals"中的"good"一词对于语义的影响并不大,可起到强调作用。

因此,在这两项译文中做进一步筛选。根据《布莱克法律词典》,

① "Ad-Hoc Query on the Understanding of the Notions of 'Public Policy' and 'Public Security'", European Migration Network, September 22, 2009, https://emnbelgium. be/publication/ad-hoc-query-public-order-and-public-security.

② Wang Chonghui, *The German Civil Code Translated and Annotated with an Historical Introduction and Appendices*, London: Stevens and Sons Limited, 1907, p. 31.

③ 《德国民法典》(第 4 版),陈卫佐译注,法律出版社 2015 年版,第 49 页。

④ Bryan A. Garner (eds.), *Black's Law Dictionary* (10th ed.), St. Paul: Thomson Reuters, 2014, p. 389.

"decency"意为适当的性质、状态或条件,仅从语义上来看,"moral decency"的表达似乎并无问题。但是根据 iWeb 语料库的检索结果,在库内所有文本中,"moral decency"这一表达仅出现 156 次,而"good morals"的频率则为 2990 次。可见前者并非常用搭配,在促进英语读者理解上能力不及后者。因而相比之下,"good morals"可作为"良俗"的合适译文。

综合以上分析,"公序良俗"这一表述的译文宜确定为"public policy and good morals"。该译文从形式上、语义上以及表达意图上均能够达到翻译目的,可以用作公序良俗原则的规范译文。

(二)"非法人组织"

目前,我国对于"非法人组织"的主流翻译共有两种:第一种来自于《民法总则》的官方译本,即"unincorporated organizations";而另一种则来自秘塔科技的《民法典》译本,即"unincorporated associations"。此外还有少数翻译采用苏式民法中"organizational unit without legal personality"这一译法。而其前身"其他组织"基本均翻译为"other organizations",因此不可沿用。

《元照英美法词典》对"corporation"一词的释义为"法人"[①],据此其动词形式"incorporated"可解释为"结成法人的"。而 unincorporated 作为 incorporated 的反义词,亦可对应解释为"未结成法人的",与"非法人"的定义一致,且相较之下比"without legal personality"更为简洁。

而 organization 和 association 两者均可以表示组织。在普通语境下,前者可直译为"组织",后者则为"协会",但在"按照一定的宗旨或是出于相同目的组成的团体"这一语义上,两者是一致的。《布莱克法

---

① 薛波主编:《元照英美法词典》,法律出版社 2003 年版,第 326 页。

律词典》中并未收录"organization"一词,在"association"词项下则直接导向"unincorporated association",明确将其作为该词组的简写并解释为"独立于法人之外的非法人组织"①,可见其在英美法中有相当的认知基础。值得注意的是,在英国法律语境下,"unincorporated association"特指非营利性非法人组织。② 但笔者认为直接使用"unincorporated association"不会造成理解上的偏差,原因有二:第一,在如美国等其他采用该表述的英美法系国家中,对"unincorporated association"并未做营利或者非营利的限定;第二,在我国《民法典·总则编》中,对非法人组织有较为详细的界定,并列举"个人独资企业、合伙企业、不具有法人资格的专业服务机构等"(第一百零二条第二款)以进一步阐明该术语的内涵。从这些具体的非法人组织中,已经可以清楚了解到我国法律语境中的"非法人组织"包含营利和非营利组织。因此,将"unincorporated associations"作为"非法人组织"的译文,可以在传达意义、促进理解以及精简结构三个方面做到性价比最大化。

随后,笔者使用 iWeb 语料库对两项译文分别进行检索,以做进一步验证,得到结果如下:unincorporated organization(s)在库中共出现 219 次,而 unincorporated association(s)共出现 1147 次。两者频率相差较大,后者通用程度明显较高。结合前文法律语义辨析,可认为"unincorporated association"为"非法人组织"较为合适的译文。

结合语言学、法学、翻译学相关知识和方法,本节对 1978 年至 2020 年间我国 16 部民法文本的术语变化及变化后的英译进行了探讨。根

---

① Bryan A. Garner (eds.), *Black's Law Dictionary* (*10th ed.*), St. Paul: Thomson Reuters, 2014, p. 148.

② 参见英国政府网站,https://www.gov.uk/unincorporated-associations,最后访问日期:2020 年 10 月 11 日。

据目标文本的使用状况(已失效/已修订,尚有效,未生效)进行分组、制作词表,再进行卡方检验之后的结果,本节选定"公序良俗"和"非法人组织"这两组存在显著变化的术语进行分析,认为在目标期间内,两组术语存在持续变化的原因与国家的经济体制密切相关。改革开放带来了更多更为复杂的社会经济活动,配套的法律也在不断完善。在内容变化的同时,民法在形式上也越发追求简洁、规范和统一,将原本不甚清晰的民法概念明确化。这些术语表达的改变同时带来了英译的问题。本节根据现有的翻译,从意义和功能两方面入手,运用法律词典、英语法律文本和线上语料库,确定"public policy and good morals"和"unincorporated association"分别为"公序良俗"和"非法人组织"最为契合的译文。不仅能体现从原表达到新术语形式上的改变,也能起到促进英语读者理解和接受的作用。

随着我国在国际上的影响力不断提高,国际化水平不断提升,加强涉外法律工作显得愈发重要和紧迫。立法语言的规范与否决定了法律文本能否准确反映立法者的立法意图①,而法律翻译则承担了将立法意图切实传达给其他主体的桥梁作用。因此,法律文本本身及其译文的形式安排和术语选择都值得学界关注。本节对民法术语的变迁进行了分析与讨论,并对其英文译本的相关更新提出了建议,希望能为我国法律术语规范化提供参考与帮助,为民法法律语言和法律翻译研究给予支持。

---

① 郭龙生:《浅议立法语言规范》,《语言与法律研究》2020年第1期。

第五章
智能时代法律语言与翻译研究的学理推进

第一节　语料库作为确定意义的测量工具

随着语料库语言学的发展与普及，律师和法官开始通过使用语料库来寻求证据。语料库作为一种新的文本资源和语言分析方法，对观察和发现语言运用中典型的型式和意义，尤其是基于概率判断和确立词语及搭配的常用结构和意义具有较高的参考价值。在阐释语料库对于推动法律解释方面可能做出的贡献之前，我们有必要介绍一下语料库语言分析的特质以及语料库的常用方法。

一、语料库语言学的目的

语料库语言学是系统分析真实语言数据的学科，正如保罗·贝克（Paul Baker）所言："了解语言如何工作的最好方法是分析语言的实际使用。"[①]为了弄清楚一个短语的常用含义，语料库语言学家会研究该

① Paul Baker, Andrew Hardie & Tony McEnery, *A Glossary of Corpus Llinguis*, Edinburgh: Edinburgh University Press, 2006.

短语在数据库或语料库中自然使用的大量实际例子,并结合"定量和定性分析"。[①] "语料库语言学的主要目标是研究结果的可复制性。"[②]重点是保留"比其他方法更具普遍性和有效性的研究结果"[③]。语料库语言学通过考察预置的、自然发生的语言分析,也避免了霍桑效应(Hawthorne Effect),即当人们知道自己被观察时,他们会改变自己的行为。[④] 在语言学、翻译学甚至美国及欧洲地区的法学界,语料库的建设和使用均是数字时代的题中之义,也是学界近三十年来的一个重要增长点。

二、语料库

语料库语言学家所研究的自然语言所存储在的数据库被称为语料库(corpus)。常见的语言学语料库包括报纸文章、书籍或法律文本的数据库。语料库语言学家致力于开发合适的语料库以适应不同学科领域、实践应用的需要。其中,库容的大小和是否具有代表性尤为关键。一个通用语料库旨在代表一个广泛的语言社区,比如整个国家;而一个特殊目的语料库则是收集一种更为有限的语言群体的语言,例如在一

---

① D. Biber, "Corpus-Based and Corpus-driven Analyses of Language Variation and Use", in Bernd Heine, Heiko Narrog (eds.), *The Oxford Handbook of Linguistic Analysis*, New York: Oxford University Press, 2010, p. 160.

② Tony McEnery, Andrew Hardie, *Corpus Linguistics: Method, Theory and Practice*, Cambridge: Cambridge University Press, 2011, p. 66.

③ D. Biber, "Corpus-Based and Corpus-Driven Analyses of Language Variation and Use", in Bernd Heine, Heiko Narrog (eds.), *The Oxford Handbook of Linguistic Analysis*, New York: Oxford University Press, 2010, p. 159.

④ Henry A. Landsberger, *Hawthorne Revisited: Management and the Worker, Its Critics, and Developments in Human Relations in Industry*, New York: Cornell University Press, 1958.

个地区或说同一语言的人之间所说的话语,又或是某个专业群体中所使用的语言,如律师、法官的法言法语等等。

　　语料库可以是静态的,也可以是动态的。历史语料库(historical corpus)是静态的,它收集特定时期的语言使用示例。相比之下,监控语料库(monitor corpus)是一个动态的语料库,它不断地更新,以反映语言使用的不断发展。语料库可以包含嵌入的语言元数据。例如,一个句法分析(parsed)语料库,包含单词的句法属性元数据;标注(tagged)语料库包含了语料库中每个切分单位所承载的词类元数据;而生(raw)语料库则不包含任何语言元数据,只包含单词或汉字。根据不同的研究目的,由研究人员自主确定建设、使用何种语料库。

三、方法

　　语言学家通过对这些数据库的系统检索,开发了分析语言用法和意义的工具与方法。这些工具可以分析出"仅凭人类语言直觉"通常不可能产生的认识。他们通过分析频率数据,可以评估一个词在一定时段、不同体裁或语域中的使用频率,[①]也可以分析给定单词或短语的不同意义。通过将语料库中一个词或短语不同意义的相对频率制表,语言学家可以完成词典所不能做到的事情:在给定的语言环境中辨别出某个术语的更多常用含义。

　　频率数据的列表需要"标注",或对检索结果进行分类。在语料库

---

① Tony McEnery, Andrew Wilson, *Corpus Linguistics: An Introduction* (2d ed.), Edinburgh: Edinburgh University Press, 2001, p. 82.

语言学中,标注越来越多地借鉴调查和内容分析方法中的原则和实践。① 第一步是在语料库中进行检索,来核查目标单词或短语的每个例证。在例证相对较少(大约100个)的情况下,标注人员可以分析每个索引行;在示例较多的情况下,则分析查看其中的随机样本。②

　　通过观察语料库中文本的索引行,语言学家可以研究自然语言中给定术语或短语的大量例子。这使得语言学家收集的信息比仅从字典中获得的信息多得多。这样可以产生一个广泛的、有代表性的样本,而不是一组孤立的、择优挑拣的句子。意义分布标注(来自索引行分析)可以说是语料库最重要的用途;其他工具在本质上是探索性大过证实性(或者最多只能提供无力的意义证据)。这种标注在本质上也是最定性的,因此需要做的工作最多。

　　语料库语言学家还通过分析词的搭配(collocation)来分析词义或用法。搭配是指中心词的邻词,即与中心词常出现在一起的词语。一个词或短语与另一个词或短语的搭配可以告诉我们一些关于意义或交际内容的有效信息。这是一种法律早已接受的语言现象。我们解释法律长期以来一直信奉"文字上的推理"(noscitur a socialis canon of construction),"从上下文而断其意"③。这反映在语言分析中,即"应该通过搭配,去了解一个词"④。

① See James C. Phillips, Jesse Egbert, "Advancing Law and Corpus Linguistics: Importing Principles and Practices from Survey and Content-Analysis Methodologies to Improve Corpus Design and Analysis", *BYU Law Review*, No. 6, 2017, p. 1589.
② 参见 Earl Babbie, *The Practice of Social Research* (12th ed.), Cambridge: Wadsworth Publishing, 2010, pp. 206-208,其中探讨了采样过程。
③ "Noscitur a Sociis", in Bryan A. Garner (eds.), *Black's Law Dictionary* (10th ed.), St. Paul: Thomson Reuters, 2014.
④ J. R. Firth, "A Synopsis of Linguistic Theory, 1930-1955", in J. R. Firth, et al. (eds.), *Studies in Linguistic Analysis*, Oxford: Blackwell, 1957, p. 11.

　　语料库语言学分析也"观察一些固定词组的变化,(这些固定词组)通常被称为词块(lexical bundles)"①。词块通常被定义为三个或更多个词的重复序列或分组。② 在其他语言学界中,这些词块被称为 N 元模式或词丛。本部分依语料库软件中的指称,称其为词丛(如"Do you want me to"和"I don't know what"是英语会话中最常见的两个词丛③)。词丛是"不完整的短语",并且"具有统计学意义(通过大量的共现来确定)"。④

　　语料库检索不仅可以在词的层次上进行分析,还可以对多词短语进行分析。它还允许通过检查特定句法结构中的术语或短语来考虑上下文,如由特定形容词修饰的名词。以《美国宪法》的文本研究为例,针对其中概念颇具争议的"公共使用"一词(public use),⑤研究者不必求助于字典来查找"public"和"use",而是可以查找"public use"实例,因为一个短语的含义可能超过其各组成部分的总和。此外,语料库检索可以生成与实证问题相关的数据,即一个给定术语在两个(或多个)不同意义中使用的频率:可以计算出给定术语在竞争语义中的使用频率。这有力地证明了,该意义是这个术语或短语在被创造时最常被理解的方式。

　　语料库分析也带来了信息透明(transparency)。仍以美国的法学

---

　　① Gena R. Bennett, *Using Corpora in the Language Learning Classroom: Corpus Linguistics for Teachers*, Ann Arbor: The University of Michigan Press, 2010, p. 9.

　　② 参见 D. Biber, et al. , *Longman Grammar of Spoken and Written English*, New York: Pearson Education, 1999, p. 991,词块在这里定义为三个以上单词的重复序列。

　　③ D. Biber, et al. , *Longman Grammar of Spoken and Written English*, New York: Pearson Education, 1999, p. 994.

　　④ D. Biber, et al. , *Longman Grammar of Spoken and Written English*, New York: Pearson Education, 1999, p. 9.

　　⑤ See John O. McGinnis, Michael B. Rappaport, "The Constitution and the Language of the Law", *William & Mary Law Review*, Vol. 59, No. 4, 2018, pp. 1370-1374.

研究为例,大多数人没有机会接触到美国建国之初的词典,也没有机会触及在原旨主义者们的学术研究和司法意见书中晦涩的历史资料。但只要能够上网,均可查询这样的在线语料库,运行相同的检索,分析文章、摘要或观点中所依赖的相同数据。使用传统的原旨主义研究者工具,有一个要素是"我说的都是真的"。但语料库分析使调查民主化,向所有人开放数据并从中得出结论。没人会相信原旨主义研究者的话。任何人都可以看到相同的数据,并试图复制或伪造结论,这本身就是进步。①

语料库的意义更超越研究本身,而在法律实践层面产生意义,其首要的即是对法律解释学中有关平义规则(plain rule)的推动。所谓"平义",指的是制定法律文本的明确含义。换句话说,"平义"是指语词惯常或通常的含义,亦即该语言的共同体所普遍接纳的意旨。"平义解释"就是用语词惯常或通常的含义来解释。按照英美法系的观点,平义是普通人在日常生活中一般性的使用的语词之含义。也就是字义(literal meaning)规则,或曰语法(grammatical meaning)规则——就是指法律文本所使用的字、词、句的意义是普通人通常理解、共同接受的含义。比如在 *Piere v. Underwood* 案中,根据《平等审判法》(EAJA),若原告对美国政府提起诉讼并胜诉,其律师费应得到补偿,除非法院发现美国政府的立场被证明是充分正当的(substantially justified)。案件的争议点在于何为"充分正当的",美国第九巡回上诉法院对其的解释是"政府的立场有法律和事实上合理的基础"。而被告则认为"合理的"(reasonable)并不能代表"充分正当的"的立法原意。最终,联邦最高法

---

① 关于利用语料库分析研究美国建国初期形成的法律文献语言,以推动原旨主义研究的案例,可参见托马斯·李、詹姆斯·菲利普斯:《大数据驱动的原旨主义研究》,宋丽珏译,《法律方法》2020年第2期。

院基于"充分正当的"通常含义,采纳了第九巡回上诉法院做出的解释。① 这里值得关注的是,对于通常含义,英美法系法官及学者倾向于认为,"制定法的词汇,短语和句子应以其自然的、一般性的、通用的、合乎语法的意义被普通人所理解"。他们对于平义规则内容的定义,通常包含两点:第一,要使法律文本能够被全面理解,词语使用必须是以语法上的通常的、一般性的、合乎语法规则的意义被普通人所理解为要义,除非这样做出的解释会导致荒谬或明显错误的结果。第二,如果法律用词属于专门技术性用语,则必须适用其技术上的专门含义。即通常依据法律措辞的普通字面含义来理解和解释,但如果法律用语属于特殊行业的专门用语,就不可使用通常含义,而仅限于专门术语的含义。②

　　也就是说,平义规则注重语言以及语言学分析,强调语法规则和词典定义,甚至认定法律条文应在固定文类、语境下无歧义、无争议,但这几乎是无法做到的。而自斯卡利亚大法官开始,人们逐渐提出了一系列确定语言通常含义的方法。首先,考察在一部法律中出现的词语或短语在其他法律中的意义。其次,考虑该用语和整个法律相符合的可能含义(possible meaning)。③ 最后,考虑其他相关法律来确定法律的通常含义(平义)。立法者制定法律的意图是让普通人懂得其含义,进而遵守其规则,如在我国起草法律时所使用的字词句也均与通常使用的语言规则相符。例如法律规定将法庭的活动情形"写入笔录",则应当理解为以笔记的形式记录在纸张或其他载体上,而不应当简单地理解

---

　　① *Pierce v. Underwood*, 487 U. S. 552, 108 S. Ct. 2541, 101 L. Ed. 2d 490, 1988 U. S. LEXIS 2882, 56 U. S. L. W. 4806, Unemployment Ins. Rep. (CCH) P14,030.

　　② 致远:《文义解释法的具体应用规则》,《法律适用》2001 年第 9 期。

　　③ *Chan v. Korean Air Lines, Ltd.*, 490 U. S. 122, 109 S. Ct. 1676, 104 L. Ed. 2d 113, 1989 U. S. LEXIS 2026, 57 U. S. L. W. 4432.

"写"的字面含义是手持钢笔,逐字记录;"笔录"应当理解为用于以后入卷查阅的载体,而不是任何普通笔记本。因此,通常含义既不简单地等同于直接的字面含义,又不是脱离其在具体背景之下的特定含义。它必须是人们共同普遍接受的含义。[1]

平义规则历史悠久,今天依然在各国的法律制度中发生着影响。近二十年来,西方法律界一直在推行"大众法律语言"运动,要求立法者、法官、律师、学者在立法、起草法律文件、撰写判决甚至写论文时,使用普通人都能懂的语言,而尽量少用那些晦涩、专业性太强的"法言法语"。这不仅体现了社会对法律的新要求,也在一定程度上印证了文义解释法,特别是平义规则的重要意义。值得注意的是,在美国法庭庭审中,语料库用于协助"平义规则"的操作,已经成为一种趋势。而在提供诉讼证据方面,语料库也大有用武之地,[2]如在下面提及的 *FCC v. AT&T.* 案和 *United States v. Costello* 案中,即有体现。

第二节　数据驱动分析:法律和语料库语言学的诞生与发展

随着语料库在法律领域的运用,法律和语料库语言学(LCL)应运而生,该学科是隶属于法学和语言学交叉学科下一个崭新的学科方向,它基于语言使用实例的大型数据库,运用多种语料库工具(如

---

① 致远:《文义解释法的具体应用规则》,《法律适用》2001 年第 9 期。

② 梁茂成:《语料库、平义原则和美国法律中的诉讼证据》,《语料库语言学》2014 年第 1 期。

AntConc,WordSmith 等),以更好地了解法律文本(法规、宪法、合同)中单词和短语的含义等。因此,LCL 是将语料库语言工具、理论和方法应用于法律问题(尤其是法律解释问题),就像法律和经济学是将经济工具、理论和方法应用于各种法律问题一样。

一、LCL 发展历史

美国法律语言学专家劳伦斯·索兰(Lawrence Solan)2005 年在一篇法律评论文章中指出,语料库语言学有可能应用于解释法律文本,[①]这篇文章可以被视为 LCL 方向的萌芽。但将语料库语言学的工具和方法应用于法律或法律解释,则要下溯至 2010 年秋季于《杨百翰大学法律评论》(*BYU Law Review*)上发表的斯蒂芬·穆里森(Stephen Mouritsen)题为《词典并非堡垒:定义的缺陷与一种基于语料库的平义解释方法》的文章。该文章提出,一直以来,词典是法官用来确定单词和短语普通含义的主要参考工具,但这种方法存在缺陷,比如语言意义并非在语境中实现,而是存在于片段的语例中,词典有时甚至仅仅提供单词释义。基于此,穆里森建议在司法实践中使用语料库语言学方法来确定语言意义。[②] 亚当·利普塔克(Adam Liptak)后在《纽约时报》上发表的关于法律解释的文章中引用了该观点,使之广泛传播。[③]

[①]　Lawrence M. Solan, " The New Textualists' New Text ", *Loyola of Los Angeles Law Review*, Vol. 38, 2005, pp. 2027-2062.

[②]　Stephen C. Mouritsen, "The Dictionary Is Not a Fortress: Definitional Fallacies and a Corpus-Based Approach to Plain Meaning", *BYU Law Review*, No. 5, 2010, pp. 1915-1980.

[③]　Adam Liptak, "Justices Turning More Frequently to Dictionary, and Not Just for Big Words", *The New York Times*, June 13, 2011.

2011 年,LCL 得到了进一步发展的机会。在美国 *Adoption of Baby E. Z.* 案的判决中,犹他州最高法院大法官托马斯·李(Thomas Rex Lee)通过使用语料库语言学来解释"监护权的决定"(custody determination)的含义,这也是美国历史上第一个利用语料库语言学来确定法律文本含义的判决。托马斯·李大法官通过检索当代美国英语语料库(COCA)的 500 个随机样本(句子),发现"监护"常出现在"离婚"(divorce)语境下,而非"收养"(adoption)语境下。研究同时发现,"监护"与"离婚"发生搭配的可能性是"收养"的十倍。故托马斯·李大法官从检索证据得出结论,认为相关法律"所涵盖的监护权诉讼,仅限于可更改的(有条件的)离婚监护令",而不是更广泛的监护程序。

自此开始,其他相关的司法实践和法学研究随之而来。在 2015 年的 *State v. Rasabout* 案中,托马斯·李大法官使用 COCA 检索,确定与枪支(或其同义词)一起使用时,"发射"(shoot)绝大多数情况下是指单次射击,而不是指清空整个弹匣。[①] 2016 年,犹他州最高法院五位大法官中的其他四位在托马斯·李大法官的多数意见中加了一个脚注,赞扬了他在案件审理中使用语料库语言学方法(尽管法院同时认为,没有必要用这么复杂的方法去解决相关问题)。[②] 基于此,密歇根州最高法院成为第一个在多数意见中使用 COCA 作为论证来源的法院,此后案件中涉及语义确定的部分逐渐出现了语料库转向,也就是在多数意见或少数意见中均有可能通过 COCA 或其他语料库来确定词汇或短语的含义。

---

① 56 P. 3d 1258, 1281-1282(Utah 2015)(Lee, J., concurring), LexisNexis, https://advance. lexis. com/document/searchwithindocument/? pdmfid = 1000516&crid = 4bd855a1-684c-4717-b433b62794ddf3a9&pdsearchwithinterm=corpus+linguistics&pdworkfolde-rlocatorid = NOT_SAVED_IN_WORKFOLDER&ecomp = 4s9nk&prid = f77138a7-2ca6-448f-aad2-8f478be9ff61.

② *Craig v. Provo*, 2016 WL 4506309, 2016 UT 40, para. 26 n. 3., https://www. utcourts. gov/opinions/supopin/Craig%20v. %20Provo%20City20160826. pdf.

比如,在 *Muscarello v. United States* 案中,美国联邦最高法院大法官布雷耶(Stephen Breyer)通过检索 Lexis 和 Westlaw 库中报纸部分,分析了武器(weapon)、交通工具(vehicle)和携带(carry)的实用语义,并进一步确定了此案被告人在毒品交易过程中于车内携带枪支属于"携带枪支"(carry a weapon),故符合联邦法律规定的"在毒品交易途中携带枪支属于犯罪"。① 此前,被告方强调"携带"一词在日常使用中主语一般为"生命体,人"而非"物体",试图以此逃脱罪责。而在 *United States v. Costello* 案中,美国第七巡回上诉法院法官波斯纳(Richard A. Posner)批评了过分依赖词典的弊端,并应用谷歌新闻(Google News)确定案中被告并未"包庇"(harbor)贩卖毒品的外国男友。根据《美国法典》(United States Code)第 8 篇第 1324 章第(a)(1)(A)(iii)条,任何人"如果明知或无视外国人非法入境美国或非法居留美国,却将此外国人窝藏、包庇或庇护(或企图窝藏、包庇或庇护)于任何地方,包括任何建筑物或交通工具之中",将处以 5 年以下监禁,并处 25 万美元以下罚款。而此案中的被告被指控触犯《美国法典》中的"窝藏"(conceal)、"包庇"(harbor)和"庇护"(shield from detection)罪,数罪并罚。联邦地区法院法官认为,被告明知男子是非法入境者,且曾驱车到车站将男子接到自己的住所,有窝藏罪犯的企图,故判缓刑 2 年,并罚款 200 美元。后来被告提出上诉,此案提交至美国第七巡回上诉法院。而波斯纳法官认为,"窝藏"指将犯人隐藏起来,不让外人发现,而"庇护"指隔离起来,以防警方发现。从案件的基本事实看,没有证据能够证明被告犯有"窝藏"或"庇护"罪。因此,该案的关键是被告是否犯有"包庇"罪,而

---

① *Muscarello v. United States*, 524 U. S. 125 (1998),判决书中指出,"我们发现在数千例随机搜索得到的真实语言使用中,大约有三分之一的语例包含本案所涉及的内容,也就是'汽车上携带枪支'(the carring of guns of a car)"。

这正取决于 harbor 一词的常用意义。

波斯纳强烈反对通过词典来确定词汇的意义。他指出,"词典中的定义是脱离语境的,而句子的真正意义取决于语境,包括对语言产生背景的理解"。为了搞清 harbor 一词的意义,波斯纳使用了一种特殊的语料库——网络。随着互联网的不断普及和互联网数据的迅速递增,互联网上的文本数据已经成为世界上最大的语料库,从互联网上挖掘数据的方法也越来越多。西方有学者专门研究作为语料库的网络(Web as corpus)。波斯纳使用网络的方法十分简单:他在谷歌中搜索harbor 的搭配词,结果发现:harbor 之后最常见的搭配词包括"fugitives"(亡命者,50800 次)、"Jews"(犹太人,19100 次)、"refugees"(难民,4820 次)、"enemies"(敌人,4730 次)、"Quakers"(贵格会教徒,3870次)等。这些数据清楚地表明,harbor 的意思不是"为……提供住所"(这是词典中给的解释),而是"通过窝藏、转移到安全地点或提供人身保护等途径,有意识地保护某特定群体成员的安全,使其免受当局的伤害"。在波斯纳看来,本案中的被告只是想与男友独处,并无意与当局为敌,故不构成包庇。在审理此案的过程中,波斯纳不依赖传统的词典,而利用互联网上的大众语言作为证据来解决法律文本中的"平义"问题,可谓独具匠心。①

而在 2016 年的 *People v. Harris* 案中,密歇根州最高法院同样依据COCA 语料库的分析,确认了具有歧义的成文法内容,该法院七位大法官均认同语料库语言学可作为成文法解释的有利佐证。该案牵涉一位司机和三名警员,其中一位警员袭击了这位司机,而同行的其他两位警员则全程旁观,并未采取任何行动,整个过程无意间被录像机记录下

---

①　关于该案件的详细论述,可参见梁茂成:《语料库、平义原则和美国法律中的诉讼证据》,《语料库语言学》2014 年第 1 期。

来。事后三名警员做出了与录像中情形不符的虚假陈述（false statement），法庭随即就此对三位警员提出了刑事指控，罪名是"攻击和殴打"（assult and battery），包括普通法上重罪的渎职行为和妨碍司法。但根据密歇根州立法《执法人员信息披露法》（DLEOA），其严禁在任何刑事诉讼中使用执法人员所做的非自愿陈述（involuntary statement）以及从该非自愿陈述中得出的任何信息（information）来指控该执法人员。该案的争议点即在于，"信息"这一语词，是否同时包括真实信息（accurate information）和虚假信息（false infromation）。判决中的多数意见参考了 COCA 的检索发现，即"信息"这一词汇虽然应包含真实信息和虚假信息，但该案的主审法官马克曼大法官（Stephen Markman）观察到，鲜少有类似"准确""无误"或类似的形容词出现在"信息"前面用以说明信息是否是真实的。换言之，当信息前并未搭配修饰语时，一般均表示是"真实信息"。法院据此认定，由于执法人员传递了不实信息，故的确妨碍了司法公正，且不受 DLEOA 保护。①

另外一个经典案例是 *Kouichi Taniguchi v. Kan Pacific Saipan, Ltd.*，此案中原告是一名日本棒球运动员，由于在被告的度假村受伤，他无法履行合同，因此损失了收入。故此，原告起诉被告，要求赔偿医疗费用和因在度假村受伤而无法履行合同的收入损失。此案争议点在于，被告（度假村）"花钱将各种文件从日文翻译成英文"，而当地法院以简易判决（summary judgement）的方式驳回此案件时，被告提交了一份要求赔偿其支付的文件翻译费用的请求。与 *Muscarello v. United States* 案相同，此案同样涉及原义解释问题。被告的索赔基于一项联邦立法，该

① *People v. Harris*, 2016 WL 3449466, 499 Mich. 332, LexisNexis, https://advance. lexis.com/api/permalink/1b62407a-4d0e-49f0-b54d-f3869fa93787/? context=1000516.

法规允许联邦诉讼中的胜诉方收回某些费用,包括"译员"(interpreter)所产生的费用。依据词典释义,联邦最高法院的阿利托大法官(Samuel A. Alito, Jr)在撰写多数意见时提出,口译员(interpreter)与笔译员(translator)意涵并无差异,均可指文件翻译工作者。而在反对意见中,金斯伯格大法官(Ruth Bader Ginsburg)则认为在日常使用中,"interpreter"主要承担口头发言的翻译工作,偶尔负责文本翻译。[①] 而这样的争论,在语料库语言学领域可以得到更加确定的语义判定,如下图所示:

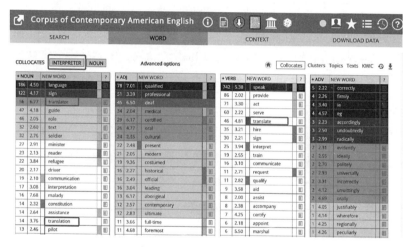

图 5-1　以 **interpreter** 作为关键词检索的搭配词分布

根据搭配信息分布,interpreter 经常与 translator 形成二项式搭配(亦即"interpreter and translator"),不难看出两者之间存在差异且常作

---

① *Kouichi Taniguchi v. Kan Pacific Saipan*, *Ltd.* 566 U. S. 560(2012), LexisNesix, https://advance. lexis. com/document/? pdmfid = 1000516&crid = e25bb349-4b5c-42bf-8347-b80844701ab1&pddocfullpath =%2Fshared%2Fdocument%2Fcases%2Furn%3AcontentItem%3A55P8-SPK1-F04K-F1JV-00000-00&pdcontentcomponentid = 6443&pdshepid = urn%3AcontentItem%3A55N5-F881-J9X5-T404-00000-00&pdteaserkey=sr0&pditab=allpods&ecomp =qzgpk&earg =sr0&prid =81e3f130-2d59-42be-936e-5dd147c486ee.

为搭配项出现。可见,语料库作为人工智能时代的话语分析工具,可以提升语义辨析的精度和效度。

从以上案例我们可以得出的结论是,法官所做的"一致的、普遍意义上的"文义解释,在很大程度上是"不确定、有分歧"的意义分析。在一些案例中(如 *Muscarello v. United States*),法官接受了与普遍意义不一致的特例,而在其他案例中(如 *Kouichi Taniguchi v. Kan Pacific Saipan, Ltd.* 和 *United States v. Costello*),普遍意义则作为直接影响判决结果的主要因素。这不仅仅是法律解释的问题,也是法治(rule of law)本身面临的问题。只不过这样的问题在人工智能日益发达的今天,有望得到更良好的解决。

在学术方面,2012 年,斯蒂芬·穆里森在《哥伦比亚科技法律评论》(*Columbia Science and Technology Law Review*)上发表了一篇文章,进一步完善和推广了使用基于语料库来确定法律歧义问题的方法。[①] 随后的 2014 年,丹尼尔·奥特纳(Daniel Ortner)发表了《仁慈的语料库:宽大处理规则、歧义和语料库语言学》。在文章中,奥特纳应用语料库语言学来确定是否存在足够的模糊解释,以"触发"联邦最高法院案件中的"宽大处理"规则。[②] 2016 年值得注意的是两篇关于法律和语料库语言学的论文:在《耶鲁法律论坛》(*The Yale Law Journal Forum*)上发表的《语料库语言学与原初公共意义:一种推动原旨主义的新实验方法》由托马斯·李法官和其他两位合著者撰写,倡导文本主义研

---

① Stephen C. Mouritsen, "Hard Cases and Hard Data: Assessing Corpus Linguistics as an Empirical Path to Plain Meaning", *Columbia Science and Technology Law Review*, Vol. 13, No. 1, 2012, p. 156.

② Daniel Ortner, "The Merciful Corpus: The Rule of Lenity, Ambiguity and Corpus Linguistics", December 1, 2014, https://papers. ssrn. com/sol3/papers. cfm? abstract_id = 2576475.

究采用语料库语言学方法,以提高文本主义分析的严谨性和准确性。①作为回应,该刊同时发表了劳伦斯·索兰的一篇题为《语料库语言学能够提高原旨主义的科学性吗?》的论文。② 2017 年同样有两篇颇具代表性的文章,其一为李·J. 斯特朗(Lee J. Strang)在《加州大学戴维斯分校法律评论》(UC Davis Law Review)上发表的《大数据如何提高原旨主义方法论的严谨性:利用语料库语言学解释语言原初语言惯例》,文章关注了语料库语言学应用于宪法原初意义确定的价值,弥补了法律解释的一些缺陷;③其二为劳伦斯·索兰和塔米·盖尔斯(Tammy Gales)在《法律话语国际期刊》(International Journal of Legal Discourse)上发表的《寻找法律的一般意义:法官、词典或是语料库?》。

在 2018 年,托马斯·李和穆里森在《耶鲁法律评论》(Yale Law Review)共同发表的《判断原初意义》可以视作是 LCL 的标志性文章,文章审视了美国判例中普遍存在的法律解释问题,首次将普通意义(ordinary meaning)进行了语言学理论化的推衍,强调了分析说话人与听话人在共同预设(presupposition)下传递的语境意义(contextual meaning)的重要性。文章还对进行此类研究的群体展开概述,分析了主流的几位文本主义者的研究范式,如理查德·法伦(Richard Fallon)、卡斯·桑斯坦(Cass Sunstein)、威尔·鲍德(Will Baude)和斯蒂芬·萨克斯(Stephen Sachs)等等。同时,文章提出了语料库法律语言学的研

---

① James C Phillips, Daniel M. Ortner & Thomas R. Lee, "Corpus Linguistics & Original Public Meaning:A New Tool to Make Originalism More Empirical", *The Yale Law Journal Forum*, Vol. 126, 2016, pp. 21-32.

② Lawrence M. Solan, "Can Corpus Linguistics Help Make Originalism Scientific?", *The Yale Law Journal Forum*, Vol. 126, 2016, pp. 57-64.

③ Lee J. Strang, "How Big Data Can Increase Originalism's Methodological Rigor: Using Corpus Linguistics to Reveal Original Language Conventions", *UC Davis Law Review*, Vol. 50, 2017, pp. 1181-1241.

究范式,回顾了四个经典案例并进行了语料库语言学分析,是 LCL 的重要奠基作品之一。① 同年,斯蒂芬·格里斯(Stefan Gries)和布莱恩·G. 斯洛克姆(Brian G. Slocum)在《杨百翰大学法律评论》上发表的《普通意义与语料库语言学》为 LCL 的发展添薪加柴。此后,斯洛克姆和斯蒂芬又在 2020 年于《南加州法律评论》(North California Law Review)上发表了《评价语料库语言学》一文,重新审视了语料库语言学在法律解释领域的应用,对之前的一些研究进行了反思,提出了更为深刻的 LCL 研究路径和方法。

然而,有关采用语料库语言学方法的合理性和准确性问题,在法律解释过程中的探讨从未停止。如 2019 年,尼尔·戈德法布(Neal Goldfarb)在第四届法律与语言学年会上发表了题为《在法律解释中的语料库语言学:何时(不)适用?》的文章,文中提到,语料库的某些数据看起来对研究本身有促进作用,实则这种表象可能会产生很多的误导,并且无法得出期待的研究结果。但在这篇文章中,对语料库的使用仍然持肯定态度,并详细分析了语料库语言学的适用范围。② 2021 年,戈德法布又在《语言学年刊》(Annual Review of Linguistics)上发表了《法律解释中的语料库语言学》,对语料库语言学在法律解释中的应用情况做了较为详尽的爬梳,同时也在文末提出了 LCL 在未来有可能面临的挑战。③

除此之外,律师和记者也注意到与法律有关的语料库语言学。早

---

① Thomas R. Lee, Stephen C. Mouritsen, "Judging Ordinary Meaning", *Yale Law Journal*, Vol. 127, No. 4, 2018, p. 788.

② Neal Goldfarb, "Corpus Linguistics in Legal Interpretation: When Is It (In) Appropriate?", February 5, 2019, https://ssrn. com/abstract = 3333512 or http://dx. doi. org/10. 2139/ssrn. 3333512.

③ Neal Goldfarb, "The Use of Corpus Linguistics in Legal Interpretation", *Annual Review of Linguistics*, No. 7, 2021, pp. 473-491.

在 2010 年,同时身兼律师的戈德法布即使用 COCA 向美国联邦最高法院提交了第一份有关法律及语料库语言学的简报,用以确定"个人"(person)的普通含义是否在 *FCC v. AT&T* 案中指代公司。本·齐默(Ben Zimmer)在为《大西洋月刊》撰稿时注意到了这一新趋势,他将法庭上的语料库语言学称为"使用类固醇加速后的词语理解"(Lexis on Steroids)[①]。

第三节　未来方案——以法律知识图谱构建为例

　　有关翻译学研究,其关注点无非是作为过程(process)或作为产品(product)的翻译,法律翻译亦隶属其中。在智能时代来临之时,以上两种层面的关注都无法脱离计算机、大数据的支持。法律翻译研究的发展进程,也是社会发展、时代变迁的历史。通过法律翻译,中国人尤其是先进知识分子,不仅获得了尊重国家主权、各国平等相处、互不干涉内政等国际法的知识和观念,也学到了西方资产阶级的法律制度和法律观念。但法律翻译研究作为一种学问,其在语言学界的发展一直落后于法学界。于法学而言,从事跨民族、跨文化的法律研究,语言障碍是最基础、最重要的问题。中国对外国法律的翻译和移植引进工作很早便已开始,从清朝初期耶稣会士卫匡国(1614—1661)到 19 世纪

---

　　① 这里是一个比喻修辞,就像人们在运动中服用类固醇以变得更强壮、更快速一样,在采用语料库语言学的分析方法后,阐释语义变得更加快速、准确。

90 年代的西方法律名词翻译活动的悄然兴起,再到沈家本奉命进行修律变法时期而后的系列国外法律著作和法典翻译,外国法中译一直是中国法学界关注的重点。与之相对,从语言学角度对于法律语言、法律翻译的研究,从 1983 年潘文国教授的第一篇学术文章发表至今,尚不足 40 年;中国法的外译实践自改革开放至今也不过 43 年——直到 1987 年,全国人大法工委才第一次组织译出《中华人民共和国法律汇编(1979—1982)》和《中华人民共和国法律汇编(1983—1986)》。但进入 20 世纪 90 年代后,特别是中国加入世贸组织前后,国家加大了对法律法规外译工作的推进力度,对外的法制交流自此成为我们与国际社会平等对话和维护我国权益的重要平台。国务院法制办公室于 2003 年起草的《国务院办公厅关于做好行政法规英文正式译本翻译、审定工作的通知(草案)》,以及于 2011 年总结并组织编写的《法规译审常用句式手册》,即可视为这一推进力度和时代要求的体现。

此外,自互联网全面发展以来,相关的科研和学术机构也开始有意识、有目的地建设各类翻译平台或语料库。比如,北京大学法学院创办的"北大法宝",绍兴文理学院外国语学院创建的"中国法律法规汉英平行语料库",汤森路透法律信息集团旗下的万律(Westlaw China)创建的智能化的"中国法律信息双语数据库"等,均是代表性案例。高质量的语料库是数据平台的生命线,但从根本上说,国内目前还并未有整合性强、专业程度高、翻译质量过硬的法律翻译数据平台问世。而未来法律翻译实践与研究的智能化进路,势必走向更加全面的"知识库"时代,此处仅做任务框架梳理。

任务一,在术语层面创建双语知识库,形成可视化比较路径;技术层面实现基于双语术语(词汇)的法律知识图谱及其使用平台,参见图 5-2:

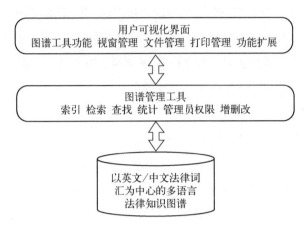

图 5-2 基于双语术语(词汇)的法律知识图谱及其使用平台图示

其中法律知识图谱的具体例子参见图 5-3,示例词条为"petition",其同义/近义词为"appeal"。

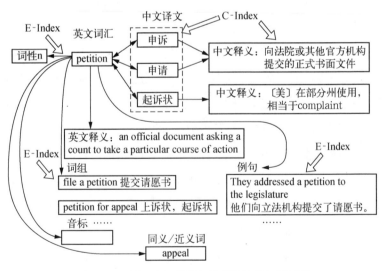

图 5-3 以"petition"词条为例的法律知识图谱

　　在图5-3中,E-Index和C-Index分别表示建立了英文和中文的词汇级索引,使得词表、短语表、例句中的同一词汇均能在检索时被查到。

　　任务二:需设计新型法律翻译机辅系统为配套技术工具,集科研数据挖掘、云端教学互动、实战质量效率提升与技能自测多功能为一体,参见图5-4。

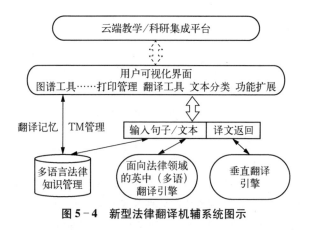

图5-4　新型法律翻译机辅系统图示

　　任务三:对应法务翻译、法条翻译、法学翻译三种类型进行分类器设计,亦可得出进行精准对标垂直领域翻译是人工智能(AI)时代翻译的发展趋势。

　　当今中国早已成为国际社会的重要参与方,包括法律在内的诸多地方、国家以及超国家层面的政策、法律法规需要翻译。大数据是提高法律翻译实践效率的良器,这亟待语言学、法学、计算机等相关领域专家的通力合作,制定符合智能时代法律翻译需求的原则和方案,形成具有可复制性、普适性参考价值的"经验"。显然,机器正在不断学习这个"经验",弱人工智能时代也终将走进量子时代。更优的法律翻译方案和更加完善的法律翻译研究,都将翻开中国法制的透明化、世界法制本土化(glocalization)的崭新一页。

参考文献

一、中文文献

（一）著作

曹建明等编：《大辞海·法学卷》（修订版），上海辞书出版社 2015 年版。

冯志杰：《汉英科技翻译指要》，中国对外翻译出版公司 1998 年版。

冯志伟：《语言与数学》，世界图书出版公司 2011 年版。

冯志伟：《自然语言处理简明教程》，上海外语教育出版社 2012 年版。

龚益：《社科术语工作的原则与方法》，商务印书馆 2009 年版。

李克兴、张新红：《法律文本与法律翻译》，中国对外翻译出版公司 2006
　　年版。

梁茂成、李文中、许家金：《语料库应用教程》，外语教学与研究出版社 2010
　　年版。

刘群：《汉英机器翻译若干关键技术研究》，清华大学出版社 2008 年版。

刘云虹、许钧主编：《翻译批评研究之路：理论、方法与途径》，南京大学出版
　　社 2015 年版。

潘庆云：《中国法律语言鉴衡》，汉语大词典出版社 2004 年版。

卫乃兴、陆军等：《对比短语学探索——来自语料库的证据》，外语教学与研
　　究出版社 2014 年版。

肖航：《语料库词义标注研究》，云南教育出版社 2016 年版。

薛波主编：《元照英美法词典》，法律出版社 2003 年版。

张德禄：《语言的功能与文体》，高等教育出版社 2005 年版。

《德国民法典》(第 4 版),陈卫佐译注,法律出版社 2015 年版。

(二) 论文

蔡新乐:《文化史就是翻译史——陈寅恪的历史发现与其翻译观初探》,《外语与外语教学》2006 年第 10 期。

程朝阳:《法律语言学导论——英美法律语言研究述介》,《中国法学教育研究》2010 年第 1 期。

戴孟勇:《法律行为与公序良俗》,《法学家》2020 年第 1 期。

戴芷宣:《公序良俗原则适用研究》,东南大学 2017 年硕士学位论文。

邓瑛:《基于语料库的英国媒体关于中国制造报道的话语分析》,上海交通大学 2011 年硕士学位论文。

董晓波:《我国立法文本规范化英译若干问题探析》,《外语教学理论与实践》2014 年第 3 期。

范晶波:《我国〈宪法〉序言的英译策略》,《中国科技翻译》2010 年第 1 期。

方琰:《法律程式化语言研究》,江西农业大学 2011 年硕士学位论文。

房宇华、胡志红:《英语法律语篇词汇特征计量化研究》,《牡丹江大学学报》2020 年第 2 期。

封鹏程:《现代汉语法律语料库的建立及其词汇计量研究》,南京师范大学 2005 年硕士学位论文。

郭龙生:《浅议立法语言规范》,《语言与法律研究》2020 年第 1 期。

郝铁川:《论逻辑思维与法律思维》,《现代法学》1997 年第 3 期。

黄文煌:《民法典编纂中的法条表达技术——对〈中华人民共和国民法典(草案)〉条文的梳理》,《暨南学报(哲学社会科学版)》2020 年第 1 期。

靳光瑾、肖航、富丽、章云帆:《现代汉语语料库建设及深加工》,《语言文字应用》2005 年第 2 期。

金可可:《德国民法上的请求权概念》,《求索》2007 年第 3 期。

康传彪:《法律英语中程式化语言结构及其应用》,《湖北经济学院学报(人文社会科学版)》2006 年第 6 期。

李更春:《程式语研究的理论突破及其对外语教学的启示》,《现代教育科学》
　　2013 年第 5 期。

李文中:《平行语料库设计及对应单位识别》,《当代外语研究》2010 年第
　　9 期。

梁茂成:《语料库、平义原则和美国法律中的诉讼证据》,《语料库语言学》
　　2014 年第 1 期。

刘金龙:《中西法律文化交流视角下的翻译史研究——〈从词典出发:法律术
　　语译名统一与规范化的翻译史研究〉评述》,《中国翻译》2014 年第 3 期。

柳经纬:《改革开放以来民法学的理论转型——百年中国民法学之考察之
　　二》,《中国政法大学学报》2010 年第 3 期。

柳经纬:《民法总则不应是〈民法通则〉的"修订版"》,《法学》2016 年第
　　10 期。

柳经纬:《迈向意思自治的民事法律行为制度——评〈中华人民共和国民法
　　总则〉第六章"民事法律行为"》,《贵州省党校学报》2017 年第 3 期。

柳经纬:《改革开放与民法变迁——以民法观念变迁为主线》,《贵州省党校
　　学报》2018 年第 4 期。

柳经纬:《改革开放四十年民法之变迁》,《中国法律评论》2018 第 5 期。

刘瑞玲:《试论法律术语翻译的精确性》,《外语学刊》2010 第 4 期。

龙卫球:《我国民法基本原则的内容嬗变与体系化意义——关于〈民法总则〉
　　第一章第 3—9 条的重点解读》,《法治现代化研究》2017 年第 2 期。

陆军、卫乃兴:《扩展意义单位模型下的英汉翻译对等型式构成研究》,《外语
　　教学与研究》2012 年第 3 期。

彭楚秋、陶友兰:《构建基于语料库的中国"法律术语社区"——以"调解"一
　　词为例》,《当代外语研究》2017 年第 1 期。

濮建忠:《语料库驱动的翻译研究:意义单位、翻译单位和对应单位》,《解放
　　军外国语学院学报》2014 年第 1 期。

邱贵溪:《论法律文件翻译的若干原则》,《中国科技翻译》2000 年第 2 期。

屈文生:《法律翻译研究的视角与思路——对法律翻译若干重要方面的梳理

和理性评价》，《江西社会科学》2010 年第 2 期。

屈文生：《中国法律术语对外翻译面临的问题与成因反思——兼谈近年来我国法律术语译名规范化问题》，《中国翻译》2012 年第 6 期。

石宏：《民法典合同编的重要发展和创新》，《中国人大》2020 第 15 期。

孙宪忠、谢鸿飞：《中国民法学六十年：1949—2009 年》，《私法研究》2010 年第 1 期。

孙莹：《我国民法调整对象的继受与变迁》，西南政法大学 2011 年博士学位论文。

谭启平：《论民事主体意义上"非法人组织"与"其他组织"的同质关系》，《四川大学学报（哲学社会科学版）》2017 年第 4 期。

托马斯·李、詹姆斯·菲利普斯：《大数据驱动的原旨主义研究》，宋丽珏译，《法律方法》2020 年第 2 期。

王利明：《民法典：国家治理体系现代化的保障》，《中外法学》2020 年第 4 期。

王利明：《中国民法学七十年：回顾与展望》，《政法论坛》2020 年第 1 期。

王轶：《民法典编纂争议问题的类型区分》，《清华法学》2020 年第 3 期。

王轶：《民法典之"变"》，《东方法学》2020 年第 4 期。

卫乃兴：《再探经典短语学的要旨和方法：模型、概念与问题》，《外语与外语教学》2011 年第 3 期。

吴苌弘：《法律翻译教学信息化研究——基于语料库和数据库检索系统的实践探索》，《外语电化教学》2014 年第 6 期。

武光军、王克非：《基于英语类比语料库的翻译文本中的搭配特征研究》，《中国外语》2011 年第 5 期。

武光军：《基于语料库的翻译文本中的搭配特征研究：回顾与评价》，《北京第二外国语学院学报》2012 年第 10 期。

肖海军：《非法人组织在民法典中的主体定位及其实现》，《法商研究》2016 年第 2 期。

肖航：《现代汉语通用平衡语料库建设与应用》，《华文世界》（台湾）2010 年第 106 期。

谢鸿飞、涂燕辉:《民法典中非营利法人制度的创新及评价》,《社会治理》
　　2020 年第 7 期。

谢鸿飞:《公序良俗原则的功能及其展开》,《探索与争鸣》2020 年第 5 期。

杨立新:《〈民法总则〉规定的非法人组织的主体地位与规则》,《求是学刊》
　　2017 年第 3 期。

张春祥:《基于短语对齐的汉-英翻译知识自动获取》,哈尔滨工业大学 2006
　　年博士学位论文。

张法连:《英美法律术语汉译策略探究》,《中国翻译》2016 年第 2 期。

张潇剑:《国际私法上的公共政策机制之剖析》,《法学评论》2005 年第 4 期。

张新宝、张红:《中国民法百年变迁》,《中国社会科学》2011 第 6 期。

张新宝:《中国民法和民法学的现状与展望》,《法学评论》2011 年第 3 期。

致远:《文义解释法的具体应用规则》,《法律适用》2001 年第 9 期。

周亚祥:《科技术语译名的统一问题》,《中国科技期刊研究》2001 年第 4 期。

二、外文文献

(一) 著作

Asher, R., *The Encyclopedia of Language and Linguistics*, Oxford: Oxford
　　University Press, 1993.

Babbie, Earl, *The Practice of Social Research* (*12th ed.*), Cambridge: Wadsworth
　　Publishing, 2010.

Baker, Paul, Andrew Hardie, Tony McEnery, *A Glossary of Corpus Llinguis*,
　　Edinburgh: Edinburgh University Press, 2006.

Bennett, Gena R., *Using Corpora in the Language Learning Classroom: Corpus
　　Linguistics for Teachers*, Ann Arbor: The University of Michigan
　　Press, 2010.

Biber, D., S. Conrad, R. Reppen, *Corpus Linguistics: Investigating Language
　　Structure and Use*, Cambridge: Cambridge University Press, 1998.

Biber, D. , et al. , *Longman Grammar of Spoken and Written English*, New York: Pearson Education, 1999.

Coode, G. , *On Legislative Expression or Language of Written Law*, *Introduction to a Digest of the Poor Laws*, Appendixed to the 1843 Report of the Poor Law Commission, 1843. Reproduced in Elmer A. Driedger, *The Composition of Legislation*, Ottawa: Queen's Printer and Controller of Stationery, 1957.

Cowie, A. P. , *Phraseology: Theory, Analysis, and Application*, Oxford: Clarendo Press, 1998.

Culicover, W. , *Simpler Syntax*, Oxford: Oxford University, 1999.

Garner, Bryan A. (eds.), *Black's Law Dictionary (10th ed.)*, St. Paul: Thomson Reuters, 2014.

Halliday, M. , C. Matthiessen, *An Introduction to Functional Grammar*, London: Edward Arnold / Beijing: Foreign Language Teaching and Research Press, 1994/2000.

Landsberger, Henry A. , *Hawthorne Revisited: Management and the Worker, Its Critics, and Developments in Human Relations in Industry*, New York: Cornell University Press, 1958.

Langacker, R W. , *The Foundations of Cognitive Grammar: Theoretical Prerequisites* v. 1, Redwood City: Stanford University Press, 1987.

Lewis, M. , *The Lexical Approach: The State of ELT and a Way Forward*, London: Language Teaching Publications, 1993.

McEnery, Tony, Andrew Wilson, *Corpus Linguistics: An Introduction (2d ed.)*, Edinburgh: Edinburgh University Press, 2001.

McEnery, Tony, Andrew Hardie, *Corpus Linguistics: Method, Theory and Practice*, Cambridge: Cambridge University Press, 2011.

Nattinger,J. , J. DeCarrico, *Lexical Phrases and Language Teaching*, Shanghai: Shanghai Foreign Language education Press, 1992.

Reis, K. , H. Vermeer, *Groundwork for a General Theory of Translation*, Berlin:

Walter de Gruyter, 1984.

Šarcevic, Susan, *New Approach to Legal Translation*, The Hague: Kluwer Law International, 1997.

Sinclair, J. , *Corpus, Concordance, Collocation*, Oxford: Oxford University Press, 1991.

Sinclair, J. , et al. , *Collins COBUILD Grammar Patterns 1: Verbs* , London: Harper-Collins Publishers, 1996.

Sinclair, J. , et al. , *English Collocation Studies: The OSTI Report*, London: Continuum, 2004.

Sinclair, J. , *Trust the Text*, London: Routledge, 2004.

Wang Chonghui, *The German Civil Code Translated and Annotated with an Historical Introduction and Appendices*, London: Stevens and Sons Limited, 1907.

Wray, A. , *Formulaic Language and the Lexicon*, Cambridge: Cambridge University Press, 2002.

Wray, A. , *Formulaic Language: Pushing the Boundaries*, Oxford: Oxford University Press, 2008.

(二) 论文

Altenberg, B. , "Adverbial Connectors in English and Swedish: Semantic and Lexical Correspondences", in H. Hasselgård, S. Oksefjell (eds.), *Out of Corpora: Studies in Honour of Stig Johansson*, New York: Rodopi, 1999.

Baker, M. , "Corpus Linguistics and Translation Studies", in M. Baker, G. Francis & E. Tognini-Bonelli (eds.), *Text and Technology*, Amsterdam: John Benjamins, 1993.

Biber, D. , "A Corpus-Driven Approach to Formulaic Language in English: Multi-word Patterns in Speech and Writing", *International Journal of Corpus Linguistics*, Vol. 14, No. 3, 2009.

Biber, D. , "Corpus-Based and Corpus-Driven Analyses of Language Variation and Use", in Bernd Heine, Heiko Narrog (eds.), *The Oxford Handbook of Linguistic Analysis*, New York: Oxford University Press, 2010.

Brown, P. F. , J. C. Lai & R. L. Mercer, "Aligning Sentences in Parallel Corpora", in *Proceedings of the 29th Annual Meeting of the ACL, 1991*.

Chen, S. F. , " Aligning Sentences in Bilingual Corpora Using Lexical Information", in *Proceedings of the 31st Annual Meeting of the ACL, 1993*.

Church, Gale, " A Program for Aligning Sentences in Bilingual Corpora ", *Computational Linguisties*, Vol. 19, No. 1, 1991.

Church, Kenneth Ward, Patrick Hanks, " Word Association Norms, Mutual Information, and Lexicography", *Computational Linguistics*, Vol. 16, No. 1, 1990.

Conklin, K. , N. Schmitt, "Formulaic Sequences: Are They Processed More Quickly than Nonformulaic Language by Native and Nonnative Speakers?" *Applied Linguistics*, Vol. 29, No. 1, 2008.

Cowie, A. P. , " Speech Formulae in English: Problems of Analysis and Dictionary Treatment", in G. Meer, A. Meulen (eds.), *Making Sense: from Lexeme to Discourse*, Centre for Language and Cognition, 2001.

Culicover, P. W. , *Simpler Syntax*, Oxford: Oxford University Press, 1999.

De Cock, S. , " A Recurrent Word Combination Approach to the Study of Formulae in the Speech of Native and Non-Native Speakers of English", *International Journal of Corpus Linguistics*, Vol. 3, No. 1, 1998.

Firth, J. R. , "A Synopsis of Linguistic Theory, 1930-1955", in J. R. Firth, et al. (eds.), *Studies in Linguistic Analysis*, Oxford: Blackwell, 1957.

Erman, B. , B. Warren, "The Idiom Principle and the Open Choice Principle", *Text* , Vol. 20, No. 1, 2000.

Gale, C. A. , " Program for Aligning Sentences in Bilingual Corpora ", *Computational Linguisties*, Vol. 19, No. 1, 1991.

Geries, S. , "Corpus Linguistics and Theoretical Linguistics: A Love-Hate Realtionshi? Not Necessarily ", *International Journal of Corpus Linguistics*, Vol. 15, No. 3, 2010.

Goldfarb, Neal, "The Use of Corpus Linguistics in Legal Interpretation", *Annual Review of Linguistics*, No. 7, 2021.

Granger, S. , "The Corpus Approach: A Common Way Forward for Contrastive Linguistics and Translationstudies?", in S. Granger, J. Lerot & S. Petch-Tyson (eds.), *Corpus-based Approaches to Contrastive Linguistics and Translation Studie*, Amsterdam & New York: Rodopi, 2003.

Granger, S. , M. Paquot, "Dissentangling the Phraseological Web", in S. Granger, F. Meunier (eds.), *Phraseology: An Interdisciplinary Perspective*, Amsterdam/Philadelphia: John Benjamins, 2008.

Johansson, S. , "Contrastive Linguistics and Corpora", in S. Granger, L. Jacques & P. T. Stephaine (eds.), *Corpus Based Approaches to Contrastive Linguistics and Translation Studies*, Amsterdam & New York: Rodopi, 2003.

Kay, M. , K. Röescheisen, "Text-Translation Alignment", *Computational Linguistics*, Vol. 19, No. 1, 1993.

Lee, Thomas R. , Stephen C. Mouritsen, "Judging Ordinary Meaning", *Yale Law Journal*, Vol. 127, No. 4, 2018.

Mauranen, A. , "Strange Strings in Translated Language: A Study of Corpora", in M. Olohan (ed.), *Intercultural Faultlines: Research Models in Translation Studies I*, Manchester: St. Jerome, 2000.

McGinnis, John O. , Michael B. Rappaport, "The Constitution and the Language of the Law", *William & Mary Law Review*, Vol. 59, No. 4, 2018.

Mouritsen, Stephen C. , "The Dictionary Is Not a Fortress: Definitional Fallacies and a Corpus-Based Approach to Plain Meaning", *BYU Law Review*, No. 5, 2010.

Mouritsen, Stephen C. , "Hard Cases and Hard Data: Assessing Corpus

Linguistics as an Empirical Path to Plain Meaning", *Columbia Science and Technology Law Review*, Vol. 13, No. 1, 2012.

Pérez-Llantada, C. , "Formulaic Language in L1 and L2 Expert Academic Writing: Convergent and Divergent Usage", *Journal of English for Academic Purposes*, Vol. 14, 2014.

Phillips, James C. , Daniel M. Ortner & Thomas R. Lee, "Corpus Linguistics & Original Public Meaning: A New Tool to Make Originalism More Empirical", *The Yale Law Journal Forum*, Vol. 126, 2016.

Phillips, James C. , Jesse Egbert, "Advancing Law and Corpus Linguistics: Importing Principles and Practices from Survey and Content-Analysis Methodologies to Improve Corpus Design and Analysis", *BYU Law Review*, No. 6, 2017.

Sinclair, J. , "Corpus, Concordance, Collocation", *Modern Language Journal*, Vol. 78, No. 3, 1991.

Sinclair, J. , "The Search for Units of Meaning", *Textus*, No. 9, 1996.

Solan, Lawrence M. , "The New Textualists' New Text", *Loyola of Los Angeles Law Review*, Vol. 38, 2005.

Solan, Lawrence M. , "Can Corpus Linguistics Help Make Originalism Scientific?", *The Yale Law Journal Forum*, Vol. 126, 2016.

Strang, Lee J. , "How Big Data Can Increase Originalism's Methodological Rigor: Using Corpus Linguistics to Reveal Original Language Conventions", *UC Davis Law Review*, Vol. 50, 2017.

Teubert, W. , "Corpus Linguistics and Lexicography", *International Journal of Corpus Linguistics*, 2001 (Special Issue).

Teubert, W. , "Directions in Corpus Linguistics", in M. Halliday, W. Teubert, C. Yalop & A. Germakova (eds.), *Lexicology & Corpus Linguistics*, London & New York: Continuum, 2004.

Tiersma, P. , "A Message in a Bottle: Text, Autonomy, and Statutory

Interpretation", *Tulane Law Review*, Vol. 76, No. 2, 2001.

Wray, A. , M. Perkins, "The Functions of Formulaic Language: An Integrated Model", *Language and Communication*, Vol. 20, No. 1, 2000.

Wu Dekai, "Aligning a Parallel English-Chinese Corpus Statistically with Lexical Criteria", in *Proceedings of the 32nd Annual Meeting of the ACL*, *1994*.

Xiao, R. , L. He & M. Yue, "In Pursuit of the Third Code: Using the ZJU Corpus of Translational Chinese in Translation Studies", in R. Xiao (ed.), *Using Corpora in Contrastive and Translation Studies*, Newcastle: Cambridge Scholars Publishing, 2010.

附 录

重要汉英民法术语及扩展翻译单位列表^①

序号	术语原文	参考译文	原文例句	译文例句
1	安全保障措施	security measure	物业服务企业等建筑物管理人应当采取必要的安全保障措施防止前款规定情形的发生；未采取必要的安全保障措施的，应当依法承担未履行安全保障义务的侵权责任。	The manager of a building such as the property management service enterprise shall take necessary security measures to prevent the occurrence of the incident specified in the preceding paragraph. Where no necessary security measures are taken, it shall bear tort liability for failure to perform the obligation of providing security measures in accordance with law.

续表

序号	术语原文	参考译文	原文例句	译文例句
2	安全保障义务	obligation of providing security	物业服务企业等建筑物管理人应当采取必要的安全保障措施防止前款规定情形的发生；未采取必要的安全保障措施的，应当依法承担未履行安全保障义务的侵权责任。	The manager of a building such as the property management service enterprise shall take necessary security measures to prevent the occurrence of the incident specified in the preceding paragraph. Where no necessary security measures are taken, it shall bear tort liability for failure to perform the obligation of providing security measures in accordance with law.
3	安置补助费	resettlement subsidies	征收集体所有的土地，应当依法及时足额支付土地补偿费、安置补助费以及农村村民住宅、其他地上附着物和青苗等的补偿费用，并安排被征地农民的社会保障费用，保障被征地农民的生活，维护被征地农民的合法权益。	In the case of expropriation of collectively-owned land, land compensation fees, resettlement subsidies, and compensation fees for rural villagers' dwellings and other ground attachments as well as young crops shall be paid in full in a timely manner in accordance with law, and social security premiums of the farmers whose land has been expropriated shall be arranged, their lives secured, and their lawful rights and interests safeguarded.

续表

序号	术语原文	参考译文	原文例句	译文例句
4	按份共有	co-ownership by shares	共有包括按份共有和共同共有。	Co-ownership consists of co-ownership by shares and joint co-ownership.
5	保理合同	factoring contract	第十六章　保理合同	Chapter XVI Factoring Contracts
6	保密义务	confidentiality obligation	前款规定的保密义务，不限制许可人申请专利，但是当事人另有约定的除外。	The confidentiality obligations provided in the preceding paragraph may not restrict the licensor's ability to file an application for a patent, unless otherwise agreed by the parties.
7	保险合同	insurance contract	第一千二百一十三条 机动车发生交通事故造成损害，属于该机动车一方责任的，先由承保机动车强制保险的保险人在强制保险责任限额范围内予以赔偿；不足部分，由承保机动车商业保险的保险人按照保险合同的约定予以赔偿；仍然不足或者没有投保商业保险的，由侵权人赔偿。	Article 1213 Where damage is caused to another person as a result of a traffic accident and the liability is attributed to the motor vehicle driver, compensation shall be made first by the insurer that underwrites the compulsory motor vehicle insurance within the limit of the insured liability. The deficiencies shall be paid by the insurer that underwrites the commercial motor vehicle insurance in accordance with the stipulations of the insurance contract. Any remaining balance or the part not covered by any commercial motor vehicle insurance shall be paid by the tortfeasor.

续表

序号	术语原文	参考译文	原文例句	译文例句
8	保证责任	suretyship liability	连带责任保证的债权人未在保证期间请求保证人承担保证责任的,保证人不再承担保证责任。	Where a creditor of a suretyship with joint and several liability fails to request the surety to undertake his suretyship liability within the term of suretyship, the surety no longer bears the suretyship liability.
9	背景资料	background information	与履行合同有关的技术背景资料,可行性论证和技术评价报告,项目任务书和技术计划书,技术标准,技术规范,原始设计和工艺文件,以及其他技术文档,按照当事人的约定可以作为合同的组成部分。	Materials such as technological background information, the feasibility studies and technological evaluation reports, the project task paper and plans, technology standards, technology norms, original design and technical documents, as well as other technical documents which are relevant to the performance of the contract may, as agreed by the parties, be component parts of the contract.
10	必要协助	necessary assistance	(二)承租人行使索赔权利时,未及时提供必要协助。	(2) when the lessee exercises the right to claim, the lessor fails to provide necessary assistance in a timely manner.

续表

序号	术语原文	参考译文	原文例句	译文例句
11	标的物	subject matter	电子合同的标的物为采用在线传输方式交付的,合同标的物进入对方当事人指定的特定系统且能够检索识别的时间为交付时间。	Where the subject matter of the said electronic contract is delivered by online transmission, the time of delivery is the time when the subject matter of the contract enters the specific system designated by the other party and can be searched and identified.
12	表决程序	voting method	法人、非法人组织依照法律或者章程规定的议事方式和表决程序作出决议的,该决议行为成立。	Where a legal person or an unincorporated organization makes a resolution in accordance with the procedure and voting method provided by law or stipulated in its articles of association, such a resolution isaccomplished as a civil juristic act.
13	补充协议	supplementary agreement	第五百一十条 合同生效后,当事人就质量、价款或者报酬、履行地点等内容没有约定或者约定不明确的,可以协议补充;不能达成补充协议的,按照合同相关条款或者交易习惯确定。	Article 510 After a contract becomes effective, where the parties have not agreed on such contents as the quality, price or remuneration, or the place of performance, and the like, or the relevant agreement is unclear, the parties may make a supplementary agreement; where the parties fail to reach a supplementary agreement, such contents shall be determined according to the relevant clauses of the contract or the course of dealing.

续表

序号	术语原文	参考译文	原文例句	译文例句
14	不当得利	unjust enrichment	债权是因合同、侵权行为、无因管理、不当得利以及法律的其他规定，权利人请求特定义务人为或者不为一定行为的权利。	A right in personam is the right of an obligee to request a specific obligor to do or not to do a certain act, as arising from a contract, a tortious act, a negotiorum gestio, or unjust enrichment, or otherwise arising by operation of law.
15	不动产	immovable property	国家对不动产实行统一登记制度。	The State implements a unified registration system with respect to immovable property.
16	不动产登记	registration of immovable property	第一节 不动产登记	Section 1 Registration of Immovable Property
17	不利影响	adversely affect	抵押权人与抵押人可以协议变更抵押权顺位以及被担保的债权数额等内容。但是，抵押权的变更未经其他抵押权人书面同意的，不得对其他抵押权人产生不利影响。	A mortgagee and the mortgagor may reach an agreement to change such things as the mortgagee's priority order in the line of the mortgagees and the amount of the secured claim, provided that any change to the mortgage may not adversely affect the other mortgagees without their written consent.

续表

序号	术语原文	参考译文	原文例句	译文例句
18	财产安全	property safety	第一千一百六十七条 侵权行为危及他人人身、财产安全的,被侵权人有权请求侵权人承担停止侵害、排除妨碍、消除危险等侵权责任。	Article 1167 Where a tortious act endangers another person's personal or property safety, the infringed person has the right to request the tortfeasor to bear tort liability such as cessation of the infringement, removal of the nuisance, or elimination of the danger.
19	财产权利	proprietary rights	第三条 民事主体的人身权利,财产权利以及其他合法权益受法律保护,任何组织或者个人不得侵犯。	Article 3 The personal rights, proprietary rights, and other lawful rights and interests of the persons of the civil law are protected by law and free from infringement by any organization or individual.
20	财产权益	proprietary interests	第四十三条 财产代管人应当妥善管理失踪人的财产,维护其财产权益。	Article 43 A custodian shall properly manage the missing person's property and safeguard his proprietary interests.
21	财务状况	financial condition	第六百六十九条 订立借款合同,借款人应当按照贷款人的要求提供与借款有关的业务活动和财务状况的真实情况。	Article 669 Upon concluding a loan contract, a borrower shall, as required by the lender, provide true information about his business activities and financial conditions related to the borrowing to the lender.

续表

序号	术语原文	参考译文	原文例句	译文例句
22	裁判文书	judgment	行为人拒不承担前款规定的民事责任的，人民法院可以采取在报刊、网络等媒体上发布公告或者公布生效裁判文书等方式执行，产生的费用由行为人负担。	Where an actor refuses to bear civil liability as provided in the preceding paragraph, the people's court may take such measures as making an announcement, publishing the final judgment, or the like, through media, such as newspapers, periodicals, or online websites, and any expenses thus incurred shall be borne by the actor.
23	采矿权	the right to mine minerals	第三百二十九条 依法取得的探矿权、采矿权、取水权和使用水域、滩涂从事养殖、捕捞的权利受法律保护。	Article 329 The right to explore and mine minerals, to draw water, and to use waters and mudflats to engage in aquaculture or fishing that are acquired in accordance with law is protected by law.
24	采取补救措施	take remedial measure	第五百七十七条 当事人一方不履行合同义务或者履行合同义务不符合约定的，应当承担继续履行、采取补救措施或者赔偿损失等违约责任。	Article 577 Where a party fails to perform the contractual obligations or the performance does not conform to the agreement, it shall bear default liability such as continuing to perform the obligations, taking remedial measures, or compensating for losses.

续表

序号	术语原文	参考译文	原文例句	译文例句
25	仓储合同	warehousing contract	第九百零四条　仓储合同是保管人储存存货人交付的仓储物,存货人支付仓储费的合同。	Article 904 A warehousing contract is a contract under which a warehouser stores the goods delivered by a depositor for which the depositor pays the warehousing fee.
26	产品价格	price of the product	约定提成支付的,可以按照产品价格、实施专利和使用技术秘密后新增的产品价值、利润或者产品销售额的一定比例提成,也可以按照约定的其他方式计算。	Where the parties agree to adopt a method of commission payment, the commission may be drawn at a specific percentage from the price of the product, the newly-increased output value and profits attained from the exploitation of patents and the utilization of technological know-how, or the sales revenue of the product, or be calculated by other methods as agreed by the parties.
27	产品责任	product liability	第四章　产品责任	Chapter IV Product Liability

续表

序号	术语原文	参考译文	原文例句	译文例句
28	产生的费用	expensesfor	第九百七十八条 合伙合同终止后，合伙财产在支付因终止而产生的费用以及清偿合伙债务后有剩余的，依据本法第九百七十二条的规定进行分配。	Article 978 Upon termination of a partnership contract, after paying the expenses for termination and discharging the partnership debts, the residual assets of the partnership property, if any, shall be distributed in accordance with the provisionsof Article 972 of this Code.
29	撤销	revoke	第一百五十条 一方或者第三人以胁迫手段，使对方在违背真实意思的情况下实施的民事法律行为，受胁迫方有权请求人民法院或者仲裁机构予以撤销。	Article 150 Where a party performs a civil juristic act against its true intention owing to duress of the other party or a third person, the coerced party has the right to request the people's court or an arbitration institution to revoke the civil juristic act.
30	撤销权	right to revoke	第一百五十二条 有下列情形之一的，撤销权消灭：	Article 152 A party's right to revoke a civil juristic act is extinguished under any of the following circumstances:
31	成年子女	adult children	成年子女对父母负有赡养、扶助和保护的义务。	Adult children have the duty to support, assist, and protect their parents.

续表

序号	术语原文	参考译文	原文例句	译文例句
32	诚信原则	the principle of good faith	第七条　民事主体从事民事活动,应当遵循诚信原则,秉持诚实、恪守承诺。	Article 7 When conducting a civil activity, a person of the civil law shall, in compliance with the principle of good faith, uphold honesty and honor commitments.
33	承包地	contracted land	(二)个别土地承包经营权人之间承包地的调整;	(2) adjustment to the contracted land among the persons who have the right to contractual management of land;
34	承担法律责任	bear legal liability	监护人不履行监护职责或者侵害被监护人合法权益的,应当承担法律责任。	A guardian who fails to perform his duties or infringes upon the lawful rights or interests of the ward shall bear legal liability.
35	承揽合同	work contract	第七百七十条　承揽合同是承揽人按照定作人的要求完成工作,交付工作成果,定作人支付报酬的合同。	Article 770 A work contract is a contract under which a contractor, in accordance with the requirements of a client, completes a work and delivers the work product to the client who pays remuneration in return.

续表

序号	术语原文	参考译文	原文例句	译文例句
36	惩罚性赔偿	punitive damages	第一千二百零七条　明知产品存在缺陷仍然生产、销售，或者没有依据前条规定采取有效补救措施，造成他人死亡或者健康严重损害的，被侵权人有权请求相应的惩罚性赔偿。	Article 1207 Where a manufacturer or seller manufactures or sells a product knowing that the product is defective, or failing to take remedial measures in accordance with the provisions of the preceding Article, so that death or serious physical harm is caused to another person, the infringed person has the right to request for the corresponding punitive damages.
37	出生时间	the time of birth	第十五条　自然人的出生时间和死亡时间，以出生证明、死亡证明记载的时间为准；没有出生证明、死亡证明的，以户籍登记或者其他有效身份登记记载的时间为准。	Article 15 The time of birth and time of death of a natural person are determined by the time recorded on his birth or death certificate as applied, or, if there is no birth or death certificate, by the time recorded in the natural person's household registration or other valid identity certificate. If there is sufficient evidence overturning the time recorded in the aforementioned documents, the time that is established by such evidence shall prevail.

续表

序号	术语原文	参考译文	原文例句	译文例句
38	初步证据	preliminary evidence	收货人在约定的期限或者合理期限内对货物的数量、毁损等未提出异议的,视为承运人已经按照运输单证的记载交付的初步证据。	Where the consignee does not raise any objection on the quantity, destruction, damage, or loss of the goods within the agreed time limit or a reasonable period of time, the silence is deemed as preliminary evidence that the carrier has delivered the goods in accordance with the transport documents.
39	村民委员会	villagers' committee	本条规定的有关组织包括:居民委员会、村民委员会、学校、医疗机构、妇女联合会、残疾人联合会、依法设立的老年人组织、民政部门等。	A relevant organization referred to in this Article includes a residents' committee, a villagers' committee, a school, a medical institution, the women's federation, the disabled person's federation, a legally established organization for senior people, the civil affairs departments, and the like.
40	代理人	agent	(三)代理人丧失民事行为能力;	(3) the agent loses his capacity for performing civil juristic acts;
41	担保合同	security contract	主合同解除后,担保人对承担的民事债务人应当承担担保责任仍应当承担担保责任,但是担保合同另有约定的除外。	After the principal contract is rescinded, a security provider shall still be obligated to secure the debtor's liability, unless otherwise agreed in the security contract.

续表

序号	术语原文	参考译文	原文例句	译文例句
42	道德义务	moral obligation	经过公证的赠与合同或者依法不得撤销的具有救灾、扶贫、助残等公益、道德义务性质的赠与合同，不适用前款规定。	The provisions of the preceding paragraph do not apply to a notarized gift contract, or a gift contract with a purpose of serving a public interest or performing a moral obligation that shall in accordance with law not be revoked, such as a gift contract for disaster-relief, poverty-relief, disability-relief, or the like purposes.
43	道路交通安全法律	laws on road traffic safety	第一千二百零八条　机动车发生交通事故造成损害的，依照道路交通安全法律和本法的有关规定承担赔偿责任。	Article 1208 Where a motor vehicle is involved in a traffic accident which causes damage, the liability for compensation shall be assumed in accordance with the relevant provisions of the laws on road traffic safety and this Code.
44	登记	register	受让人取得从权利不因该从权利未办理转移登记手续或者未转移占有而受到影响。	Failure to register the assignment of the accessory right or failure to change the possession thereof does not affect the acquisition of the accessory right by the assignee.

续表

序号	术语原文	参考译文	原文例句	译文例句
45	登记机关	registration authority	第一千零七十七条 自婚姻登记机关收到离婚登记申请之日起三十日内，任何一方不愿意离婚的，可以向婚姻登记机关撤回离婚登记申请。	Article 1077 Where either party is unwilling to divorce, he may withdraw the divorce registration application within thirty days after such an application is received by the marriage registration authority.
46	登记事项	items for registration	（二）就有关登记事项询问申请人；	(2) to inquire of the applicant regarding the relevant items for registration;
47	登记证书	registration certificate	（四）法人依法被吊销营业执照、登记证书，被责令关闭或者被撤销；	(4) the legal person's business license or registration certificate is legally revoked, or the legal person has received an order of closure or been dissolved;
48	低价转让	transferring something at low prices	违反国有财产管理规定，在企业改制、合并分立、关联交易等过程中，低价转让、合谋私分，擅自以其他方式造成国有财产损失的，应当依法承担法律责任。	A person, who causes losses to the State-owned property by transferring it at low prices, secretly distributing it in conspiracy with other persons, creating a security interest on it without authorization, or by other means in the course of enterprise restructuring, merger or division, affiliated transactions, and the like, in violation of the provisions on the administration of the State-owned property, shall bear legal liability in accordance with law.

续表

序号	术语原文	参考译文	原文例句	译文例句
49	抵押合同	mortgage contract	担保合同包括抵押合同、质押合同和其他具有担保功能的合同。	Security contracts include mortgage contracts, pledge contracts, and other contracts with a function of security.
50	地上附着物	ground attachments	征收集体所有的土地，应当依法及时足额支付土地补偿费、安置补助费以及农村村民住宅、其他地上附着物和青苗等的补偿费用，并安排被征地农民的社会保障费用，保障被征地农民的生活，维护被征地农民的合法权益。	In the case of expropriation of collectively-owned land, land compensation fees, resettlement subsidies, and compensation fees for rural villagers' dwellings and other ground attachments as well as young crops shall be paid in full in a timely manner in accordance with law, and social security premiums of the farmers whose land has been expropriated shall be arranged, their lives secured, and their lawful rights and interests safeguarded.
51	第一顺序继承人	successor(s) first in order	继承开始后，由第一顺序继承人继承，第二顺序继承人不继承；没有第一顺序继承人继承的，由第二顺序继承人继承。	When succession opens, the successor(s) first in order shall inherit to the exclusion of the successor(s) second in order. The successor(s) second in order shall inherit the estate in default of any successor first in order.

续表

序号	术语原文	参考译文	原文例句	译文例句
52	电力设施	electric power facilities	铁路、公路、电力设施、电信设施和油气管道等基础设施，依照法律规定为国家所有的，属于国家所有。	Infrastructures such as railways, roads, electric power facilities, telecommunication facilities, as well as oil and gas pipelines that are provided by law to be owned by the State are owned by the State.
53	电子合同	electronic contract	第五百一十二条　通过互联网等信息网络订立的电子合同的标的为交付商品并采用快递物流方式交付的，收货人的签收时间为交付时间。	Article 512 Where the object of an electronic contract concluded through internet or other information network is the delivery of goods and the goods are to be delivered by express delivery services, the time of delivery is the time of acknowledging receipt of the goods by the recipient.
54	电子数据交换	electronic data interchange	以电子数据交换、电子邮件等方式能够有形地表现所载内容，并可以随时调取查用的数据电文，视为书面形式。	A data message in any form, such as electronic data interchange and e-mails, that renders the content contained therein capable of being represented in a tangible form and accessible for reference and use at any time is deemed as a writing.

续表

序号	术语原文	参考译文	原文例句	译文例句
55	订立合同	conclude a contract	第四百六十九条 当事人订立合同,可以采用书面形式、口头形式或者其他形式。	Article 469 The parties may conclude a contract in writing, orally, or in other forms.
56	定金合同	earnest money contract	定金合同自实际交付定金时成立。	An earnest money contract is formed upon actual delivery of the earnest money.
57	动产	movable property	第二百四十条 所有权人对自己的不动产或者动产,依法享有占有、使用、收益和处分的权利。	Article 240 An owner is entitled to possess, use, benefit from, and dispose of his own immovable or movable property in accordance with law.
58	独立地位	independent status	营利法人的出资人不得滥用法人独立地位和出资人有限责任损害法人债权人的利益;滥用法人独立地位和出资人有限责任,逃避债务,严重损害法人债权人的利益的,应当对法人债务承担连带责任。	A capital contributor of a for-profit legal person may not abuse the legal person's independent status and his own limited liability status to harm the interests of the legal person's creditors. A capital contributor abusing the legal person's independent status or its own limited liability status to evade repayment of debts and thus severely harming the interests of the legal person's creditors shall be jointly and severally liable for the legal person's obligations.

续表

序号	术语原文	参考译文	原文例句	译文例句
59	多式联运	multi-modal transport	第八百三十八条　多式联运经营人负责履行或者组织履行多式联运合同,对全程运输享有承运人的权利,承担承运人的义务。	Article 838 An operator of multi-modal transport is responsible for performing or organizing the performance of a multi-modal transport contract, and enjoys the rights and assumes the obligations of a carrier throughout the entire transport.
60	儿童福利机构	children's welfare institution	(二)儿童福利机构;	(2) a children's welfare institution;
61	发展权利	development rights	国家实行社会主义市场经济,保障一切市场主体的平等法律地位和发展权利。	The state implements the socialist market economy, and safeguards the equal legal status and development rights of all market players.
62	法定代理人	legal representative	第十九条　八周岁以上的未成年人为限制民事行为能力人,实施民事法律行为由其法定代理人代理或者经其法定代理人同意、追认;但是,可以独立实施纯获利益的民事法律行为或者与其年龄、智力相适应的民事法律行为。	Article 19 A minor aged eight or above has limited capacity for performing civil juristic acts and may perform a civil juristic act through or upon consent or ratification of his legal representative, except that such a minor may independently perform a civil juristic act that is purely beneficial to him or that is appropriate to his age and intelligence.

续表

序号	术语原文	参考译文	原文例句	译文例句
63	法定货币	lawful currency	第五百一十四条　以支付金钱为内容的债，除法律另有规定或者当事人另有约定外，债权人可以请求债务人以实际履行地的法定货币币履行。	Article 514 Where an obligation is payment of money, unless otherwise provided by law or agreed by the parties, the creditor may request the debtor to perform the obligation by the lawful currency of the place of actual performance.
64	法定孳息	civil fruits	第四百一十二条　债务人不履行到期债务或者发生当事人约定的实现抵押权的情形，致使抵押财产被人民法院依法扣押的，自扣押之日起，抵押权人有权收取该抵押财产的天然孳息或者法定孳息，但是抵押权人未通知应当清偿法定孳息义务人的除外。	Article 412 Where a debtor fails to perform his obligation due or an event upon the occurrence of which a mortgage is to be enforced as agreed upon by the parties occurs, resulting in the seizure of the mortgaged property by the people's court in accordance with law, the mortgagee is entitled to collect the natural fruits or civil fruits accrued from the mortgaged property as of the date of the seizure, unless the mortgagee fails to notify the person who is obligated to pay off the civil fruits.

续表

序号	术语原文	参考译文	原文例句	译文例句
65	受法律保护	be protected by law	第三条　民事主体的人身权利、财产权利以及其他合法权益受法律保护，任何组织或者个人不得侵犯。	Article 3 The personal rights, proprietary rights, and other lawful rights and interests of the persons of the civil law are protected by law and free from infringement by any organization or individual.
66	法律地位	legal status	第四条　民事主体在民事活动中的法律地位一律平等。	Article 4 All persons of the civil law are equal in legal status when conducting civil activities.
67	法律法规	laws and regulations	对物业服务区域内违反有关治安、环保、消防等法律法规的行为，物业服务人应当及时采取合理措施制止，向有关行政主管部门报告并协助处理。	For any violation of the relevant laws or regulations on public security, environmental protection, fire protection, and the like in theproperty management service area, the property management service provider shall, in a timely manner, take reasonable measures to stop the violation, make a report to the competent department, and render assistance to the department in handling the violation.

续表

序号	术语原文	参考译文	原文例句	译文例句
68	法律关系	juristic relationship	第五条　民事主体从事民事活动，应当遵循自愿原则，按照自己的意思设立、变更、终止民事法律关系。	Article 5 When conducting a civil activity, a person of the civil law shall, in compliance with the principle of voluntariness, create, alter, or terminate a civil juristic relationship according to his own will.
69	法律规定	provided by law	第一百二十九条　民事权利可以依据民事法律行为，事实行为，法律规定的事件或者法律规定的其他方式取得。	Article 129 Civil-law rights may be acquired through the performance of a civil juristic act, the occurrence of an act de facto, the occurrence of an event as provided by law, or by other means provided by law.
70	法律后果	legal consequences	第七十五条　设立人为设立法人从事的民事活动，其法律后果由法人承受；法人未成立的，其法律后果由设立人承受，设立人为二人以上的，享有连带债权，承担连带债务。	Article 75 The legal consequences of the civil activities conducted by an incorporator for the purpose of establishing a legal person shall be assumed by the legal person; or, in the event that no legal person is successfully established, by the incorporator, or the incorporators jointly and severally if there are two or more of them.

续表

序号	术语原文	参考译文	原文例句	译文例句
71	法律文书	legal document	第二百二十九条 因人民法院、仲裁机构的法律文书或者人民政府的征收决定等，导致物权设立、变更、转让或者消灭的，自法律文书或者征收决定等生效时发生效力。	Article 229 Where a real right is created, altered, transferred, or extinguished as a result of a legal document issued by the people's court or an arbitration institution, or based on an expropriation decision made by the people's government, the creation, alteration, transfer, or extinguishment of the real right becomes effective at the time when the legal document or expropriation decision enters into effect.
72	法律约束力	be legally binding on	第一百一十九条 依法成立的合同，对当事人具有法律约束力。	Article 119 A contract formed in accordance with law is legally binding on the parties to the contract.
73	法律约束力	legal effect	第五百四十二条 债务人影响债权人的债权实现的行为被撤销的，自始没有法律约束力。	Article 542 Where an act of the debtor adversely affecting the enforcement of the creditor's claim is revoked, such an act does not have legal effect *ab initio*.
74	法人	legal person	第五十八条 法人应当依法成立。	Article 58 A legal person shall be established in accordance with law.

续表

序号	术语原文	参考译文	原文例句	译文例句
75	返还财产	return of property	（二）不动产物权和登记的动产物权的权利人请求返还财产；	(2) a claim for return of property of a personwho has a real right in immovable or registered movable property;
76	返还原物	return the original thing	该遗失物通过转让被他人占有的，权利人有权向无处分权人请求损害赔偿，或者自知道或者应当知道受让人之日起二年内向受让人请求返还原物；但是，受让人通过拍卖或者向具有经营资格的经营者购得该遗失物的，权利人请求返还原物时应当支付受让人所付的费用。	Where the lost thing is possessed by another person by way of transfer, the right holder has the right to claim damages against the person who disposes of the thing without the right to disposition, or to request the transferee to return the original thing within two years from the date on which the right holder knows or should have known of the transferee; provided, however, that where the transferee has acquired the lost thing at auction or from a qualified business operator, the right holder shall, at the time of requesting the return of the original thing, reimburse the expenses that have been paid by the transferee.
77	犯罪记录	criminal record	（四）无不利于被收养人健康成长的违法犯罪记录；	(4) having no criminal record unfavorable to the healthy growth of the adoptee;

续表

序号	术语原文	参考译文	原文例句	译文例句
78	非法拘禁	illegal detention	第一千零一十一条　以非法拘禁等方式剥夺、限制他人的行动自由，或者非法搜查他人身体的，受害人有权依法请求行为人承担民事责任。	Article 1011 A person, whose freedom of movement has been deprived of or restricted by illegal detention or the like measures, or whose body has been illegally searched, has the right to request the actor to bear civil liability in accordance with law.
79	非法人组织	unincorporated organizations	第四章　非法人组织	Chapter IV Unincorporated Organizations
80	非法占有	illegally possess	第一千二百四十二条　非法占有高度危险物造成他人损害的，由非法占有人承担侵权责任。	Article 1242 Where damage is caused to another person by an ultra-hazardous thing that is illegally possessed, the illegal possessor of the ultra-hazardous thing shall bear tort liability.
81	非婚生子女	children born out of wedlock	本编所称子女，包括婚生子女、非婚生子女、养子女和有扶养关系的继子女。	"Children" referred to in this Book include children born in or out of wedlock, and adopted children, as well as stepchildren who were raised up by the decedent.

续表

序号	术语原文	参考译文	原文例句	译文例句
82	分立	division	违反国有财产管理规定，在企业改制、合并分立、关联交易等过程中，低价转让、合谋私分、擅自担保或者以其他方式造成国有财产损失的，应当依法承担法律责任。	A person, who causes losses to the State-owned property by transferring it at low prices, secretly distributing it in conspiracy with other persons, creating a security interest on it without authorization, or by other means in the course of enterprise restructuring, merger or division, affiliatedtransactions, and the like, in violation of the provisions on the administration of the State-owned property, shall bear legal liability in accordance with law.
83	分支机构	branch	第七十四条　法人可以依法设立分支机构。	Article 74 A legal person may establish branches in accordance with law.
84	夫妻共同财产	community property	（一）一方有隐藏、转移、变卖、毁损、挥霍夫妻共同财产或者伪造夫妻共同债务等严重损害夫妻共同财产利益的行为；	(1) the other spouse has concealed, transferred, sold, destructed or damaged, or squandered the community property, created a false community debt, or committed other acts that seriously infringe upon the interests of the community property;

续表

序号	术语原文	参考译文	原文例句	译文例句
85	扶养义务	obligation to support	(二)对赠与人有扶养义务而不履行;	(2) having an obligation to support the donor but failing to perform that obligation;
86	服务标准	service standard	第八百二十一条 承运人擅自降低服务标准的,应当根据旅客的请求退票或者减收票款;提高服务标准的,不得加收票款。	Article 821 A carrier who unilaterally downgrades the service standard shall, upon the passenger's request, refund his ticket or reduce the fare. A carrier who upgrades the service standard may not charge extra fare.
87	服务承诺	commitment of service	物业服务人公开作出的有利于业主的服务承诺,为物业服务合同的组成部分。	A commitment of service made publicly by a property management service provider in favor of the property owners shall be a component part of the property management service contract.
88	服务费用	service fee	第九百三十八条 物业服务合同的内容一般包括服务事项、服务质量、服务费用的标准和收取办法、维修资金的使用、服务用房的管理和使用、服务期限、服务交接等条款。	Article 938 A property management service contract generally contains clauses specifying the contents of the services, the services quality, the rates and the collection methods of the service fee, the use of the maintenance funds, the management and use of the service premises, the term of service, the service handover, and the like.

续表

序号	术语原文	参考译文	原文例句	译文例句
89	服务类型	type of service	网络服务提供者接到通知后，应当及时将该通知转送相关网络用户，并根据构成侵权的初步证据和服务类型采取必要措施；未及时采取必要措施的，对损害的扩大部分与该网络用户承担连带责任。	After receiving the notice, the network service provider shall timely forward the notice to the relevant network user and take necessary measures based on the preliminary evidence establishing the tort and the type of service complained about. Where it fails to take necessary measures in time, it shall assume joint and several liability for the aggravated part of the damage with the network user.
90	服务区域	service area	第九百四十二条　物业服务人应当按照约定和物业的使用性质，妥善维修、养护、清洁、绿化和经营管理物业服务区域内的业主共有部分，维护物业服务区域内的基本秩序，采取合理措施保护业主的人身、财产安全。	Article 942 A property management service provider shall, in accordance with the contract and the nature of the use of theproperty, properly repair, maintain, clean, grow plants in, and manage the common space of the property management service area co-owned by the owners, maintain the basic order in the property management service area, and take reasonable measures to protect the owners' personal and property safety.

续表

序号	术语原文	参考译文	原文例句	译文例句
91	服务组织	service provider	第九百四十一条 物业服务人将物业服务区域内的部分专项服务事项委托给其他专业性服务组织或者第三人的，应当就该部分专项服务事项向业主负责。	Article 941 Where a property management service provider authorizes a specialized service entity or any other third person to handle some specialized services in the property management service area, the property management service provider shall be responsible to the owners in terms of the specialized services.
92	父母子女	parents and children	当事人所生的子女，适用本法关于父母子女的规定。	The provisions of this Code on parents and children shall apply to the children born by the parties to a void or annulled marriage.
93	附属设施	ancillary facility	紧急情况下需要维修建筑物及其附属设施的，业主大会或者业主委员会可以依法申请使用建筑物及其附属设施的维修资金。	Where a building and its auxiliary facilities need to be maintained in an emergency situation, the owners' assembly or the owners' committee may, in accordance with law, apply for the use of the maintenance funds for the building and its auxiliary facilities.

续表

序号	术语原文	参考译文	原文例句	译文例句
94	高致病性（物）	highly pathogenicthing	第一千二百三十九条 占有或者使用易燃、易爆、剧毒、高放射性、强腐蚀性、高致病性等高度危险物造成他人损害的，占有人或者使用人应当承担侵权责任；但是，能够证明损害是因受害人故意或者不可抗力造成的，不承担责任。	Article 1239 Where the possession or use of flammable, explosive, highly toxic, highly radioactive, strongly corrosive, highly pathogenic, or other ultrahazardous things causes damage to another person, the possessor or user thereof shall bear tort liability, except that such a possessor or user does not assume any liability if it can be proven that the damage was intentionally caused by the victim or caused by *force majeure*.
95	格式条款	standard clause	第四百九十六条 格式条款是当事人为了重复使用而预先拟定，并在订立合同时未与对方协商的条款。	Article 496 A standard clause refers to a clause formulated in advance by a party for repeated use which has not been negotiated with the other party when concluding the contract.
96	工程建设标准	construction standard	第二百九十三条 建造建筑物，不得违反国家有关工程建设标准，不得妨碍相邻建筑物的通风、采光和日照。	Article 293 The construction of a building may not violate the relevant constructionstandards of the State or obstruct the ventilation, lighting, or sunlight of the adjacent buildings.

续表

序号	术语原文	参考译文	原文例句	译文例句
97	工程质量	project quality	第七百九十五条 施工合同的内容一般包括工程范围、建设工期、中间交工工程的开工和竣工时间、工程质量、工程造价、技术资料的交付时间、材料和设备供应责任、拨款和结算、竣工验收、质量保修范围和质量保证期、相互协作等条款。	Article 795 A construction contract generally contains clauses specifying the scope of the project, the period for construction, the time of commencement and completion of the project to be delivered in midcourse, project quality, costs, delivery time of technical materials, the responsibility for the supply of materials and equipment, fund allocation and settlement, project inspection and acceptance upon its completion, range and period of quality warranty, cooperation, and the like.
98	公共道路	public road	第二百七十四条 建筑区划内的道路,属于业主共有,但是属于城镇公共道路的除外。	Article 274 Roads within the construction zone are co-owned by all unit owners, except for those that are part of the urban public roads.
99	公共绿地	public green space	建筑区划内的绿地,属于业主共有,但是属于城镇公共绿地或者明示属于个人的除外。	Green spaces within the construction zone are co-owned by all unit owners, except for those that are part of the urban public green spaces and those expressly indicated to be owned by private individuals.

续表

序号	术语原文	参考译文	原文例句	译文例句
100	公平原则	the principle of fairness	第六条　民事主体从事民事活动，应当遵循公平原则，合理确定各方的权利和义务。	Article 6 When conducting a civil activity, a person of the civil law shall, in compliance with the principle of fairness, reasonably establish the rights and obligations of each party.
101	公序良俗	public order or good morals	第八条　民事主体从事民事活动，不得违反法律，不得违背公序良俗。	Article 8 When conducting a civil activity, no person of the civil law may violate the law, or offend public order or good morals.
102	共同共有	joint co-ownership	共有包括按份共有和共同共有。	Co-ownership consists of co-ownership by shares and joint co-ownership.
103	共同利益	common interest	第九十条　具备法人条件，基于会员共同意愿，为公益目的或者会员共同利益等非营利目的设立的社会团体，经依法登记成立，取得社会团体法人资格；依法不需要办理法人登记的，从成立之日起，具有社会团体法人资格。	Article 90 A social organization established upon the common will of its members for a non-profit purpose, such as public welfare or the common interest of all members, attains the status of a social-organization legal person if it satisfies the requirements for being a legal person and is legally registered as such. Where the law does not require such a social organization to be registered, it attains the status of a social-organization legal person from the date of its establishment.

续表

序号	术语原文	参考译文	原文例句	译文例句
104	共有	co-ownership	第八章　共有	Chapter VIII Co-ownership
105	供电质量标准	standard for power supply	第六百五十一条　供电人应当按照国家规定的供电质量标准和约定安全供电。	Article 651 A supplier of electricity shall safely supply electricity in accordance with the quality standard for power supply set by the State and in the agreement.
106	股份有限公司	a joint stock company limited by shares	第二百六十八条　国家、集体和私人依法可以出资设立有限责任公司、股份有限公司或者其他企业。	Article 268 The State, collectives, and private individuals may establish companies with limited liabilities, joint stock companies limited by shares, or other enterprises through making capital contributions in accordance with law.
107	固体废物	solid wastes	第二百九十四条　不动产权利人不得违反国家规定弃置固体废物，排放大气污染物、水污染物、土壤污染物、噪声、光辐射、电磁辐射等有害物质。	Article 294 A person entitled to the real rights in immovable property may not, in violation of the regulations of the State, discard solid wastes or emit harmful substances such as atmospheric pollutants, water pollutants, soil pollutants, noises, light radiation, or electromagnetic radiation.

续表

序号	术语原文	参考译文	原文例句	译文例句
108	故意犯罪	intentional crime	第三十八条 被监护人的父母或者子女被人民法院撤销监护人资格后,除对被监护人实施故意犯罪的外,经其申请,人民法院确有悔改表现的,可以在尊重被监护人真实意愿的前提下,视情况恢复其监护人资格,人民法院指定的监护人与被监护人的监护关系同时终止。	Article 38 Where a ward's parent or child, who has been disqualified as a guardian by the people's court for reasons other than having committed an intentional crime against the ward, and who has truly repented and mended his ways, applies to the people's court for reinstatement, the people's court may, upon considering the actual situation and upon the satisfaction of the prerequisite that the true will of the ward is respected, reinstate the guardian, and the guardianship between the ward and the guardian appointed by the people's court after the disqualification of the original guardian shall thus be terminated simultaneously.

续表

序号	术语原文	参考译文	原文例句	译文例句
109	关联交易	affiliated transactions	违反国有财产管理规定，在企业改制、合并分立、关联交易等过程中，低价转让，合谋私分，擅自担保或者以其他方式造成国有财产损失的，应当依法承担法律责任。	A person, who causes losses to the State-owned property by transferring it at low prices, secretly distributing it in conspiracy with other persons, creating a security interest on it without authorization, or by other means in the course of enterprise restructuring, merger or division, affiliated transactions, and the like, in violation of the provisions on the administration of the State-owned property, shall bear legalliability in accordance with law.
110	管理措施	management measure	物业服务企业或者其他管理人应当执行政府依法实施的应急处置措施和其他管理措施，积极配合开展相关工作。	The property management service enterprise or other managers shall carry out emergency measures and other management measures implemented by the government in accordance with law and actively cooperate in the performance of the relevant work.

续表

序号	术语原文	参考译文	原文例句	译文例句
111	管理和使用	management and use	第九百三十八条　物业服务合同的内容一般包括服务事项、服务质量、服务费用的标准和收取办法、维修资金的使用、服务用房的管理和使用、服务期限、服务交接等条款。	Article 938 A property management service contract generally contains clauses specifying the contents of the services, the service quality, the rates and the collection methods of the service fee, the use of the maintenance funds, the management and use of the service premises, the term of service, the service handover, and the like.
112	管理人	manager	（四）选聘和解聘物业服务企业或者其他管理人；	（4）to employ and remove the property management service enterprise or other managers;
113	国际货物买卖合同	contract for the international sale of goods	第五百九十四条　因国际货物买卖合同和技术进出口合同争议提起诉讼或者申请仲裁的时效期间为四年。	Article 594 The limitation period for filing a lawsuit or arbitration on a dispute arising from a contract for international sale of goods and a contract for the import and export of technology is four years.

续表

序号	术语原文	参考译文	原文例句	译文例句
114	国际经济组织	international economic organization	第六百八十三条　机关法人不得为保证人，但是经国务院批准为使用外国政府或者国际经济组织贷款进行转贷的除外。	Article 683 No State-organ legal person may act as a surety, except that such a State organ may, upon approval of the State Council, act as a surety in re-lending of the loans granted by a foreign government or an international economic organization.
115	国家利益	interests of the state	第一百三十二条　民事主体不得滥用民事权利损害国家利益、社会公共利益或者他人合法权益。	Article 132 No person of the civil law shall abuse his civil-law rights and harm the interests of the State, the public interests, or the lawful rights and interests of others.
116	行动自由	freedom of movement	自然人的身体完整和行动自由受法律保护。	A natural person's corporeal integrity and freedom of movement are protected by law and free from infringement by any organization or individual.
117	行纪人	broker	第九百五十四条　委托物交付给行纪人时有瑕疵或者容易腐烂、变质的，经委托人同意，行纪人可以处分该物；不能与委托人及时取得联系的，行纪人可以合理处分。	Article 954 If the commissioned article has a defect at the time when it is delivered to a broker, or if it is perishable, the broker may dispose of the article upon the client's consent; if the broker is unable to make prompt contact with the client, the broker may dispose of the article in a proper manner.

续表

序号	术语原文	参考译文	原文例句	译文例句
118	行使权利	exercise of rights	所有权人不得干涉用益物权人行使权利。	The owner may not interfere with the exercise of such rights by the usufructuary.
119	行业标准	industrial standard	(一)质量要求不明确的,按照强制性国家标准履行;没有强制性国家标准的,按照推荐性国家标准履行;没有推荐性国家标准的,按照行业标准履行;没有国家标准、行业标准的,按照通常标准或者符合合同目的的特定标准履行。	(1) where the quality requirements are not clearly stipulated, the contract shall be performed in accordance with a mandatory national standard, or a recommendatory national standard in the absence of a mandatory national standard, or the standard of the industry in the absence of a recommendatory national standard. In the absence of any national or industrial standard, the contract shall be performed in accordance with the general standard or a specific standard conforming to the purpose of the contract.
120	行政许可	administrative license	第七百三十八条　依照法律、行政法规的规定,对于租赁物的经营使用应当取得行政许可的,出租人未取得行政许可不影响融资租赁合同的效力。	Article 738 Where the operation or use of a leased object requires an administrative license in accordance with the provision of laws or administrative regulations, the failure of the lessor to obtain such administrative license does not affect the validity of the contract for financing lease.

续表

序号	术语原文	参考译文	原文例句	译文例句
121	行政主管部门	administrative department	业主或者其他行为人拒不履行相关义务的,有关当事人可以向有关行政主管部门报告或者投诉,有关行政主管部门应当依法处理。	Where a unit owner or an actor refuses to perform the relevant duties, the party concerned may make a report to, or lodge a complaint with the competent administrative department, which shall handle the case in accordance with law.
122	行政主管部门	administrative authority	第五百三十四条 对当事人利用合同实施危害国家利益、社会公共利益行为的,市场监督管理和其他有关行政主管部门依照法律、行政法规的规定负责监督处理。	Article 534 Where the parties take advantage of the contract to commit an act that endangers the State's interests or public interests, the market regulatory authority and other relevant administrative authorities shall be responsible for supervising and handling it in accordance with the provisions of laws and administrative regulations.
123	合并	merger	违反国有财产管理规定,在企业改制、合并分立、关联交易等过程中,遭自担保或者以其他方式造成国有财产损失的,应当依法承担法律责任。	A person, who causes losses to the State-owned property by transferring it at low prices, secretly distributing it in conspiracy with other persons, creating a security interest on it without authorization, or by other means in the course of enterprise restructuring, merger or division, affiliated transactions, and the like, in violation of the provisions on the administration of the State-owned property, shall bear legal liability in accordance with law.

续表

序号	术语原文	参考译文	原文例句	译文例句
124	合法财产	the property lawfully owned by	第二百六十七条　私人的合法财产受法律保护,禁止任何组织或者个人侵占、哄抢、破坏。	Article 267 The property lawfully owned by a private individual is protected by law, and no organization or individual may misappropriate, loot, or destruct such property.
125	合伙财产	partnership property	第九百六十九条　合伙人的出资、因合伙事务依法取得的收益和其他财产,属于合伙财产。	Article 969 The capital contributions made by the partners and the proceeds thereof and other property acquired in accordance with law in the course of the partnership business are partnership property.
126	合理补偿	reasonable compensation	当事人约定租赁期限届满租赁物归出租人所有,因租赁物毁损、灭失或者附合、混合于他物致使承租人不能返还的,出租人有权请求承租人给予合理补偿。	Where the parties agree that the lessor shall have the ownership over the leased object upon expiration of the term of the lease, and the lessee is unable to return the leased object due to destruction, damage, or loss of the leased object, or because the leased object has been attached to or mixed with another thing, the lessor has the right to request the lessee to make reasonable compensation.

续表

序号	术语原文	参考译文	原文例句	译文例句
127	合理成本	reasonable costs	第二百八十二条　建设单位、物业服务企业或者其他管理人等利用业主的共有部分产生的收入，在扣除合理成本之后，属于业主共有。	Article 282 The income generated from the space co-owned by the unit owners that is received by the developer, the property management service enterprise, or other managers is co-owned by all unit owners after reasonable costs are deducted.
128	合理措施	reasonable measures	第九百四十二条　物业服务人应当按照约定和物业的使用性质，妥善维修、养护、清洁、绿化和经营管理物业服务区域内的业主共有部分，维护物业服务区域内的基本秩序，采取合理措施保护业主的人身、财产安全。	Article 942 A property management service provider shall, in accordance with the contract and the nature of the use of the property, properly repair, maintain, clean, grow plants in, and manage the common space of the property management service area co-owned by the owners, maintain the basic order in the property management service area, and take reasonable measures to protect the owners' personal and property safety.
129	合理费用	reasonable expenses	当事人因防止损失扩大而支出的合理费用，由违约方负担。	The reasonable expenses incurred by a party in preventing the aggravation of the loss shall be borne by the breaching party.

续表

序号	术语原文	参考译文	原文例句	译文例句
130	合理价款	reasonable price	第四百零四条 以动产抵押的,不得对抗正常经营活动中已经支付合理价款并取得抵押财产的买受人。	Article 404 A mortgage on movable property may not be asserted against a buyer who has paid a reasonable purchase price and acquired the mortgaged property in the ordinary course of business.
131	合理期限	reasonable period of time	其他共有人应当在合理期限内行使优先购买权。	The other co-owners shall exercise their right of pre-emption within a reasonable period of time.
132	合理要求	reasonable demand	前款规定的协议或者判决,不妨碍子女在必要时向父母任何一方提出超过协议或者判决原定数额的合理要求。	The agreement or judgment provided in the preceding paragraph may not preclude the child, when necessary, from making reasonable demand of payment on either parent in excess of the amount specified in the agreement or judgment.
133	合谋私分	secretly distributing something in conspiracy with other persons	违反国有财产管理规定,在企业改制、合并分立、关联交易等过程中,擅自转让、合谋私分、低价保或者以其他方式造成国有财产损失的,应当依法承担法律责任。	A person, who causes losses to the State-owned property by transferring it at low prices, secretly distributing it in conspiracy with other persons, creating a security interest on it without authorization, or by other means in the course of enterprise restructuring, merger or division, affiliated transactions, and the like, in violation of the provisions on the administration of the State-owned property, shall bear legal liability in accordance with law.

续表

序号	术语原文	参考译文	原文例句	译文例句
134	合同关系	contractual relationship	第四百五十八条　基于合同关系等产生的占有，有关不动产或者动产的使用、收益、违约责任等，按照合同约定；合同没有约定或者约定不明确的，依照有关法律规定。	Article 458 In the case of possession of immovable or movable property based on a contractual relationship, matters such as the use of the immovable or movable property, the benefits therefrom, and the default liability shall be subject to the agreement in the contract; where there is no agreement thereon in the contract or the relevant agreement is unclear, the relevant provisions of laws shall be followed.
135	合同解除	contract be rescinded	第五百六十六条　合同解除后，尚未履行的，终止履行；已经履行的，根据履行情况和合同性质，当事人可以请求恢复原状或者采取其他补救措施，并有权请求赔偿损失。	Article 566 After a contract is rescinded, where an obligation has not yet been performed, the performance shall cease; where an obligation has already been performed, the parties may, taking into account the performance status and the nature of the contract, request restoration to the original status or other remedial measures taken, and have the right to request for compensation for the losses.

续表

序号	术语原文	参考译文	原文例句	译文例句
136	合同性质	nature of the contract	第五百六十六条　合同解除后，尚未履行的，终止履行；已经履行的，根据履行情况和合同性质，当事人可以请求恢复原状或者采取其他补救措施，并有权请求赔偿损失。	Article 566 After a contract is rescinded, where an obligation has not yet been performed, the performance shall cease; where an obligation has already been performed, the parties may, taking into account the performance status and the nature of the contract, request restoration to the original status or other remedial measures taken, and have the right to request for compensation for the losses.
137	合同义务	contractual obligations	第八百八十四条　技术服务合同的委托人不履行合同义务或者履行合同义务不符合约定，影响工作进度和质量，不接受或者逾期接受工作成果的，支付的报酬不得追回，未支付的报酬应当支付。	Article 884 Where a client to a technology service contract fails to perform the contractual obligations or performs the obligations in a manner inconsistent with the contract, thus affecting the progress and quality of the work, or fails to accept the work product or delays the acceptance, the client may not request for refund of the paid remuneration, and shall pay any unpaid remuneration.

续表

序号	术语原文	参考译文	原文例句	译文例句
138	合作经济组织法人	cooperative economic organizations legal person	第九十六条　本节规定的机关法人、农村集体经济组织法人、城镇农村的合作经济组织法人、基层群众性自治组织法人，为特别法人。	Article 96 For the purposes of this Section, State-organ legal persons, rural economic collective legal persons, urban and rural cooperative economic organization legal persons, and primary-level self-governing organization legal persons are special types of legal persons.
139	核材料	nuclear material	第一千二百三十七条　民用核设施或者运入运出核设施的核材料发生核事故造成他人损害的，民用核设施的营运单位应当承担侵权责任；但是，能够证明损害是因战争、武装冲突、暴乱等情形或者受害人故意造成的，不承担责任。	Article 1237 Where a nuclear accident occurs at a civil nuclear facility or when nuclear materials are transported into or out of a civil nuclear facility and damage is thus caused to another person, the operator of the facility shall bear tort liability, except that the operator does not assume such liability if it can be proven that the damage is caused by a war, an armed conflict, a riot, or other like circumstances, or the damage is intentionally caused by the victim.

续表

序号	术语原文	参考译文	原文例句	译文例句
140	核事故	nuclear accident	第一千二百三十七条 民用核设施或者运入运出核设施的核材料发生核事故造成他人损害的，民用核设施的营运单位应当承担侵权责任；但是，能够证明损害是因战争、武装冲突、暴乱等情形或者受害人故意造成的，不承担责任。	Article 1237 Where a nuclear accident occurs at a civil nuclear facility or when nuclear materials are transported into or out of a civil nuclear facility and damage is thus caused to another person, the operator of the facility shall bear tort liability, except that the operator does not assume such liability if itcan be proven that the damage is caused by a war, an armed conflict, a riot, or under other like circumstances, or the damage is intentionally caused by the victim.
141	互谅互让	mutual understanding and accommodation	第一千一百三十二条 继承人应当本着互谅互让、和睦团结的精神，协商处理继承问题。	Article 1132 Any issue arising from succession shall be dealt with through consultation by and among the successors in the spirit of amity, unity, mutual understanding, and accommodation.
142	婚生子女	children born in wedlock	第一千零七十一条 非婚生子女与婚生子女同等的权利，任何组织或者个人不得加以危害和歧视。	Article 1071 Children born out of wedlock have equal rights as children born in wedlock, and no organization or individual may harm or discriminate against them.

续表

序号	术语原文	参考译文	原文例句	译文例句
143	婚姻家庭关系	marital or familial relationship	第一百一十二条　自然人因婚姻家庭关系等产生的人身权利受法律保护。	Article 112 The personal rights of a natural person arising from a marital or familial relationship are protected by law.
144	婚姻自主权	right to freedom of marriage	第一百一十条　自然人享有生命权、身体权、健康权、姓名权、肖像权、名誉权、荣誉权、隐私权、婚姻自主权等权利。	Article 110 A natural person enjoys the right to life, the right to corporeal integrity, the right to health, the right to name, the right to likeness, the right to reputation, the right to honor, the right to privacy, and the right to freedom of marriage.
145	机动车交通事故	motor vehicle traffic accident	第五章　机动车交通事故责任	Chapter V Liability for Motor Vehicle Traffic Accidents
146	基层群众性自治组织法人	primary-level self-governing organization legal person	第九十六条　本节规定的机关法人、农村集体经济组织法人、城镇农村的合作经济组织法人、基层群众性自治组织法人，为特别法人。	Article 96 For the purposes of this Section, State-organ legal persons, rural economic collective legal persons, urban and rural cooperative economic organization legal persons, and primary-level self-governing organization legal persons are special types of legal persons.

续表

序号	术语原文	参考译文	原文例句	译文例句
147	基础资料	basic materials	第七百九十四条　勘察、设计合同的内容一般包括提交有关基础资料和概预算等文件的期限，质量要求，费用以及其他协作条件等条款。	Article 794 A prospecting or designing contract generally contains clauses specifying the time limit for submission of documents relating to the basic materials and budget, quality requirements, expenses and other cooperative conditions, and the like.
148	集成电路布图设计	layout designs of integrated circuits	（六）集成电路布图设计；	(6) layout designs of integrated circuits;
149	集体行使所有权	the ownership be exercised collectively	（一）属于村农民集体所有的，由村集体经济组织或者村民委员会依法代表集体行使所有权；	(1) where they are owned by the farmer collective of a village, the ownership shall be exercised collectively by the collective economic organization of the village or the villagers' committee on behalf of the collective in accordance with law;
150	集体所有权	collective ownership	第五章　国家所有权和集体所有权，私人所有权	Chapter V State Ownership, Collective Ownership, and Private Ownership

续表

序号	术语原文	参考译文	原文例句	译文例句
151	计算机软件著作权	computer software copyright	第八百七十六条　集成电路布图设计专有权、植物新品种权、计算机软件著作权等其他知识产权的转让和许可，参照适用本节的有关规定。	Article 876 The relevant provisions of this Section shall be applied *mutatis mutandis* to the transfer and licensing of the exclusive rights to layout-designs of integrated circuits, rights to new plant varieties, computer software copyrights, and other intellectual property rights.
152	计算利息	calculate interest	利息预先在本金中扣除的，应当按照实际借款额返还借款并计算利息。	Where the interest is deducted from the principal in advance, the loan shall be repaid and the interest shall be calculated according to the actual amount of money provided.
153	技术标准	technical standard	与履行合同有关的技术背景资料、可行性论证和技术评价报告、项目任务书和技术计划书、技术标准、技术规范、原始设计和工艺文件，以及其他技术文档，按照当事人的约定可以作为合同的组成部分。	Materials such as technological background information, the feasibility studies and technological evaluation reports, the project task paper and plans, technology standards, technology norms, original design and technical documents, as well as other technical documents which are relevant to the performance of the contract may, as agreed by the parties, be component parts of the contract.

续表

序号	术语原文	参考译文	原文例句	译文例句
154	技术服务合同	technical service contract	技术服务合同是当事人一方以技术知识为对方解决特定技术问题所订立的合同,不包括承揽合同和建设工程合同。	A technology service contract is a contract under which one party uses his technological knowledge to solve specific technological problems for the other party. Technology service contracts does not include work contracts or contracts for construction project.
155	技术合同	technology contract	第八百四十三条　技术合同是当事人就技术开发、转让、许可、咨询或者服务订立的确立相互之间权利和义务的合同。	Article 843　A technology contract is a contract concluded by the parties to establish their rights and obligations for technology development, transfer, licensing, consultation, or service.
156	技术开发合同	technology development contract	第八百五十七条　作为技术开发合同标的的技术已经由他人公开,致使技术开发合同的履行没有意义的,当事人可以解除合同。	Article 857　Where a technology which is the object of a technology development contract is revealed to the public by others, thus rendering the performance of the contract meaningless, the parties may rescind the contract.

续表

序号	术语原文	参考译文	原文例句	译文例句
157	技术秘密转让合同	technological know-how transfer contract	第八百六十八条 技术秘密转让合同的让与人和技术秘密使用许可合同的许可人应当按照约定提供技术资料,进行技术指导,保证技术的实用性,可靠性,承担保密义务。	Article 868 A transferor under atechnological know-how transfer contract or a licensor under a technological know-how licensing contract shall, in accordance with the agreement, provide technological materials, give technological guidance, guarantee the practical applicability and reliability of the technology, and perform confidentiality obligations.
158	技术培训合同	technical training contract	第八百八十七条 法律、行政法规对技术中介合同、技术培训合同另有规定的,依照其规定。	Article 887 Where there are laws or administrative regulations providing otherwise on technology intermediary contracts and technology training contracts, the relevant provisions shall be followed.
159	技术文档	technical document	与履行合同有关的技术背景资料,可行性论证和技术评价报告,项目任务书和技术计划书,技术标准,技术规范,原始设计和工艺文件,以及其他技术文档,按照当事人的约定可以作为合同的组成部分。	Materials such as technological background information, the feasibility studies and technological evaluation reports, the project task paper and plans, technology standards, technology norms, original design and technical documents, as well as other technical documents which are relevant to the performance of the contract may, as agreed by the parties, be component parts of the contract.

续表

序号	术语原文	参考译文	原文例句	译文例句
160	技术问题	technological problem	第八百八十三条 技术服务合同的受托人应当按照约定完成服务项目，解决技术问题，保证工作质量，并传授解决技术问题的知识。	Article 883 An entrusted person in a technology service contract shall, in accordance with the agreement, complete the services, solve the technological issues, guarantee the quality of the work, and impart the knowledge for solving the technological problems.
161	技术性能	technical performance	第七百三十六条 融资租赁合同的内容一般包括租赁物的名称、数量、规格、技术性能、检验方法，租赁期限、租金构成及其支付期限和方式，租赁期限届满租赁物的归属等条款。	Article 736 A contract for financing lease generally contains clauses specifying the name, quantity, specifications, technical performance, and inspection method of the leased object, the term of the lease, the composition of rent, the period, method, and currency of payment of the rent, the ownership over the leased object upon expiration of the term, and the like.
162	技术许可	technology licensing	第三节 技术转让合同和技术许可合同	Section 3 Technology Transfer Contracts and Technology Licensing Contracts
163	技术要求	technical requirement	第七百七十六条 承揽人发现定作者提供的图纸或者技术要求不合理的，应当及时通知定作人。	Article 776 A contractor shall promptly notify the client if he finds that the drawings or technical requirements provided by the client are unreasonable.

续表

序号	术语原文	参考译文	原文例句	译文例句
164	技术转让合同	technology transfer contract	第八百六十二条　技术转让合同是合法拥有技术的权利人,将现有特定的专利、专利申请,技术秘密的相关权利让与他人所订立的合同。	Article 862 A technology transfer contract is a contract under which a lawful right holder of a technology assigns to another person the relevant rights in respect of a specific patent, application for a patent, or technological know-how.
165	技术咨询合同	technology consultation contract	第八百七十八条　技术咨询合同是当事人一方以技术知识为对方就特定技术项目提供可行性论证、技术预测、专题技术调查、分析评价报告等所订立的合同。	Article 878 A technology consultation contract is a contract under which one party uses technological knowledge to provide the other party with the feasibility study, technological forecast, special technological investigation, and analysis and evaluation report on a specific technological project.
166	技术资料	technical material	第七百八十条　承揽人完成工作的,应当向定作人交付工作成果,并提交必要的技术资料和有关质量证明。	Article 780 Upon completion of his work, a contractor shall deliver to the client the work product and provide the client with the necessary technical materials and related quality certificates.
167	家庭关系	domestic relations	第三章　家庭关系	Chapter III Domestic Relations

续表

序号	术语原文	参考译文	原文例句	译文例句
168	家庭美德	family virtues	第一千零四十三条　家庭应当树立优良家风，弘扬家庭美德，重视家庭文明建设。	Article 1043 Families shall establish good family values, promote family virtues, and enhance family civility.
169	监护人	guardian	未成年人的父母已经死亡或者没有监护能力的，由下列有监护能力的人按顺序担任监护人：	Where the parents of a minor are deceased or incompetent to be his guardians, the following persons, if competent, shall act as his guardians in the following order:
170	检验报告	test report	第一千二百二十五条　医疗机构及其医务人员应当按照规定填写并妥善保管住院志、医嘱单、检验报告、手术及麻醉记录、病理资料、护理记录等病历资料。	Article 1225 Medical institutions and their medical staff shall properly enter and maintain medical records such as hospitalization logs, medical orders, test reports, surgical and anesthesia records, pathological data, and nursing records in accordance with the regulations.
171	建设工程	construction project	承包人不得将其承包的全部建设工程转包给第三人或者将其承包的全部建设工程支解以后以分包的名义分别转包给第三人。	A contractor may not delegate the whole of the contracted construction project to a third person or break up the contracted construction project into several parts and delegate them separately to third persons in the name of subcontracting.

续表

序号	术语原文	参考译文	原文例句	译文例句
172	建设工程合同	contract for construction project	第七百八十八条 建设工程合同是承包人进行工程建设,发包人支付价款的合同。	Article 788 A contract for construction project is a contract under which a contractor carries out the construction of a project andthe contract-offering party pays the price in return.
173	交通运输工具	vehicles for transport	(六)交通运输工具;	(6) vehicles for transport;
174	交易合同	transaction contract	第七百六十二条 保理合同的内容一般包括业务类型、服务范围、服务期限、基础交易合同情况、应收账款信息、保理融资款或者服务报酬及其支付方式等条款。	Article 762 A factoring contract generally contains clauses specifying the business type, scope of service, term of service, information on the underlying transaction contract and the accounts receivable, the financing funds through factoring, the service remuneration, the methods of payment thereof, and the like.

续表

序号	术语原文	参考译文	原文例句	译文例句
175	教育机构	educational institution	第一千二百零一条 无民事行为能力人或者限制民事行为能力人在幼儿园、学校或者其他教育机构学习、生活期间，受到幼儿园、学校或者其他教育机构以外的第三人人身损害的，由第三人承担侵权责任；幼儿园、学校或者其他教育机构未尽到管理职责的，承担相应的补充责任。幼儿园、学校或者其他教育机构承担补充责任后，可以向第三人追偿。	Article 1201 Where a person with no or limited capacity for performing civil juristic acts, while studying or living in a kindergarten, school, or any other educational institution, suffers personal injury caused by a third person other than the kindergarten, school, or the educational institution, the third person shall bear tort liability, and the kindergarten, school, or the educational institution shall assume the corresponding supplementary liability if it fails to fulfill its responsibilities in management. After assuming the supplementary liability, the kindergarten, school, or the educational institution may claim indemnification against the third person.

续表

序号	术语原文	参考译文	原文例句	译文例句
176	节约资源	save resources	对包装方式没有约定或者约定不明确，依据本法第五百一十条的规定仍不能确定的，应当按照通用的方式包装；没有通用方式的，应当采取足以保护标的物且有利于节约资源、保护生态环境的包装方式。	Where there is no agreement between the parties on the packaging method or the relevant agreement is unclear, if the packaging method cannot be determined according to the provisions of Article 510 of this Code, the subject matter shall be packaged in a general way, or, in the absence of a general way, in a manner sufficient to protect the subject matter and conducive to saving resources and protecting the ecological environment.
177	解决争议	dispute resolution	（八）解决争议的方法。	(8) the means of dispute resolution.
178	界址	metes and bounds	第二百一十一条　当事人申请登记，应当根据不同登记事项提供权属证明和不动产界址、面积等必要材料。	Article 211 When applying for registration of immoveable property, an applicant shall, in light of the different items to be registered, provide necessary materials such as the proof of real rights, metes and bounds, and the area of the immoveable property.

续表

序号	术语原文	参考译文	原文例句	译文例句
179	进出口合同	contract for the import and export	第五百九十四条　因国际货物买卖合同和技术进出口合同争议提起诉讼或者申请仲裁的时效期间为四年。	Article 594 The limitation period for filing a lawsuit or arbitration on a dispute arising from a contract for international sale of goods and a contract for the import and export of technology is four years.
180	近亲属	close relatives	第一千一百一十七条　收养关系解除后，养父母与养子女以及其他近亲属间的权利义务关系即行消除，与生父母以及其他近亲属间的权利义务关系是否恢复，可以协商确定。但是，成年养子女与生父母间的权利义务关系自行恢复。	Article 1117 Upon dissolution of an adoptive relationship, the rights and duties between an adoptee and his adoptive parents as well as the latter's other close relatives shall be terminated, and the rights and duties between the adoptee and his natural parents as well as the latter's other close relatives shall be automatically restored. However, while an adopted child has become an adult, whether the rights and duties between such an adoptee and his natural parents as well as the latter's other close relatives are to be restored may be decided through consultation.

续表

序号	术语原文	参考译文	原文例句	译文例句
181	经济社会发展需要	the needsfor economic and social development	第八十八条　具备法人条件,为适应经济社会发展需要,提供公益服务设立的事业单位,经依法登记成立,取得事业单位法人资格;依法不需要办理法人登记的,从成立之日起,具有事业单位法人资格。	Article 88 A public institution established for the purpose of providing public services to meet the needs for economic and social development attains the status of a public-institution legal person if it satisfies the requirements for being a legal person and is legally registered as such; where the law does not require such a public institution to be registered, it attains the status of a public-institution legal person from the date of its establishment.
182	经济秩序	economic order	第一条　为了保护民事主体的合法权益,调整民事关系,维护社会和经济秩序,适应中国特色社会主义发展要求,弘扬社会主义核心价值观,根据宪法,制定本法。	Article 1 This Code is formulated in accordance with the Constitution of the People's Republic of China for the purposes of protecting the lawful rights and interests of the persons of the civil law, regulating civil-law relations, maintaining social and economic order, meeting the needs for developing socialism with Chinese characteristics, and carrying forward the core socialist values.

续表

序号	术语原文	参考译文	原文例句	译文例句
183	经营范围	scope of business	第五百零五条 当事人超越经营范围订立的合同的效力，应当依照本法第一编第六章第三节和本节的有关规定确定，不得仅以超越经营范围确认合同无效。	Article 505 Where the parties conclude a contract beyond their scope of business, the validity of the contract shall be determined according to the relevant provisions in Section 3 of Chapter VI of Book One of this Code and this Book, and the contract may not be determined as invalid solely on the ground that it is beyond their scope of business.
184	精神健康状况	mental status	第二十二条 不能完全辨认自己行为的成年人为限制民事行为能力人，实施民事法律行为由其法定代理人代理或者经其法定代理人同意、追认；但是，可以独立实施纯获利益的民事法律行为或者与其智力、精神健康状况相适应的民事法律行为。	Article 22 An adult unable to fully comprehend his own conduct has limited capacity for performing civil juristic acts and may perform a civil juristic act through or upon consent or ratification of his legal representative, except that such an adult may independently perform a civil juristic act that is purely beneficial to him or that is appropriate to his intelligence and mental status.

续表

序号	术语原文	参考译文	原文例句	译文例句
185	精神损害赔偿	compensation for mental distress	第九百九十六条　因当事人一方的违约行为，损害对方人格权并造成严重精神损害，受损害方选择请求其承担违约责任的，不影响受损害方请求精神损害赔偿。	Article 996 Where the personality rights of a party are harmed by the other party's breach of contract and the injured party thus suffers severe mental distress, if the injured party elects to request the other party to bear liability based on breach of contract, his right to claim for compensation for mental distress is not affected.
186	居民委员会	residents' committee	本条规定的有关组织包括:居民委员会、村民委员会、学校、医疗机构、妇女联合会、残疾人联合会、依法设立的老年人组织、民政部门等。	A relevant organization referred to in this Article includes a residents' committee, a villagers' committee, a school, a medical institution, the women's federation, the disabled person's federation, a legally established organization for senior people, the civil affairs departments, and the like.

续表

序号	术语原文	参考译文	原文例句	译文例句
187	勘探开发	exploration and exploitation	在中华人民共和国境内履行的中外合资经营企业合同、中外合作经营企业合同、中外合作勘探开发自然资源合同，适用中华人民共和国法律。	The laws of the People's Republic of China shall apply to the contracts of Sino-foreign equity joint venture, contracts of Sino-foreign contractual joint venture, or contracts of Sino-foreign cooperation in the exploration and exploitation of natural resources, that are to be performed within the territory of the People's Republic of China.
188	科研活动	scientific research activity	第一千零九条 从事与人体基因、人体胚胎等有关的医学和科研活动，应当遵守法律、行政法规和国家有关规定，不得危害人体健康，不得违背伦理道德，不得损害公共利益。	Article 1009 A medical and scientific research activity related to human genes, embryos, or the like shall be done in accordance with the relevant provisions of laws, administrative regulations, and the regulations of the State, and may not endanger human health, offend ethics and morals, or harm public interests.
189	客运合同	passenger transport contract	第八百一十四条 客运合同自承运人向旅客出具客票时成立，但是当事人另有约定或者另有交易习惯的除外。	Article 814 A passenger transport contract is formed at the time when the carrier issues a ticket to the passenger, unless otherwise provided by the parties or in accordance with the course of dealing.

续表

序号	术语原文	参考译文	原文例句	译文例句
190	控股出资人	controlling capital contributor	第八十四条　营利法人的控股出资人、实际控制人、董事、监事、高级管理人员不得利用其关联关系损害法人的利益；利用关联关系造成法人损失的，应当承担赔偿责任。	Article 84　The controlling capital contributors, actual controllers, directors, supervisors, and senior management officers of a for-profit legal person may not harm the legal person's interests by taking advantage of any affiliated relations, and shall compensate for any loss thus caused to the legal person.
191	宽限期	grace period	债权人与债务人对主债务履行期限没有约定或者约定不明确的，保证期间自债权人请求债务人履行债务的宽限期届满之日起计算。	Where a creditor and a debtor fail to agree on the period of performance of the principal obligation or the relevant agreement is unclear, the term of suretyship shall be counted from the date when the grace period for the creditor to request the debtor to perform the obligation expires.

续表

序号	术语原文	参考译文	原文例句	译文例句
192	劳务派遣	labor dispatch	劳务派遣期间,被派遣的工作人员因执行工作任务造成他人损害的,由接受劳务派遣的用工单位承担侵权责任;劳务派遣单位有过错的,承担相应的责任。	Where, during the period of labor dispatch, a dispatched employee causes damage to another person in connection with the performance of his work, the employer receiving the dispatched employee shall assume tort liability. If the employer dispatching the employee is at fault, it shall assume the corresponding liability.
193	老年人组织	a legally established organization for senior people	本条规定的有关组织包括:居民委员会,村民委员会,学校,医疗机构,妇女联合会,残疾人联合会,依法设立的老年人组织,民政部门等。	A relevant organization referred to in this Article includes a residents' committee, a villagers' committee, a school, a medical institution, the women's federation, the disabled person's federation, a legally established organization for senior people, the civil affairs departments, and the like.

续表

序号	术语原文	参考译文	原文例句	译文例句
194	利害关系人	interested person	利害关系人隐瞒真实情况,致使他人被宣告死亡而取得其财产的,除应当返还财产外,还应当对由此造成的损失承担赔偿责任。	Where an interested person conceals the true information and causes a natural person to be declared dead so as to obtain the latter's property, the interested person shall, in addition to returning the wrongfully obtained property, make compensation for any loss thus caused.
195	临时措施	temporary measures	第三十六条　监护人有下列情形之一的,人民法院根据有关个人或者组织的申请,撤销其监护人资格,安排必要的临时监护措施,并按照最有利于被监护人的原则依法指定监护人:	Article 36 Where a guardian has performed any of the following acts, the people's court shall, upon request of a relevant individual or organization, disqualify the guardian, adopt necessary temporary measures, and appoint a new guardian in the best interest of the ward in accordance with law:
196	临时监护人	temporary guardian	依据本条第一款规定指定监护人前,被监护人的人身权利、财产权利以及其他合法权益处于无人保护状态的,由被监护人住所地的居民委员会、村民委员会或者法律规定的有关组织或者民政部门担任临时监护人。	Where the personal, proprietary, and other lawful rights and interests of a ward are not under any protection before a guardian is appointed in accordance with the first paragraph of this Article, the residents' committee, the villagers' committee, a relevant organization designated by law, or the civil affairs department in the place where the ward's domicile is located shall act as a temporary guardian.

续表

序号	术语原文	参考译文	原文例句	译文例句
197	伦理委员会	ethics committee	第一千零八条　为研制新药,医疗器械或者发展新的预防和治疗方法,需要进行临床试验的,应当依法经相关主管部门批准并经伦理委员会审查同意,向受试者或者受试者的监护人告知试验目的,用途和可能产生的风险等详细情况,并经其书面同意。	Article 1008 Where a clinical trial is needed for developing new drugs and medical devices or developing new prevention and treatment methods, upon approval of the relevant competent authorities and the examination and approval of the ethics committee in accordance with law, the participants or their guardians shall be informed of the details including the purposes, methods, and the possible risks of the trial, and their written consent must be obtained.
198	履行地点	place of performance	第六百五十条　供用电合同的履行地点,按照当事人约定;当事人没有约定或者约定不明确的,供电设施的产权分界处为履行地点。	Article 650 The place of performance of a contract for the supply and consumption of electricity shall be agreed by the parties; if there is no agreement between the parties or the relevant agreement is unclear, the place of demarcation of the property rights in the electricity supply facilities is the place of performance.

续表

序号	术语原文	参考译文	原文例句	译文例句
199	履行监护职责	performance of the duty of guardian	监护人依法履行监护职责产生的权利，受法律保护。	A guardian's rights arising from performance of his duties as required by law are protected by law.
200	履行债务	perform the obligation	第五百二十四条 债务人不履行债务，第三人对履行该债务具有合法利益的，第三人有权向债权人代为履行；但是，根据债务性质、按照当事人约定或者依照法律规定只能由债务人履行的除外。	Article 524 Where a debtor fails to perform an obligation and a third person has a lawful interest in the performance of the obligation, the third person is entitled to perform it to the creditor on behalf of the debtor, unless the obligation may only be performed by the debtor based on the nature of the obligation, as agreed by the parties, or as provided by law.
201	履行债务	perform obligation	第四百三十六条 债务人履行债务或者出质人提前清偿所担保的债权的，质权人应当返还质押财产。	Article 436 A pledgee shall return the pledged property after the debtor has performed his obligation or the pledgor has paid the secured claim before it is due.

续表

序号	术语原文	参考译文	原文例句	译文例句
202	履行职责	perform one's duties	第一千一百四十八条 遗产管理人应当依法履行职责，因故意或者重大过失造成继承人、受遗赠人、债权人损害的，应当承担民事责任。	Article 1148 An administrator of an estate shall perform his duties in accordance with law, and shall bear civil liability if any successor, donee-by-will, or creditor of the decedent suffers damage caused by his intentional act or gross negligence.
203	麻醉记录	anesthesia record	第一千二百二十五条 医疗机构及其医务人员应当按照规定填写并妥善保管住院志、医嘱单、检验报告、手术及麻醉记录、病理资料、护理记录等病历资料。	Article 1225 Medical institutions and their medical staff shall properly enter and maintain medical records such as hospitalization logs, medical orders, test reports, surgical and anesthesia records, pathological data, and nursing records in accordance with the regulations.
204	买卖合同	sales contract	（一）出租人与出卖人订立的买卖合同解除、被确认无效或者被撤销，且未能重新订立买卖合同；	(1) the sales contract between the lessor and the seller is rescinded or determined as void or revoked, and the parties fail to conclude a sales contract anew;

续表

序号	术语原文	参考译文	原文例句	译文例句
205	买卖婚姻	mercenary marriage	第一千零四十二条 禁止包办、买卖婚姻和其他干涉婚姻自由的行为。	Article 1042 Arranged marriages, mercenary marriages, and other acts interfering with the freedom of marriage are prohibited.
206	免责条款	exculpatory clause	第五百零六条 合同中的下列免责条款无效：	Article 506 An exculpatory clause in a contract exempting the following liabilities are void:
207	民事法律关系	civil juristic relationship	捐助法人的决策机构、执行机构或者法定代表人作出决定的程序违反法律、行政法规、法人章程，或者决定内容违反法人章程的，捐助人等利害关系人或者主管机关可以请求人民法院撤销该决定。但是，捐助法人依据该决定与善意相对人形成的民事法律关系不受影响。	Where a decision is made by the decision-making body, executive body, or the legal representative of a donation-funded legal person, if the decision-making procedure is in violation of the laws, administrative regulations, or the legal person's articles of association, or, if the content of the decision violates the articles of association, a donor or any other interested person, or the competent authority may request the people's court to revoke the decision. Provided, however, that any civil juristic relationship already formed between the donation-funded legal person and a *bona fide* counterparty based on such a decision may not be affected.

续表

序号	术语原文	参考译文	原文例句	译文例句
208	民事法律行为	civil juristic act	第二十条 不满八周岁的未成年人为无民事行为能力人,由其法定代理人代理实施民事法律行为。	Article 20 A minor under the age of eight has no capacity for performing civil juristic acts, and may perform a civil juristic act only through his legal representative.
209	民事关系	civil-law relations	第一条 为了保护民事主体的合法权益,调整民事关系,维护社会和经济秩序,适应中国特色社会主义发展要求,弘扬社会主义核心价值观,根据宪法,制定本法。	Article 1 This Code is formulated in accordance with the Constitution of the People's Republic of China for the purposes of protecting the lawful rights and interests of the persons of the civil law, regulating civil-law relations, maintaining social and economic order, meeting the needs for developing socialism with Chinese characteristics, and carrying forward the core socialist values.
210	民事行为能力	capacity for performing civil juristic acts	第一节 民事权利能力和民事行为能力	Section 1 Capacity for Enjoying Civil-law Rights and Capacity for Performing Civil Juristic Acts
211	民事活动	civil activities	第四条 民事主体在民事活动中的法律地位一律平等。	Article 4 All persons of the civil law are equal in legal status when conducting civil activities.

续表

序号	术语原文	参考译文	原文例句	译文例句
212	民事权利	civil-law rights	第五章　民事权利	Chapter V Civil-law Rights
213	民事权利能力	capacity for enjoying civil-law rights	第一节　民事权利能力和民事行为能力	Section 1 Capacity for Enjoying Civil-law Rights and Capacity for Performing Civil Juristic Acts
214	民事权益	civil rights and interests	第一百二十条　民事权益受到侵害的,被侵权人有权请求侵权人承担侵权责任。	Article 120 Where a person's civil-law rights and interests are infringed upon due to a tortious act, the person is entitled to request the tortfeasor to bear tort liability.
215	民事义务	civil-law obligations	第一百七十六条　民事主体依照法律规定或者按照当事人约定,履行民事义务,承担民事责任。	Article 176 A person of the civil law shall perform civil-law obligations and bear civil liability in accordance with law or the agreement of the parties.
216	民事主体	person of the civil law	第一条　为了保护民事主体的合法权益,调整民事关系,维护社会和经济秩序,适应中国特色社会主义发展要求,弘扬社会主义核心价值观,根据宪法,制定本法。	Article 1 This Code is formulated in accordance with the Constitution of the People's Republic of China for the purposes of protecting the lawful rights and interests of the persons of the civil law, regulating civil-law relations, maintaining social and economic order, meeting the needs for developing socialism with Chinese characteristics, and carrying forward the core socialist values.

续表

序号	术语原文	参考译文	原文例句	译文例句
217	民用航空器	civil aircraft	第一千二百三十八条　民用航空器造成他人损害的,民用航空器的经营者应当承担侵权责任;但是,能够证明损害是因受害人故意造成的,不承担责任。	Article 1238 Where a civil aircraft causes damage to another person, the operator of the aircraft shall bear tort liability, except that the operator does not assume any liability if it can be proven that the damage is intentionally caused by the victim.
218	民用核设施	civil nuclear facility	第一千二百三十七条　民用核设施或者运入运出核设施的核材料发生核事故造成他人损害的,民用核设施的营运单位应当承担侵权责任;但是,能够证明损害是因战争、武装冲突、暴乱等情形或者受害人故意造成的,不承担责任。	Article 1237 Where a nuclear accident occurs at a civil nuclear facility or when nuclear materials are transported into or out of a civil nuclear facility and damage is thus caused to another person, the operator of the facility shall bear tort liability, except that the operator does not assume such liability if it can be proven that the damage is caused by a war, an armed conflict, a riot, or under other like circumstances, or the damage is intentionally caused by the victim.
219	名称权	right to entity name	第三章　姓名权和名称权	Chapter III Rights to Name and Rights to Entity Name

续表

序号	术语原文	参考译文	原文例句	译文例句
220	名誉权	right to reputation	第五章　名誉权和荣誉权	Chapter V Rights to Reputation and Rights to Honor
221	明确同意	express consent	需要实施手术、特殊检查、特殊治疗的，医务人员应当及时向患者具体说明医疗风险、替代医疗方案等情况，并取得其明确同意；不能或者不宜向患者说明的，应当向患者的近亲属说明，并取得其明确同意。	Where a surgery, a special examination, or a special treatment is needed, the medical staff shall explain to the patient the medical risks, alternative treatment plans, and other information in a timely manner and obtain his express consent. Where it is impossible or inappropriate to do so, the medical staff shall explain it to the patient's close relatives and get their express consent.
222	明示	make an expression of intent expressly	第一百四十条　行为人可以明示或者默示做出意思表示。	Article 140 A person performing a civil juristic act may make an expression of intent either expressly or implicitly.
223	默示	make an expression of intent implicitly		
224	内部管理机构	internal management structure	执行机构行使召集权力机构会议，决定法人的经营计划和投资方案，决定法人内部管理机构的设置，以及法人章程规定的其他职权。	The executive body has the authority to convene meetings of the governing body, decide on business and investment plans, establish internal management structure, and perform other responsibilities stipulated in the articles of association of the legal person.

续表

序号	术语原文	参考译文	原文例句	译文例句
225	农村承包经营户	rural-land contractual management households	第四节 个体工商户和农村承包经营户	Section 4 Individual-run Industrial and Commercial Households and Rural-land Contractual Management Households
226	农村集体经济组织	rural economic collective	第五十五条 农村集体经济组织的成员,依法取得农村土地承包经营权,从事家庭承包经营的,为农村承包经营户。	Article 55 Members of a rural economic collective who, in accordance with law, have been granted an original contract to operate a lot of rural land and engage in the operation of the land on a household basis form a rural-land contractual management household.
227	农村土地	rural land	第五十五条 农村集体经济组织的成员,依法取得农村土地承包经营权,从事家庭承包经营的,为农村承包经营户。	Article 55 Members of a rural economic collective who, in accordance with law, have been granted an original contract to operate a lot of rural land and engage in the operation of the land on a household basis form a rural-land contractual management household.

续表

序号	术语原文	参考译文	原文例句	译文例句
228	农村(土地)承包经营户	rural-land contractual management household	第五十五条　农村集体经济组织的成员，依法取得农村土地承包经营权，从事家庭承包经营的，为农村承包经营户。	Article 55 Members of a rural economic collective who, in accordance with law, have been granted an original contract to operate a lot of rural land and engage in the operation of the land on a household basis form a rural-land contractual management household.
229	农村土地承包经营权	contract to operate a lot of rural land	第五十五条　农村集体经济组织的成员，依法取得农村土地承包经营权，从事家庭承包经营的，为农村承包经营户。	Article 55 Members of a rural economic collective who, in accordance with law, have been granted an original contract to operate a lot of rural land and engage in the operation of the land on a household basis form a rural-land contractual management household.
230	农用地	agricultural land	第二百四十四条　国家对耕地实行特殊保护，严格限制农用地转为建设用地，控制建设用地总量。	Article 244 The State provides special protection to cultivated land, strictly restricts the conversion of agricultural land into land used for construction purposes, and controls the overall volume of the land used for construction purposes.

序号	术语原文	参考译文	原文例句	译文例句
231	排放污染物	discharge pollutants	业主大会或者业主委员会,对任意弃置垃圾,排放污染物或者噪声,违反规定饲养动物,违章搭建,侵占通道,拒付物业费等损害他人合法权益的行为,有权依照法律、法规以及管理规约,请求行为人停止侵害,排除妨碍,消除危险,恢复原状,赔偿损失。	With respect to an act impairing the lawful rights and interests of others, such as arbitrarily discarding garbage, discharging pollutants or noises, feeding and keeping animals in violation of the regulations, constructing structures against rules and regulations, encroaching on passages, and refusing to pay property management fees, the owners' assembly or the owners' committee has the right to request the actor to discontinue such infringements, remove the nuisance, eliminate the danger, restore to the original condition, and compensate for the losses thus caused.
232	赔偿损失	bear the liability for compensating	第七百八十七条 定作人在承揽人完成工作前可以随时解除承揽合同,造成承揽人损失的,应当赔偿损失。	Article 787 The client may rescind the work contract at any time before the contractor completes his work and shall bear the liability for compensating any loss thus caused to the contractor.

续表

序号	术语原文	参考译文	原文例句	译文例句
233	赔偿责任	be liable for compensation	财产代管人因故意或者重大过失造成失踪人财产损失的,应当承担赔偿责任。	A custodian who, intentionally or due to gross negligence, causes damage to the property of the missing person shall be liable for compensation.
234	凭样品买卖	sale by sample	第六百三十五条 凭样品买卖的当事人应当封存样品,并可以对样品质量予以说明。	Article 635 The parties to a sale by sample shall seal up the sample and may make specifications of its quality.
235	破产	bankrupt	(二)法人被宣告破产;	(2) the legal person is declared bankrupt;
236	破产案件	bankruptcy petition	(二)人民法院已经受理债务人破产案件;	(2) the people's court has accepted the debtor's bankruptcy petition;
237	破产清算	bankruptcy liquidation	第七十三条 法人被宣告破产的,依法进行破产清算并完成法人注销登记时,法人终止。	Article 73 A legal person declared bankrupt is terminated upon completion of the bankruptcy liquidation and de-registration in accordance with law.
238	期限	term	第四节 民事法律行为的附条件和附期限	Section 4 A Civil Juristic Act Subject to a Condition or a Term

续表

序号	术语原文	参考译文	原文例句	译文例句
239	企业改制	enterprise restructuring	违反国有财产管理规定，在企业改制，合并分立，低价转让、合谋私分，擅自担保或者以其他方式造成国有财产损失的，应当依法承担法律责任。	A person, who causes losses to the State-owned property by transferring it at low prices, secretly distributing it in conspiracy with other persons, creating a security interest on it without authorization, or by other means in the course of enterprise restructuring, merger or division, affiliated transactions, and the like, in violation of the provisions on the administration of the State-owned property, shall bear legal liability in accordance with law.
240	弃置垃圾	arbitrarily discarding garbage	业主大会或者业主委员会，对任意弃置垃圾、排放污染物或者噪声、违反规定饲养动物、违章搭建、侵占通道、拒付物业费等损害他人合法权益的行为，有权依照法律、法规以及管理规约，请求行为人停止侵害、排除妨碍、消除危险、恢复原状、赔偿损失。	With respect to an act impairing the lawful rights and interests of others, such as arbitrarily discarding garbage, discharging pollutants or noises, feeding and keeping animals in violation of the regulations, constructing structures against rules and regulations, encroaching on passages, and refusing to pay property management fees, the owners' assembly or the owners' committee has the right to request the actor to discontinue such infringements, remove the nuisance, eliminate the danger, restore to the original condition, and compensate for the losses thus caused.

续表

序号	术语原文	参考译文	原文例句	译文例句
241	强制性标准	mandatory standard	发包人提供的主要建筑材料、建筑构配件和设备不符合强制性标准或者不履行协助义务，致使承包人无法施工，经催告后在合理期限内仍未履行相应义务的，承包人可以解除合同。	Where the main construction materials, construction components and accessories, and equipment provided by the contract-offering party fail to conform to the mandatory standard, or the contract-offering party fails to perform the obligation of providing assistance, so that the contractor cannot undertake the construction work, if the contract-offering party still fails to perform the corresponding obligations within a reasonable period of time after being demanded, the contractor may rescind the contract.
242	侵权责任	tort liability	第七编 侵权责任	Book Seven Tort Liability
243	青苗	young crop	征收集体所有的土地，应当依法及时足额支付土地补偿费、安置补助费以及农村村民住宅、其他地上附着物和青苗等的补偿费用，并安排被征地农民的社会保障费用，维护被征地农民的生活，维护被征地农民的合法权益。	In the case of expropriation of collectively-owned land, land compensation fees, resettlement subsidies, and compensation fees for rural villagers' dwellings and other ground attachments as well as young crops shall be paid in full in a timely manner in accordance with law, and social security premiums of the farmers whose land has been expropriated shall be arranged, their lives secured, and their lawful rights and interests safeguarded.

续表

序号	术语原文	参考译文	原文例句	译文例句
244	清算义务人	the persons with the duty of liquidation	第七十条　法人解散的，除合并或者分立的情形外，清算义务人应当及时组成清算组进行清算。	Article 70 Where a legal person is dissolved for reasons other than a merger or division, a liquidation committee shall be formed in a timely manner by the persons with the duty of liquidation to liquidate the legal person.
245	清算组	liquidation committee	第七十条　法人解散的，除合并或者分立的情形外，清算义务人应当及时组成清算组进行清算。	Article 70 Where a legal person is dissolved for reasons other than a merger or division, a liquidation committee shall be formed in a timely manner by the persons with the duty of liquidation to liquidate the legal person.
246	请求权	right to request	占有人返还原物的请求权，自侵占发生之日起一年内未行使的，该请求权消灭。	The possessor's right to request for restitution is extinguished if such a right has not been exercised within one year from the date the trespass or conversion occurs.

续表

序号	术语原文	参考译文	原文例句	译文例句
247	权利义务	rights and obligations	第五百三十七条　人民法院认定代位权成立的，由债务人的相对人向债权人履行义务，债权人接受履行后，债权人与债务人、债务人与相对人之间相应的权利义务终止。	Article 537 Where the people's court determines that the right of subrogation has been established, the counterparty of the debtor shall perform the obligation to the creditor. After the performance is accepted by the creditor, the corresponding rights and obligations between the creditor and the debtor, and those between the debtor and the counterparty, are terminated.
248	权属证明	the proof of real rights	第二百一十一条　当事人申请登记，应当根据不同登记事项提供权属证明和不动产界址、面积等必要材料。	Article 211 When applying for registration of immoveable property, an applicant shall, in light of the different items to be registered, provide necessary materials such as the proof of real rights, metes and bounds, and the area of the immovable property.
249	人格权	personality rights	第四编　人格权	Book Four Personality Rights
250	人身关系	personal relationships	第二条　民法调整平等主体的自然人、法人和非法人组织之间的人身关系和财产关系。	Article 2 The civil law regulates personal and proprietary relationships among the persons of the civil law, namely, natural persons, legal persons, and unincorporated organizations that are equal in status.

续表

序号	术语原文	参考译文	原文例句	译文例句
251	人身权利	personal rights	第三条　民事主体的人身权利,财产权利以及其他合法权益受法律保护,任何组织或者个人不得侵犯。	Article 3 The personal rights, proprietary rights, and other lawful rights and interests of the persons of the civil law are protected by law and free from infringement by any organization or individual.
252	人体基因	human gene	第一千零九条　从事与人体基因、人体胚胎等有关的医学和科研活动,应当遵守法律、行政法规和国家有关规定,不得危害人体健康,不得违背伦理道德,不得损害公共利益。	Article 1009 A medical and scientific research activity related to human genes, embryos, or the like shall be done in accordance with the relevant provisions of laws, administrative regulations, and the regulations of the State, and may not endanger human health, offend ethics and morals, or harm public interests.
253	人体胚胎	human embryo	第一千零九条　从事与人体基因、人体胚胎等有关的医学和科研活动,应当遵守法律、行政法规和国家有关规定,不得危害人体健康,不得违背伦理道德,不得损害公共利益。	Article 1009 A medical and scientificresearch activity related to human genes, embryos, or the like shall be done in accordance with the relevant provisions of laws, administrative regulations, and the regulations of the State, and may not endanger human health, offend ethics and morals, or harm public interests.

续表

序号	术语原文	参考译文	原文例句	译文例句
254	人体器官	human organ	第一千零六条　完全民事行为能力人有权依法自主决定无偿捐献其人体细胞、人体组织、人体器官、遗体。	Article 1006 A person with full capacity for performing civil juristic acts has the right to make a voluntary decision in accordance with law to donate his cells, tissues, organs, and remains.
255	人体细胞	human cell	第一千零六条　完全民事行为能力人有权依法自主决定无偿捐献其人体细胞、人体组织、人体器官、遗体。	Article 1006 A person with full capacity for performing civil juristic acts has the right to make a voluntary decision in accordance with law to donate his cells, tissues, organs, and remains.
256	荣誉权	right to honor	第五章　名誉权和荣誉权	Chapter V Rights to Reputation and Rights to Honor
257	融资租赁合同	contracts for financing lease	第十五章　融资租赁合同	Chapter XV Contracts for Financing Lease
258	善意第三人	*bona fide* third person	第二百二十五条　船舶、航空器和机动车等物权的设立、变更、转让和消灭，未经登记，不得对抗善意第三人。	Article 225 The creation, alteration, transfer, or extinguishment of the real rights in vessels, aircrafts, motor vehicles, and the like, that have not been registered, is not effective against a *bona fide* third person.

续表

序号	术语原文	参考译文	原文例句	译文例句
259	善意相对人	*bona fide* counterparty	第六十五条　法人的实际情况与登记的事项不一致的,不得对抗善意相对人。	Article 65 The actual situation of a legal person, which is inconsistent with what is recorded upon registration, may not be asserted against a *bona fide* counterparty.
260	擅自担保	creating a security interest on something without authorization	违反国有财产管理规定,在企业改制、合并分立、关联交易等过程中,擅自担保或者以其他方式造成国有财产损失的,应当依法承担法律责任。	A person, who causes losses to the State-owned property by transferring it at low prices, secretly distributing it in conspiracy with other persons, creating a security interest on it without authorization, or by other means in the course of enterprise restructuring, merger or division, affiliated transactions, and the like, in violation of the provisions on the administration of the State-owned property, shall bear legal liability in accordance with law.
261	商品住宅	commercial residential	工业、商业、旅游、娱乐和商品住宅等经营性用地以及同一土地有两个以上意向用地者的,应当采取招标、拍卖等公开竞价的方式出让。	The bidding, auction, or other means of public bidding shall be adopted in transferring a lot of land used for businesspurposes, such as for industrial, commercial, tourism, recreational, and commercial residential purposes, or where there are two or more intended users competing for the right to use the same lot of land.

续表

序号	术语原文	参考译文	原文例句	译文例句
262	商业道德	commercial ethics	第八十六条　营利法人从事经营活动,应当遵守商业道德,维护交易安全,接受政府和社会的监督,承担社会责任。	Article 86 A for-profit legal person shall, when engaging in operational activities, observe commercial ethics, maintain the security of transactions, subject itself to the supervision of the government and the public, and assume social responsibilities.
263	商业秘密	trade secret	(五)商业秘密;	(5) trade secrets;
264	商业信誉	good will of business	(三)丧失商业信誉;	(3) the good will of its business has been lost;
265	设计费	designing fee	第八百条　勘察、设计的质量不符合要求或者未按照期限提交勘察、设计文件拖延工期,造成发包人损失的,勘察人、设计人应当继续完善勘察、设计,减收或者免收勘察、设计费并赔偿损失。	Article 800 Where losses are caused to a contract-offering party due to the fact that the prospecting or designing does not conform to the quality requirements or that the prospecting or designing documents are not submitted as scheduled, so that the period for construction is delayed, the prospecting or designing party shall continue on perfecting the prospecting or designing, reduce or waive the prospecting or designing fees, and make compensation for the losses.

续表

序号	术语原文	参考译文	原文例句	译文例句
266	社会保障	social security	征收集体所有的土地,应当依法及时足额支付土地补偿费、安置补助费以及农村村民住宅、其他地上附着物和青苗等的补偿费用,并安排被征地农民的社会保障费用,保障被征地农民的生活,维护被征地农民的合法权益。	In the case of expropriation of collectively-owned land, land compensation fees, resettlement subsidies, and compensation fees for rural villagers' dwellings and other ground attachments as well as young crops shall be paid in full in a timely manner in accordance with law, and social security premiums of the farmers whose land has been expropriated shall be arranged, their lives secured, and their lawful rights and interests safeguarded.
267	社会服务机构	social service institutions	非营利法人包括事业单位、社会团体、基金会、社会服务机构等。	Non-profit legal persons include public institutions, social organizations, social foundations, social service institutions, and the like.
268	社会公共利益	public interests	第一百三十二条 民事主体不得滥用民事权利损害国家利益、社会公共利益或者他人合法权益。	Article 132 No person of the civil law shall abuse his civil-law rights and harm the interests of the State, the public interests, or the lawful rights and interests of others.

续表

序号	术语原文	参考译文	原文例句	译文例句
269	社会责任	social responsibilities	第八十六条 营利法人从事经营活动,应当遵守商业道德,维护交易安全,接受政府和社会的监督,承担社会责任。	Article 86 A for-profit legal person shall, when engaging in operational activities, observe commercial ethics, maintain the security of transactions, subject itself to the supervision of the government and the public, and assume social responsibilities.
270	社会主义核心价值观	core socialist values	第一条 为了保护民事主体的合法权益,调整民事关系,维护社会经济秩序,适应中国特色社会主义发展要求,弘扬社会主义核心价值观,根据宪法,制定本法。	Article 1 This Code is formulated in accordance with the Constitution of the People's Republic of China for the purposes of protecting the lawful rights and interests of the persons of the civil law, regulating civil-law relations, maintaining social and economic order, meeting the needs for developing socialism with Chinese characteristics, and carrying forward the core socialist values.
271	社会主义市场经济	socialist market economy	国家实行社会主义市场经济,保障一切市场主体的平等法律地位和发展权利。	The State implements a socialist market economy and protects the equal legal status and development rights of all market participants.

续表

序号	术语原文	参考译文	原文例句	译文例句
272	社会主义市场经济体制	the system of socialist market economy	第二百零六条　国家坚持和完善公有制为主体、多种所有制经济共同发展,按劳分配为主体、多种分配方式并存,社会主义市场经济体制等社会主义基本经济制度。	Article 206 The State upholds and improves the fundamental socialist economic systems, such as the ownership system under which diverse forms of ownership co-develop with public ownership as the mainstay, the distribution system under which multiple forms of distribution co-exist with distribution according to work as the mainstay, as well as the system of socialist market economy.
273	申请登记	applying for registration	第二百一十一条　当事人申请登记,应当根据不同登记事项提供权属证明和不动产界址、面积等必要材料。	Article 211 When applying for registration of immoveable property, an applicant shall, in light of the different items to be registered, provide necessary materials such as the proof of real rights, metes and bounds, and the area of the immovable property.
274	申请号	application number	技术合同涉及专利的,应当注明发明创造的名称、专利申请人和专利权人、申请日期、申请号、专利号以及专利权的有效期限。	Where a technology contract involves a patent, it shall indicate the designation of the invention, the applicant and the patentee thereof, the date of application, the application number, the patent number, and the term of the patent rights.

续表

序号	术语原文	参考译文	原文例句	译文例句
275	申请仲裁	apply for arbitration	第六百九十三条　一般保证的债权人未在保证期间对债务人提起诉讼或者申请仲裁的，保证人不再承担保证责任。	Article 693 Where a creditor of a general suretyship fails to file a lawsuit or apply for arbitration against the debtor within the term of suretyship, the surety no longer bears the suretyship liability.
276	申请专利的权利	right to apply for patent	第八百五十九条　委托开发完成的发明创造，除法律另有规定或者当事人另有约定外，申请专利的权利属于研究开发人。	Article 859 Where an invention is accomplished through commissioned development, the right to apply for patent on the invention belongs to the researcher-developer, unless otherwise provided by law or agreed by the parties.
277	生产设备	production equipment	（四）生产设备、原材料、半成品、产品；	(4) production equipment, raw materials, work in process, and finished products;
278	生产设施	production facilities	（二）集体所有的建筑物、生产设施、农田水利设施；	(2) the buildings, production facilities, and farmland water conservancy facilities that are owned by collectives;
279	生命权	rights to life	第二章　生命权、身体权和健康权	Chapter II Rights to Life, Rights to Corporeal Integrity, and Rights to Health
280	生态环境损害	damage to the ecological environment	（三）生态环境损害调查、鉴定评估等费用；	(3) expenses for investigation, appraisal, and assessment of the damage to the ecological environment;

续表

序号	术语原文	参考译文	原文例句	译文例句
281	施工合同	construction contract	第七百九十五条　施工合同的内容一般包括工程范围、建设工期、中间交工工程的开工和竣工时间、工程质量、工程造价、技术资料交付时间、材料和设备供应责任、拨款和结算、竣工验收、质量保修范围和质量保证期、相互协作等条款。	Article 795 A construction contract generally contains clauses specifying the scope of the project, the period for construction, the time of commencement and completion of the project to be delivered in midcourse, project quality, costs, delivery time of technical materials, the responsibility for the supply of materials and equipment, fund allocation and settlement, project inspection and acceptance upon its completion, range and period of quality warranty, cooperation, and the like.
282	施工图纸	construction drawing	第七百九十九条　建设工程竣工后，发包人应当根据施工图纸及说明书、国家颁发的施工验收规范和质量检验标准及时进行验收。	Article 799 Upon completion of a construction project, the contract-offering party shall promptly undertake the inspection for acceptance in accordance with the construction drawings and descriptions, as well as the rules of inspection and acceptance of construction projects and the standards for quality inspection issued by the State.

续表

序号	术语原文	参考译文	原文例句	译文例句
283	实际价值	actual value	第一千一百六十一条 继承人以所得遗产实际价值为限清偿被继承人依法应当缴纳的税款和债务。超过遗产实际价值部分,继承人自愿偿还的不在此限。	Article 1161 A successor shall pay the taxes and debts legally payable or owed by the decedent to the extent of the actual value of the portion of the estate he inherits, unless the successor pays voluntarily in excess of such limit.
284	实际控制人	actual controller	第八十四条 营利法人的控股出资人、实际控制人、董事、监事、高级管理人员不得利用其关联关系损害法人的利益;利用关联关系造成法人损失的,应当承担赔偿责任。	Article 84 The controlling capital contributors, actual controllers, directors, supervisors, and senior management officers of a for-profit legal person may not harm the legal person's interests by taking advantage of any affiliated relations, and shall compensate for any loss thus caused to the legal person.
285	实用新型	new utility models	(二)发明、实用新型、外观设计;	(2) inventions, new utility models, or appearance designs;

续表

序号	术语原文	参考译文	原文例句	译文例句
286	市场利率	market interest rate	借款合同对支付利息约定不明确，当事人不能达成补充协议的，按照当地或者当事人的交易方式、交易习惯，市场利率等因素确定利息；自然人之间借款的，视为没有利息。	Where the agreement in a loan contract is unclear on the payment of interest, if the parties are unable to reach a supplementary agreement, the interest shall be determined by taking account of the practices in the local area or between the parties such as the method of transaction, course of dealing, the market interest rate, and the like. Where such a loan is between natural persons, the loan is deemed as bearing no interest.
287	事业单位法人	public-institution legal person	第八十八条　具备法人条件，为适应经济社会发展需要，提供公益服务设立的事业单位，经依法登记成立，取得事业单位法人资格；依法不需要办理法人登记的，从成立之日起，具有事业单位法人资格。	Article 88 A public institution established for the purpose of providing public services to meet the needs for economic and social development attains the status of a public-institution legal person if it satisfies the requirements for being a legal person and is legally registered as such; where the law does not require such a public institution to be registered, it attains the status of a public-institution legal person from the date of its establishment.

续表

序号	术语原文	参考译文	原文例句	译文例句
288	试用买卖	sale on trial use	第六百三十七条 试用买卖的当事人可以约定标的物的试用期限。	Article 637 The parties to a sale on trial use may agree on a period for trial use of the subject matter.
289	收养协议	adoption agreement	收养关系当事人愿意签订收养协议的,可以签订收养协议。	The parties to an adoptive relationship may enter into an adoption agreement on a voluntary basis.
290	书面合同	contract concluded in writing	第六百八十五条 保证合同可以是单独订立的书面合同,也可以是主债权债务合同中的保证条款。	Article 685 A suretyship contract may be a contract concluded separately in writing or a guarantee clause in a principal claim-obligation contract.
291	书面同意	written consent	第三百九十一条 第三人提供担保,未经其书面同意,债权人允许债务人转移全部或者部分债务的,担保人不再承担相应的担保责任。	Article 391 Where a third person provides security and the creditor allows the debtor totransfer all or part of the secured obligations without the third person's written consent, the security provider is no longer liable for securing the part of the obligations so transferred.

续表

序号	术语原文	参考译文	原文例句	译文例句
292	书面协议	written agreement	收养人应当提供由其所在国有权机构出具的有关其年龄、婚姻、职业、财产、健康、有无受过刑事处罚等状况的证明材料，并与送养人签订书面协议，亲自向省、自治区、直辖市人民政府民政部门登记。	The foreign adopter shall submit documents issued by the competent authorities of his country of residence certifying such personal information as his age, marital status, occupation, financial situation, physical condition, and whether he has criminal record. The foreign adopter shall conclude a written agreement with the person who places the child for adoption and register the adoption in person with the civil affairs department of the people's government at the level of provinces, autonomous regions, or municipalities directly under the State Council.
293	书面形式	writing	书面形式是合同书、信件、电报、电传、传真等可以有形地表现所载内容的形式。	A writing refers to any form that renders the content contained therein capable of being represented in a tangible form, such as a written agreement, letter, telegram, telex, facsimile, or the like.
294	数据电文	electronic data message	当事人对采用数据电文形式的意思表示的生效时间另有约定的，按照其约定。	Where the parties have agreed otherwise on the effective time of the expression of intent made in the form of an electronic data message, such an agreement shall prevail.

续表

序号	术语原文	参考译文	原文例句	译文例句
295	水利设施	water conservancy facilities	（二）集体所有的建筑物、生产设施、农田水利设施；	(2) the buildings, production facilities, and farmland water conservancy facilities that are owned by collectives;
296	私人所有权	private ownership	第五章 国家所有权、集体所有权、私人所有权	Chapter V State Ownership, Collective Ownership, and Private Ownership
297	死亡宣告	declaration of death	死亡宣告被撤销的，婚姻关系自撤销死亡宣告之日起自行恢复。但是，其配偶再婚或者向婚姻登记机关书面声明不愿意恢复的除外。	Where the declaration of death is revoked, the aforementioned marital relationship shall be automatically resumed from the date the declaration of death is revoked, unless the spouse has married to someone else or states in writing to the marriage registration authority the unwillingness to resume the marriage.
298	诉讼时效	limitation of action	第九章 诉讼时效	Chapter IX Limitation of Action
299	损害赔偿金	compensatory damages	第三百八十九条 担保物权的担保范围包括主债权及其利息、违约金、损害赔偿金、保管担保财产和实现担保物权的费用。	Article 389 Unless otherwise agreed by the parties, the scope covered by a security interest includes the principal claim and its interests based on the principal contract, liquidated damages, compensatory damages, and the expenses arising from safekeeping the collateral and enforcing the security interests.

续表

序号	术语原文	参考译文	原文例句	译文例句
300	索赔权	right to claim	第七百四十二条 承租人对出卖人行使索赔权利，不影响其履行支付租金的义务。	Article 742 A lessee's exercise of the right to claim against the seller does not affect his performance of the obligation to pay the rent.
301	他人合法权益	lawful rights and interests of others	第一百三十二条 民事主体不得滥用民事权利损害国家利益、社会公共利益或者他人合法权益。	Article 132 No person of the civil law shall abuse his civil-law rights and harm the interests of the State, the public interests, or the lawful rights and interests of others.
302	特别规定	special provisions	第十一条 其他法律对民事关系有特别规定的，依照其规定。	Article 11 Where there are other laws providing special provisions regulating civil-law relations, such provisions shall be followed.
303	特定个人	specific individual	第一千零三十八条 信息处理者不得泄露或者篡改其收集、存储的个人信息；未经自然人同意，不得向他人非法提供其个人信息，但是经过加工无法识别特定个人且不能复原的除外。	Article 1038 An information processor may not disclose or tamper with the personal information he collects and stores, and may not illegally provide to others the personal information of a natural person without the latter's consent, unless the information, after being processed, cannot be used to identify any specific individual and cannot be restored to its original status.

续表

序号	术语原文	参考译文	原文例句	译文例句
304	特殊保护	special protection	第二百四十四条　国家对耕地实行特殊保护,严格限制农用地转为建设用地,控制建设用地总量。	Article 244 The State provides special protection to cultivated land, strictly restricts the conversion of agricultural land into land used for construction purposes, and controls the overall volume of the land used for construction purposes.
305	特殊困难	special difficulty	对生活有特殊困难又缺乏劳动能力的继承人,分配遗产时,应当予以照顾。	When distributing an estate, due consideration shall be given to a successor who has special financial difficulties and is unable to work.
306	特殊情况	special circumstances	但是,自权利受到损害之日起超过二十年的,人民法院不予保护,有特殊情况的,人民法院可以根据权利人的申请决定延长。	However, no protection to a right is to be granted by the people's court if 20 years have lapsed since the date when the injury occurs, except that the people's court may, upon request of the right holder, extend the limitation period under special circumstances.
307	提供担保	provide security	第三人为债务人向债权人提供担保的,可以要求债务人提供反担保。	Where a third person provides security to the creditor for the debtor, the debtor may be requested to provide a counter-security.

续表

序号	术语原文	参考译文	原文例句	译文例句
308	提供技术资料	provide technological materials	第八百六十八条　技术人与受让人按照许可合同的约定提供技术资料,进行技术指导,保证技术的实用性,可靠性,承担保密义务。	Article 868 A transferor under a technological know-how transfer contract or a licensor under a technological know-how licensing contract shall, in accordance with the agreement, provide technological materials, give technological guidance, guarantee the practical applicability and reliability of the technology, and perform confidentiality obligations.
309	提供劳务	provide services	提供劳务期间,因第三人的行为造成提供劳务一方损害的,提供劳务一方有权请求第三人承担侵权责任,也有权请求接受劳务一方给予补偿。	Where an act of a third person causes damage to the service-providing party when such services are provided, the service-providing party has the right to request the third person to bear tort liability, or to request the service-receiving party to make compensation.
310	天然孳息	natural fruit	第三百二十一条　天然孳息,由所有权人取得;既有所有权人又有用益物权人的,由用益物权人取得。	Article 321 Unless otherwise agreed by the parties, the natural fruits of a thing shall be acquired by the owner of the thing, or by a usufructuary if there are both an owner and a usufructuary of the thing.

续表

序号	术语原文	参考译文	原文例句	译文例句
311	条件成就	condition be fulfilled	第一百五十八条　民事法律行为可以附条件,但是根据其性质不得附条件的除外。附条件的民事法律行为,自条件成就时生效。附解除条件的民事法律行为,自条件成就时失效。	Article 158 A condition may be attached to a civil juristic act unless the nature of the act denies such an attachment. A civil juristic act subject to a condition precedent becomes effective when the condition is fulfilled. A civil juristic act subject to a condition subsequent becomes invalid when the condition is fulfilled.
312	同一合同	the same contract	(二)债务人的债权与转让的债权是基于同一合同产生。	(2) the debtor's claim and the assigned claim are generated on the basis of the same contract.
313	统一登记	unified registration	国家对不动产实行统一登记制度。	The State implements a unified registration system with respect to immovable property.
314	投资计划	investment plan	第七百九十二条　国家重大建设工程合同,应当按照国家规定的程序和国家批准的投资计划,可行性研究报告等文件订立。	Article 792 Contracts for major construction projects of the State shall be concluded in accordance with the procedures set forth by the State and such documents as investment plans and feasibility study reports approved by the State.

续表

序号	术语原文	参考译文	原文例句	译文例句
315	土地承包	land contracting	（一）土地承包方案以及将土地发包给本集体以外的组织或者个人承包;	(1) land contracting schemes, and the contracting of land to any organization or individual outside this collective;
316	土地承包经营	contractual management of land	农民集体所有和国家所有由农民集体使用的耕地、林地、草地以及其他用于农业的土地,依法实行土地承包经营制度。	A system of contractual management of land is adopted in accordance with law for cultivated land, forestland, grassland, and other land used for agricultural purposes which are owned by farmers collectively, or owned by the State and used by farmers collectively.
317	土地承包经营权	right to contractual management of land	登记机构应当向土地承包经营权人发放土地承包经营权证、林权证等证书,并登记造册,确认土地承包经营权。	The registration authority shall issue a certificate, such as a certificate of the right to contractual management of land, a certificate of the right to forestry, and the like, to the person entitled to the respective right to contractual management of land, and establish a register for this purpose to record and confirm such rights.

续表

序号	术语原文	参考译文	原文例句	译文例句
318	土地所有权	ownership of the land	第四百一十八条 以集体所有有土地的使用权依法抵押的,实现抵押权后,未经法定程序,不得改变土地所有权的性质和土地用途。	Article 418 Where a right to use a lot of land owned by a collective is mortgaged in accordance with law, the nature of the ownership and the purpose of use of the land may not be altered without going through statutory procedures after the mortgage is enforced.
319	土地所有权	land ownership	(一)土地所有权;	(1) Land ownership;
320	土地用途	use of the lot	第三百四十六条 设立建设用地使用权,应当符合节约资源,保护生态环境的要求,遵守法律,行政法规规定的关于土地用途的规定,不得损害已经设立的用益物权。	Article 346 The right to use a lot of land for construction purposes shall be created in conformity with the requirements for conservation of resources and protection of the ecological environment, and in compliance with the provisions of laws and administrative regulations on the planned use of the lot, and may not impair the rights to usufruct already created thereon.
321	外国政府	foreign government	第六百八十三条 机关法人不得为保证人,但是经国务院批准为使用外国政府或者国际经济组织贷款进行转贷的除外。	Article 683 No State-organ legal person may act as a surety, except that such a State organ may, upon approval of the State Council, act as a surety in re-lending of the loans granted by a foreign government or an international economic organization.

续表

序号	术语原文	参考译文	原文例句	译文例句
322	外墙	exterior wall	第二百八十一条　建筑物及其附属设施的维修资金，属于业主共有。经业主共同决定，可以用于电梯、屋顶、外墙、无障碍设施等共有部分的维修、更新和改造。	Article 281 The maintenance funds for buildings and their auxiliary facilities are co-owned by the unit owners. The funds may, upon joint decision of the unit owners, beused for the maintenance, renewal, and renovation of the co-owned spaces, such as elevators, roofs, exterior walls, and barrier-free facilities.
323	完全民事行为能力人	a person with full capacity for performing civil juristic acts	第一千一百九十条　完全民事行为能力人对自己的行为暂时没有意识或者失去控制造成他人损害有过错的，应当承担侵权责任；没有过错的，根据行为人的经济状况对受害人适当补偿。	Article 1190 Where a person with full capacity for performing civil juristic acts is at fault for causing damage to another person due to temporary loss of consciousness or loss of control, he shall bear tort liability. Where he is not at fault, he shall make appropriate compensation to the victim according to his financial situation.
324	网络虚拟财产	online virtual assets	第一百二十七条　法律对数据、网络虚拟财产的保护有规定的，依照其规定。	Article 127 Where there are laws particularly providing for the protection of data and online virtual assets, such provisions shall be followed.

续表

序号	术语原文	参考译文	原文例句	译文例句
325	危害人体健康	endanger human health	第一千零九条　从事与人体基因、人体胚胎等有关的医学和科研活动，应当遵守法律、行政法规和国家有关规定，不得危害人体健康，不得违背伦理道德，不得损害公共利益。	Article 1009 A medical and scientific research activity related to human genes, embryos, or the like shall be done in accordance with the relevant provisions of laws, administrative regulations, and the regulations of the State, and may not endanger human health, offend ethics and morals, or harm public interests.
326	违反法律	violation of laws	第二百七十九条　业主不得违反法律、法规以及管理规约，将住宅改变为经营性用房。	Article 279 No unit owner may turn a dwelling space into a space used for operating businesses in violation of laws, regulations, or the covenants on management.
327	违约方	breaching party	合同因违约解除的，解除权人可以请求违约方承担违约责任，但是当事人另有约定的除外。	Where a contract is rescinded due to a default, the party with the right to rescind the contract may request the breaching party to bear default liability, unless otherwise agreed by the parties.

续表

序号	术语原文	参考译文	原文例句	译文例句
328	违约金	liquidated damages	第三百八十九条 担保物权的担保范围包括主债权及其利息、违约金、损害赔偿金、保管担保财产和实现担保物权的费用。	Article 389 Unless otherwise agreed by the parties, the scope covered by a security interest includes the principal claim and its interests based on the principal contract, compensatory damages, liquidated damages, and the expenses arising from safekeeping the collateral and enforcing the security interests.
329	违约责任	default liability	第五百一十条 对违约责任没有约定或者约定不明确，依据本法的规定仍不能确定的，受损害方根据标的的性质以及损失的大小，可以合理选择请求对方承担修理、重作、更换、退货、减少价款或者报酬等违约责任。	Where there is no agreement between the parties on the default liability or the relevant agreement is unclear, and if it cannot be determined according to the provisions of Article 510 of this Code, the aggrieved party may, by virtue of the nature of the object and according to the degree of the losses, reasonably request the other party to bear the default liability such as repair, redoing, replacement, return of the subject matter, decrease in price or remuneration, and the like.

续表

序号	术语原文	参考译文	原文例句	译文例句
330	维修资金	maintenance funds	第九百三十八条 物业服务合同的内容一般包括服务事项、服务质量、服务费用的标准和收取办法、维修资金的使用、服务用房的管理和使用、服务期限、服务交接等条款。	Article 938 A property management service contract generally contains clauses specifying the contents of the services, the service quality, the rates and the collection methods of the service fee, the use of the maintenance funds, the management and use of the service premises, the term of service, the service handover, and the like.
331	委托代理	agency by agreement	第一百七十三条 有下列情形之一的,委托代理终止:	Article 173 An agency by agreement is terminated under any of the following circumstances:
332	委托合同	entrustment contracts	发包人与监理人的权利和义务以及法律责任,应当依照本编委托合同以及其他有关法律、行政法规的规定。	The rights and obligations as well as the legal liabilities of the contract-offering party and the superintendent shall be defined in accordance with the provisions on entrustment contracts of this Book as well as the relevant provisions of other laws and administrative regulations.

续表

序号	术语原文	参考译文	原文例句	译文例句
333	未成年子女	minor children	第一千零五十八条　夫妻双方平等享有对未成年子女抚养、教育和保护的权利，共同承担对未成年子女抚养、教育和保护的义务。	Article 1058 Both spouses have equal rights and joint duties to raise, educate, and protect their minor children.
334	文物	cultural relics	第二百五十三条　法律规定属于国家所有的文物，属于国家所有。	Article 253 The cultural relics that are provided by law to be owned by the State are owned by the State.
335	无民事行为能力人	a person with no capacity for performing civil juristic acts	被人民法院认定为无民事行为能力人或者限制民事行为能力人的，经本人、利害关系人或者有关组织申请，人民法院可以根据其智力、精神健康恢复的状况，认定该成年人恢复为限制民事行为能力人或者完全民事行为能力人。	Where a person has been identified by the people's court as a person with no or limited capacity for performing civil juristic acts, the people's court may, upon request of the person, an interested person thereof, or a relevant organization, and based on the recovery of his intelligence and mental health, declare that the said person becomes a person with limited or full capacity for performing civil juristic acts.

续表

序号	术语原文	参考译文	原文例句	译文例句
336	无限责任	unlimited liability	第一百零四条 非法人组织的财产不足以清偿债务的,其出资人或者设立人承担无限责任。法律另有规定的,依照其规定。	Article 104 Where an unincorporated organization becomes insolvent, its capital contributors or founders shall assume unlimited liability for the debts of the organization, unless otherwise provided by law.
337	无线电频谱资源	radio-frequency spectrum resources	第二百五十二条 无线电频谱资源属于国家所有。	Article 252 Radio-frequency spectrum resources are owned by the State.
338	物权	real rights	第三章 物权的保护	Chapter III Protection of Real Rights
339	物业服务合同	contract for property management service	第九百四十条 建设单位依法与物业服务人订立的前期物业服务合同约定的服务期限届满前,业主委员会或者业主与新物业服务人订立的物业服务合同生效的,前期物业服务合同终止。	Article 940 Where a contract for property management service concluded by the owners' committee or the owners with a new property management service provider becomes effective prior to expiration of the service term as agreed in a preliminary contract for property management service concluded between the developer and the old property management service provider in accordance with law, the preliminary contract for property management service is terminated.

续表

序号	术语原文	参考译文	原文例句	译文例句
340	物业服务企业	property management service enterprise	物业服务企业等建筑物管理人应当采取必要的安全保障措施防止前款规定情形的发生；未采取必要的安全保障措施的，应当依法承担未履行安全保障义务的侵权责任。	The manager of a building such as the property management service enterprise shall take necessary security measures to prevent the occurrence of the incident specified in the preceding paragraph. Where no necessary security measures are taken, it shall bear tort liability for failure to perform the obligation of providing security measures in accordance with law.
341	物质技术条件	materials and technological resources	职务技术成果是执行法人或者非法人组织的工作任务，或者主要是利用法人或者非法人组织的物质技术条件所完成的技术成果。	A work for hire is a technological achievement that is accomplished as a result of performing the tasks assigned by a legal person or unincorporated organization or that is accomplished mainly by using the materials and technological resources of the said legal person or unincorporated organization.
342	限制民事行为能力人	a person with limited capacity for performing civil juristic acts	被人民法院认定为无民事行为能力人或者限制民事行为能力人的，经本人、利害关系人或者有关组织申请，人民法院可以根据其智力、精神健康恢复的状况，认定该成年人恢复为限制民事行为能力人或者完全民事行为能力人。	Where a person has been identified by the people's court as a person with no or limited capacity for performing civil juristic acts, the people's court may, upon request of the person, an interested person thereof, or a relevant organization, and based on the recovery of his intelligence and mental health, declare that the said person becomes a person with limited or full capacity for performing civil juristic acts.

续表

序号	术语原文	参考译文	原文例句	译文例句
343	乡镇、村企业	township or village enterprise	第三百九十八条 乡镇、村企业的建设用地使用权不得单独抵押。	Article 398 A right to use a lot of land for construction purposes of a township or village enterprise may not be mortgaged separately.
344	相关内容	pertinent part	立遗嘱后,遗嘱人实施与遗嘱内容相反的民事法律行为的,视为对遗嘱相关内容的撤回。	Where a testator who, after making a will, acts inconsistently with the content of his will, the pertinent part of the will is deemed to be revoked.
345	享有权利	have rights	第二百七十三条 业主对建筑物专有部分以外的共有部分,享有权利、承担义务;不得以放弃权利为由不履行义务。	Article 273 A unit owner has rights and assumes duties with respect to the common space other than the exclusive units of the building, and may not refuse to perform such duties on the ground that he has waived such rights.
346	项目任务	project task	与履行合同有关的技术背景资料,可行性论证和技术评价报告,项目任务书和计划书,技术标准,技术规范,原始设计和工艺文件,以及其他技术文档,按照当事人的约定可以作为合同的组成部分。	Materials such as technological background information, the feasibility studies and technological evaluation reports, the project task paper and plans, technology standards, technology norms, original design and technical documents, as well as other technical documents which are relevant to the performance of the contract may, as agreed by the parties, be component parts of the contract.

续表

序号	术语原文	参考译文	原文例句	译文例句
347	消除危险	elimination of the danger	（三）消除危险；	(3) elimination of the danger;
348	胁迫	duress of	第一百五十条 一方或者第三人以胁迫手段，使对方在违背真实意思的情况下实施的民事法律行为，受胁迫方有权请求人民法院或者仲裁机构予以撤销。	Article 150 Where a party performs a civil juristic act against its true intention owing to duress of the other party or a third person, the coerced party has the right to request the people's court or an arbitration institution to revoke the civil juristic act.
349	信息技术	information technology	第一千零一十九条 任何组织或者个人不得以丑化、污损，或者利用信息技术手段伪造等方式侵害他人的肖像权。	Article 1019 No organization or individual may infringe upon other's rights to likeness by vilifying or defacing the image thereof, or through other ways such as falsifying other's image by utilizing information technology.
350	信息网络	information network	当事人一方通过互联网等信息网络发布的商品或者服务信息符合要约条件的，对方选择该商品或者服务并提交订单成功时合同成立，但是当事人另有约定的除外。	Where the information about goods or services published by a party via information network, such as internet, satisfies the conditions for an offer, unless otherwise agreed by the parties, a contract is formed at the time when the other party selects such product or service and successfully submits the order.

序号	术语原文	参考译文	原文例句	译文例句
351	信用信息	credit information	第一千零三十条　民事主体与征信机构等信用信息处理者之间的关系，适用本编有关个人信息保护的规定和其他法律、行政法规的有关规定。	Article 1030 The provisions of this Book on the protection of personal information and the relevant provisions of other laws and administrative regulations shall be applied to the relationship between a person of the civil law and a credit information processor such as a credit reporting agency.
352	刑事处罚	criminal record	收养人应当提供其所在国有权机构出具的有关其年龄、婚姻、职业、财产、健康、有无受过刑事处罚等状况的证明材料，并与送养人签订书面协议，亲自向省、自治区、直辖市人民政府民政部门登记。	The foreign adopter shall submit documents issued by the competent authorities of his country of residence certifying such personal information as his age, marital status, occupation, financial situation, physical condition, and whether he has criminal record. The foreign adopter shall conclude a written agreement with the person who places the child for adoption and register the adoption in person with the civil affairs department of the people's government at the level of provinces, autonomous regions, or municipalities directly under the State Council.

续表

序号	术语原文	参考译文	原文例句	译文例句
353	姓名权	right to name	第三章 姓名权和名称权	Chapter III Rights to Name and Rights to Entity Name
354	许可合同	license contract	第八百六十五条 专利实施许可合同仅在该专利权的存续期限内有效。	Article 865 A patent exploitation licensing contract is valid only within the period during which the patent is valid.
355	严重精神损害	severe mental distress	第九百九十六条 因当事人一方的违约行为,损害对方人格权并造成严重精神损害,受损害方选择请求其承担违约责任的,不影响受损害方请求精神损害赔偿。	Article 996 Where the personality rights of a party are harmed by the other party's breach of contract and the injured party thus suffers severe mental distress, if the injured party elects to request the other party to bear liability based on breach of contract, his right to claim to compensation for mental distress is not affected.
356	研究开发	research and development	第八百五十二条 委托开发合同的委托人应当按照约定支付研究开发经费和报酬,提供技术资料,提出研究开发要求,完成协作事项,接受研究开发成果。	Article 852 A client of a commissioned development contract shall pay for the research and development fees and the remunerations in accordance with the agreement, provide technological materials, make proposals for research and development, complete his tasks in the cooperative work, and accept the work product of the research and development.

续表

序号	术语原文	参考译文	原文例句	译文例句
357	野生动植物资源	wild animal and plant resources	第二百五十一条 法律规定属于国家所有的野生动植物资源,属于国家所有。	Article 251 The wild animal and plant resources that are provided by law to be owned by the State are owned by the State.
358	业主大会	the owners' assembly	第二百八十条 业主大会或者业主委员会的决定,对业主具有法律约束力。	Article 280 Decisions of the owners' assembly or the owners' committee are legally binding on unit owners.
359	业主委员会	the owners' committee	第二百八十条 业主大会或者业主委员会的决定,对业主具有法律约束力。	Article 280 Decisions of the owners' assembly or the owners' committee are legally binding on unit owners.
360	一般规定	general rules	第一章 一般规定	Chapter I General Rules
361	医疗措施	treatment measures	第一千二百一十九条 医务人员在诊疗活动中应当向患者说明病情和医疗措施。	Article 1219 The medical staff shall explain the medical conditions and treatment measures to the patient when diagnosing and treating him.

续表

序号	术语原文	参考译文	原文例句	译文例句
362	医疗费用	medical expenses	（二）一方负有法定扶养义务的人患重大疾病需要医治，另一方不同意支付相关医疗费用。	(2) a person, whom one of the spouses has a statutory obligation to support, is suffering from a serious disease and needs medical treatment, but the other spouse does not agree to pay the relevant medical expenses.
363	医疗风险	medical risk	需要实施手术、特殊检查、特殊治疗的，医务人员应当及时向患者具体说明医疗风险，并说明其替代医疗方案等情况，取得其明确同意；不能或者不宜向患者说明的，应当向患者的近亲属说明，并取得其明确同意。	Where a surgery, a special examination, or a special treatment is needed, the medical staff shall explain to the patient the medical risks, alternative treatment plans, and other information in a timely manner and obtain his express consent. Where it is impossible or inappropriate to do so, the medical staff shall explain it to the patient's close relatives and get their express consent.
364	医疗机构	medical institution	本条规定的有关组织包括：居民委员会、村民委员会、学校、医疗机构，妇女联合会、残疾人联合会，依法设立的老年人组织，民政部门等。	A relevant organization referred to in this Article includes a residents' committee, a villagers' committee, a school, a medical institution, the women's federation, the disabled person's federation, a legally established organization for senior people, the civil affairs departments, and the like.

续表

序号	术语原文	参考译文	原文例句	译文例句
365	医疗机构	medical and health facilities	（三）学校、幼儿园、医疗机构等为公益目的成立的教育设施、医疗卫生设施和其他公益设施；	（3）educational facilities, medical and health facilities, and other public welfare facilities of non-profit legal persons established for public welfare purposes, such as schools, kindergartens, and medical institutions;
366	医疗器械	medical device	第一千零八条　为研制新药、医疗器械或者发展新的预防和治疗方法，需要进行临床试验的，应当依法经相关主管部门批准并经伦理委员会审查同意，向受试者或者受试者的监护人告知试验目的、用途和可能产生的风险等详细情况，并经其书面同意。	Article 1008 Where a clinical trial is needed for developing new drugs and medical devices or developing new prevention and treatment methods, upon approval of the relevant competent authorities and the examination and approval of the ethics committee in accordance with law, the participants or their guardians shall be informed of the details including the purposes, methods, and the possible risks of the trial, and their written consent must be obtained.
367	遗产管理人	administrator of estate	第九百三十五条　因委托人死亡或者被宣告破产、解散，致使委托合同终止，将损害委托人利益的，在委托人的继承人、遗产管理人或者清算人承受委托事务或者清算人承受委托事务之前，受托人应当继续处理委托事务。	Article 935 Where termination of an entrustment contract resulting from the death, declared bankruptcy, or declared dissolution of the principal is to harm the interests of the principal, the agent shall continue to handle the entrusted matter until the heirs, administrator of estate, or the liquidator of the principal takes it over.

序号	术语原文	参考译文	原文例句	译文例句
368	遗失物	lost thing	该遗失物通过转让被他人占有的，权利人有权向无处分权人请求损害赔偿，或者自知道或者应当知道受让人之日起二年内向受让人请求返还原物；但是，受让人通过拍卖或者向具有经营资格的经营者购得该遗失物的，权利人请求返还原物时应当支付受让人所付的费用。	Where the lost thing is possessed by another person by way of transfer, the right holder has the right to claim damages against the person who disposes of the thing without the right to disposition, or to request the transferee to return the original thing within two years from the date on which the right holder knows or should have known of the transferee; provided, however, that where the transferee has acquired the lost thing at auction or from a qualified business operator, the right holder shall, at the time of requesting the return of the original thing, reimburse the expenses that have been paid by the transferee. The right holder has, after having reimbursed the expenses paid by the transferee, the right to indemnification against the person who disposes of the thing without the right to disposition.

续表

序号	术语原文	参考译文	原文例句	译文例句
369	议事方式	procedure	法人、非法人组织依照法律或者章程规定的议事方式和表决程序作出决议的，该决议行为成立。	Where a legal person or an unincorporated organization makes a resolution in accordance with the procedure and voting method provided by law or stipulated in its articles of association, such a resolution is accomplished as a civil juristic act.
370	议事规则	the procedural rule	（一）制定和修改业主大会议事规则；	(1) to formulate and amend the procedural rules of the owners' assembly;
371	意思表示	intent made in the form of	当事人对采用数据电文形式的意思表示的生效时间另有约定的，按照其约定。	Where the parties have agreed otherwise on the effective time of the expression of intent made in the form of an electronic data message, such an agreement shall prevail.
372	隐蔽工程	concealed project	第七百九十八条　隐蔽工程在隐蔽以前，承包人应当通知发包人检查。	Article 798 Prior to the concealment of a concealed project, the contractor shall notify the contract-offering party to inspect it.

续表

序号	术语原文	参考译文	原文例句	译文例句
373	隐私权	right to privacy	第六章 隐私权和个人信息保护	Chapter VI Rights to Privacy and Protection of Personal Information
374	营利法人	for-profit legal person	营利法人的出资人不得滥用法人独立地位和出资人有限责任损害法人债权人的利益;滥用法人独立地位和出资人有限责任,逃避债务,严重损害法人债权人的利益的,应当对法人债务承担连带责任。	A capital contributor of a for-profit legal person may not abuse the legal person's independent status and his own limited liability status to harm the interests of the legal person's creditors. A capital contributor abusing the legal person's independent status or its own limited liability status to evade repayment of debts and thus severely harming the interests of the legal person's creditors shall be jointly and severally liable for the legal person's obligations.

续表

序号	术语原文	参考译文	原文例句	译文例句
375	应收账款	accounts receivable	第七百六十八条　应收账款债权人就同一应收账款订立多个保理合同，致使多个保理人主张权利的，已经登记的先于未登记的取得应收账款；均已经登记的，按照登记时间的先后顺序取得应收账款；均未登记的，由最先到达应收账款债务人的转让通知中载明的保理人取得应收账款；既未登记也未通知的，按照保理融资款或者服务报酬的比例取得应收账款。	Article 768 Where a creditor of an account receivable concludes multiple factoring contracts with different factors so that the factors claim their rights against the same account receivable, the account receivable shall be obtained by the factor of a registered factoring contract in priority over the factors of unregistered factoring contracts, or, where all factoring contracts are registered, by the factors in an order of priority according to the time of registration, or, where none of the factoring contracts have been registered, by the factor stated in the transfer notice which has reached the debtor of the account receivable first in time. Where none of the factoring contracts have been registered andno transfer notice has been sent, the account receivable shall be obtained by the factors on a pro rata basis on the amount of financing funds each has provided, or the service remuneration each is entitled to.

续表

序号	术语原文	参考译文	原文例句	译文例句
376	用益物权	right to usufruct	第三百一十条 两个以上组织、个人共同享有用益物权、担保物权的,参照适用本章的有关规定。	Article 310 The relevant provisions of this Chapter shall be applied mutatis mutandis to the situation where two or more organizations or individuals are jointly entitled to a right to usufruct or a security interest.
377	油气管道	oil and gas pipelines	铁路、公路、电力设施、电信设施和油气管道等基础设施,依照法律规定为国家所有的,属于国家所有。	Infrastructures such as railways, roads, electric power facilities, telecommunication facilities, as well as oil and gas pipelines that are provided by law to be owned by the State are owned by the State.
378	有偿合同	non-gratuitous contracts	第六百四十六条 法律对其他有偿合同有规定的,依照其规定;没有规定的,参照适用买卖合同的有关规定。	Article 646 Where there are provisions of laws governing other non-gratuitous contracts, such provisions shall be followed. In the absence of such a provision, the relevant provisions on sales contracts shall be applied mutatis mutandis.

续表

序号	术语原文	参考译文	原文例句	译文例句
379	有限责任	limited liability	营利法人的出资人不得滥用法人独立地位和出资人有限责任损害法人债权人的利益;滥用法人独立地位和出资人有限责任,逃避债务,严重损害法人的债权人的利益的,应当对法人债务承担连带责任。	A capital contributor of a for-profit legal person may not abuse the legal person's independent status and his own limited liability status to harm the interests of the legal person's creditors. A capital contributor abusing the legal person's independent status or its own limited liability status to evade repayment of debts and thus severely harming the interests of the legal person's creditors shall be jointly and severally liable for the legal person's obligations.
380	有限责任公司	a company with limited liabilities	第二百六十八条 国家、集体和私人依法可以出资设立有限责任公司,股份有限公司或者其他企业。	Article 268 The State, collectives, and private individuals may establish companies with limited liabilities, joint stock companies limited by shares, or other enterprises through making capital contributions in accordance with law.

续表

序号	术语原文	参考译文	原文例句	译文例句
381	预告登记	the priority notice be registered	预告登记后,未经预告登记的权利人同意,处分该不动产的,不发生物权效力。	Where, after the priority notice is registered, the immovable property is disposed of without the consent of the right holder as registered in the priority notice, the disposition is not effective in terms of the real right.
382	原租赁合同	original lease contract	第七百三十四条　租赁期限届满,承租人继续使用租赁物,出租人没有提出异议的,原租赁合同继续有效,但是租赁期限为不定期。	Article 734 Where a lessee continues to use the leased object upon expiration of the term of the lease and the lessor has not raised any objection, the original lease contract continues to be valid, except that the term of the lease becomes indefinite.
383	运输合同	transport contract	第八百零九条　运输合同是承运人将旅客或者货物从起运地点运输到约定地点,旅客、托运人或者收货人支付票款或者运输费用的合同。	Article 809 A transport contract is a contract under which a carrier transports a passenger or goods from the place of dispatch to a destination agreed by the parties, and the passenger, consignor, or consignee pays the fare or the freight.

续表

序号	术语原文	参考译文	原文例句	译文例句
384	责任人	responsible person	第一千二百五十二条 建筑物、构筑物或者其他设施倒塌、塌陷造成他人损害的，由建设单位与施工单位承担连带责任，但是建设单位与施工单位能够证明不存在质量缺陷的除外。建设单位、施工单位赔偿后，有其他责任人的，有权向其他责任人追偿。	Article 1252 Where a building, structure, or another type of facility collapses or subsides and causes damage to another person, the project owner and the constructor shall assume joint and several liability unless they can prove that there is no quality defect. Where the damage is due to the fault of another responsible person, the project owner or constructor who has made compensation has the right to indemnification against the responsible person.

续表

序号	术语原文	参考译文	原文例句	译文例句
385	责任限额	limit of liability	第一千二百一十六条 机动车驾驶人发生交通事故后逃逸,该机动车参加强制保险的,由保险人在机动车强制保险责任限额范围内予以赔偿;机动车不明,该机动车未参加强制保险或者抢救费用超过机动车强制保险责任限额,需要支付被侵权人人身伤亡的抢救、丧葬等费用的,由道路交通事故社会救助基金垫付。	Article 1216 In a hit-and-run accident, if the motor vehicle is insured by a compulsory insurance, compensation shall be paid by the insurer within the limit of the insured liability. Where the motor vehicle cannot be located, is not covered by the compulsory insurance, or the rescue expenses exceed the limit of liability of the compulsory motor vehicle insurance, and payment needs to be made against the rescue, funeral, and other expenses incurred as a result of the death or bodily injury of the infringed person, such payment shall be paid from the Social Assistance Fund for Road Traffic Accidents.

续表

序号	术语原文	参考译文	原文例句	译文例句
386	债权人	creditor	第五百二十四条 债务人不履行债务,第三人对履行该债务具有合法利益的,第三人有权向债权人代为履行;但是,按照债务性质、按照法律规定或者依照当事人约定只能由债务人履行的除外。	Article 524 Where a debtor fails to perform an obligation and a third person has a lawful interest in the performance of the obligation, the third person is entitled to perform it to the creditor on behalf of the debtor, unless theobligation may only be performed by the debtor based on the nature of the obligation, as agreed by the parties, or as provided by law.
387	债务人	debtor	第五百二十四条 债务人不履行债务,第三人对履行该债务具有合法利益的,第三人有权向债权人代为履行;但是,按照债务性质、按照法律规定或者依照当事人约定只能由债务人履行的除外。	Article 524 Where a debtor fails to perform an obligation and a third person has a lawful interest in the performance of the obligation, the third person is entitled to perform it to the creditor on behalf of the debtor, unless the obligation may only be performed by the debtor based on the nature of the obligation, as agreed by the parties, or as provided by law.

序号	术语原文	参考译文	原文例句	译文例句
388	真实身份	real identity	通知应当包括构成侵权的初步证据及权利人的真实身份信息。	The notice shall include the preliminary evidence establishing the tort and the real identity information of the right holder.
389	诊疗活动	diagnosis and treatment	第一千二百一十八条 患者在诊疗活动中受到损害，医疗机构或者其医务人员有过错的，由医疗机构承担赔偿责任。	Article 1218 Where a patient suffers damage during diagnosis and treatment, and the medical institution or its medical staff is at fault, the medical institution shall assume the liability for compensation.
390	征收	expropriation	征收集体所有的土地，应当依法及时足额支付土地补偿费、安置补助费以及农村村民住宅、其他地上附着物和青苗等的补偿费用，并安排被征地农民的社会保障费用，保障被征地农民的生活，维护被征地农民的合法权益。	In the case of expropriation of collectively-owned land, land compensation fees, resettlement subsidies, and compensation fees for rural villagers' dwellings and other ground attachments as well as young crops shall be paid in full in a timely manner in accordance with law, and social security premiums of the farmers whose land has been expropriated shall be arranged, their lives secured, and their lawful rights and interests safeguarded.

续表

序号	术语原文	参考译文	原文例句	译文例句
391	证据	evidence	不动产权属证书记载的事项，应当与不动产登记簿一致；记载不一致的，除有证据证明不动产登记簿确有错误外，以不动产登记簿记载为准。	The items recorded in the real right certificate for immovable property shall be consistent with what are recorded in the register of immovable property; in case of inconsistency between the two, what is recorded in the register of immovable property shall prevail, unless there is evidence establishing a clear error in the register of immovable property.
392	支付方式	method of payment	第六百二十六条　买受人应当按照约定的数额和支付方式支付价款。	Article 626 A buyer shall make payment in accordance with the agreed amount and method of payment.
393	支付利息	pay interest	第五百六十一条　债务人在履行主债务外，还应当支付利息和实现债权的有关费用，其给付不足以清偿全部债务的，除当事人另有约定外，应当按照下列顺序履行：	Article 561 In addition to performing the principal obligation, a debtor shall pay to the creditor interests and other expenses related to the enforcement of the obligation. Where the payment is not sufficient to discharge all of the obligations, unless otherwise agreed by the parties, the debtor shall perform the obligations in accordance with the following order of priority:

续表

序号	术语原文	参考译文	原文例句	译文例句
394	知识产权的保护	the protection of intellectual property rights	第八百四十四条 订立技术合同,应当有利于知识产权的保护和科学技术的进步,促进科学技术成果的研发、转化,应用和推广。	Article 844 The conclusion of a technology contract shall be conducive to the protection of intellectual property rights and the advance of science and technology, and shall promote the research and development, transformation, application, and dissemination of the achievements in science and technology.
395	执行董事	executive director	执行机构为董事会或者执行董事的,董事长、执行董事或者经理按照法人章程的规定担任法定代表人;未设董事会或者执行董事的,法人章程规定的主要负责人为其执行机构和法定代表人。	Where the executive body of a legal person is the board of directors or the executive director, the legal representative shall be the chairman of the board of directors, the executive director, or the manager, as is stipulated in the articles of association. Where there is no board of directors or executive director established, the person with the principal responsibilities as stipulated in the articles of association shall be the executive body and the legal representative of the legal person.

续表

序号	术语原文	参考译文	原文例句	译文例句
396	直接损失	direct loss	因解除合同造成对方损失的,除可归责于该当事人的事由外,无偿委托合同的解除方应当赔偿因解除时间不当造成的直接损失,有偿委托的解除方应当赔偿对方的直接损失和合同履行后可以获得的利益。	Where rescission of the contract by a party causes losses to the other party, the party rescinding a gratuitous entrustment contract shall compensate for the direct loss caused by the rescission at an improper time, and the party rescinding a non-gratuitous entrustment contract shall compensate for the direct loss and the expected profit obtainable had the contract been performed, unless the loss is incurred by a cause not attributable to the rescinding party.
397	直辖市人民政府	people's government municipality directly under the state council	收养人应当提供由其所在国有权机构出具的有关其年龄、婚姻、职业、财产、健康、有无受过刑事处罚等状况的证明材料,并与送养人签订书面协议,亲自到省、自治区、直辖市人民政府民政部门登记。	The foreign adopter shall submit documents issued by the competent authorities of his country of residence certifying such personal information as his age, marital status, occupation, financial situation, physical condition, and whether he has criminal record. The foreign adopter shall conclude a written agreement with the person who places the child for adoption and register the adoption in person with the civil affairs department of the people's government at the level of provinces, autonomous regions, or municipalities directly under the State Council.

续表

序号	术语原文	参考译文	原文例句	译文例句
398	指定监护人	appoint the guardian	第三十一条　对监护人的确定有争议的,由被监护人住所地的居民委员会、村民委员会或者民政部门指定监护人,有关当事人对指定监护人不服的,可以向人民法院申请指定监护人;有关当事人也可以直接向人民法院申请指定监护人。	Article 31 Where a dispute arises over the determination of a guardian, the guardian shall be appointed by the residents' committee, the villagers' committee, or the civil affairs department in the place where the ward's domicile is located, and a party not satisfied with such an appointment may request the people's court to appoint a guardian; the relevant parties may also directly request the people's court to make such an appointment.
399	质量要求	quality requirement	(一)质量要求不明确的,按照强制性国家标准履行;没有强制性国家标准的,按照推荐性国家标准履行;没有推荐性国家标准的,按照行业标准履行;没有国家标准、行业标准的,按照通常标准或者符合合同目的的特定标准履行。	(1) where the quality requirements are not clearly stipulated, the contract shall be performed in accordance with a mandatory national standard, or a recommendatory national standard in the absence of a mandatory national standard, or the standard of the industry in the absence of a recommendatory national standard. In the absence of any national or industrial standard, the contract shall be performed in accordance with the general standard or a specific standard conforming to the purpose of the contract.

续表

序号	术语原文	参考译文	原文例句	译文例句
400	质押合同	pledge contract	担保合同包括抵押合同、质押合同和其他具有担保功能的合同。	Security contracts include mortgage contracts, pledge contracts, and other contracts with a function of security.
401	治疗方法	treatment method	第一千零八条 为研制新药、医疗器械或者发展新的预防和治疗方法,需要进行临床试验的,应当依法经相关主管部门批准并经伦理委员会审查同意,向受试者或者受试者的监护人告知试验目的、用途和可能产生的风险等详细情况,并经其书面同意。	Article 1008 Where a clinical trial is needed for developing new drugs and medical devices or developing new prevention and treatment methods, upon approval of the relevant competent authorities and the examination and approval of the ethics committee in accordance with law, the participants or their guardians shall be informed of the details including the purposes, methods, and the possible risks of the trial, and their written consent must be obtained.
402	终止妊娠	termination of pregnancy	第一千零八十二条 女方在怀孕期间、分娩后一年内或者终止妊娠后六个月内,男方不得提出离婚;但是,女方提出离婚或者人民法院认为确有必要受理男方离婚请求的除外。	Article 1082 A husband may not file for divorce during his wife's pregnancy, within one year after his wife delivers, or within six months after termination of her pregnancy, unless the wife applies for divorce, or the people's court deems it necessary to hear the divorce request made by the husband.

序号	术语原文	参考译文	原文例句	译文例句
403	仲裁机构	arbitral institution	第一百四十七条　基于重大误解实施的民事法律行为,行为人有权请求人民法院或者仲裁机构予以撤销。	Article 147 Where a civil juristic act is performed based on serious misunderstanding, the person who performs the act has the right to request the people's court or an arbitration institution to revoke the act.
404	重大过失	gross negligence	财产代管人因故意或者重大过失造成失踪人财产损失的,应当承担赔偿责任。	A custodian who, intentionally or due to gross negligence, causes damage to the property of the missing person shall be liable for compensation.
405	重大决策	major decisions	国家、集体和私人所有的不动产或者动产投到企业的,由出资人按照约定或者出资比例享有资产收益、重大决策以及选择经营管理者等权利并履行义务。	Where the immovable or movable property of the State, collectives, and private individuals are invested in an enterprise, the investors are, in accordance with their agreement or in proportion to their investment, entitled to receive returns on the assets, make major decisions, and select business managers, and obligated to perform their duties.

续表

序号	术语原文	参考译文	原文例句	译文例句
406	重大误解	serious misunderstanding	第一百四十七条　基于重大误解实施的民事法律行为,行为人有权请求人民法院或者仲裁机构予以撤销。	Article 147 Where a civil juristic act is performed based on serious misunderstanding, the person who performs the act has the right to request the people's court or an arbitration institution to revoke the act.
407	重复使用	repeated use	第四百九十六条　格式条款是当事人为了重复使用而预先拟定,并在订立合同时未与对方协商的条款。	Article 496 A standard clause refers to a clause formulated in advance by a party for repeated use which has not been negotiated with the other party when concluding the contract.
408	重要事实	important fact	中介人故意隐瞒与订立合同有关的重要事实或者提供虚假情况,损害委托人利益的,不得请求支付报酬并应当承担赔偿责任。	Where a middleman intentionally conceals important facts in relation to the conclusionof the contract or provides untrue information thereof, thus harming the interests of the client, he may not request for remuneration and shall bear the liability for compensation.

续表

序号	术语原文	参考译文	原文例句	译文例句
409	主管机关	competent authority	清算义务人未及时履行清算义务,造成损害的,应当承担民事责任;主管机关或者利害关系人可以申请人民法院指定有关人员组成清算组进行清算。	The persons with the duty to liquidate the legal person who fail to perform their duties in time and thus cause damage to others shall bear civil liability; the competent authority or an interested person may request the people's court to appoint the relevant persons to form a liquidation committee to liquidate the legal person.
410	主合同	principal contract	主合同解除后,担保人对承担的民事责任仍应当承担担保责任,但是担保合同另有约定的除外。	After the principal contract is rescinded, a security provider shall still be obligated to secure the debtor's liability, unless otherwise agreed in the security contract.
411	注册商标	registered trademark	(五)可以转让的注册商标专用权、专利权、著作权等知识产权中的财产权;	(5) transferable proprietary rights consisted in intellectual property such as the right to the exclusive use of registered trademarks, patent rights, and copyrights;

续表

序号	术语原文	参考译文	原文例句	译文例句
412	专利申请	application for patent	第八百六十二条 技术转让合同是合法拥有技术的权利人,将现有特定的专利、专利申请,技术秘密的相关权利让与他人所订立的合同。	Article 862 A technology transfer contract is a contract under which a lawful right holder of a technology assigns to another person the relevant rights in respect of a specific patent, application for a patent, or technological know-how.
413	专利申请权	right to apply for patent	第八百六十条 合作开发完成的发明创造,申请专利的权利属于合作开发的当事人共有;当事人一方转让其共有的专利申请权的,其他各方享有以同等条件优先受让的权利。但是,当事人另有约定的除外。	Article 860 Where an invention is accomplished through cooperative development, the right to apply for patent thereon jointly belongs to all parties to the cooperative development. Where one party is to transfer the part of the joint patent application right he owns, the other party or parties shall have a priority right to acquire the right on equivalent conditions, unless otherwise agreed by the parties.

续表

序号	术语原文	参考译文	原文例句	译文例句
414	专利申请人	(patent) applicant	技术合同涉及专利的,应当注明发明创造的名称、专利申请人和专利权人、申请日期、申请号、专利号以及专利权的有效期限。	Where a technology contract involves a patent, it shall indicate the designation of the invention, the applicant and the patentee thereof, the date of application, the application number, the patent number, and the term of the patent rights.
415	追认	ratification	第一百六十九条 代理人需要转委托第三人代理的,应当取得被代理人的同意或者追认。	Article 169 Where an agent needs to re-delegate his authority to a third person, he shall obtain consent or ratification from the principal.
416	自然流水	natural flowing water	对自然流水的利用,应当在不动产的相邻权利人之间合理分配。	The right to utilization of natural flowing water shall be reasonably allocated among the persons entitled to the adjacent rights in the immovable property.
417	自愿原则	the principle of voluntariness	第五条 民事主体从事民事活动,应当遵循自愿原则,按照自己的意思设立、变更、终止民事法律关系。	Article 5 When conducting a civil activity, a person of the civil law shall, in compliance with the principle of voluntariness, create, alter, or terminate a civil juristic relationship according to his own will.

续表

序号	术语原文	参考译文	原文例句	译文例句
418	宗教活动	religious activities	依法设立的宗教活动场所,具备法人条件的,可以申请法人登记,取得捐助法人资格。法律、行政法规对宗教活动场所有规定的,依照其规定。	A site legally established to hold religious activities may be registered as a legal person and attains the status of a donation-funded legal person if it meets the requirements for being a legal person. Where there are laws or administrative regulations providing for the religious sites, such provisions shall be followed.
419	租金	rent	第七百二十三条　因第三人主张权利,致使承租人不能对租赁物使用、收益的,承租人可以请求减少租金或者不支付租金。	Article 723 Where a lessee is unable to use or to receive benefit from the leased object owing to a claim from a third person, the lessee may request for a reduction of or exemption from the rent.
420	租赁合同	lease contract	第七百二十五条　租赁物在承租人按照租赁合同占有期限内发生所有权变动的,不影响租赁合同的效力。	Article 725 A change in the ownership of a leased object during the period that a lessee possesses the leased object in accordance with the lease contract does not affect the validity of the lease contract.

续表

序号	术语原文	参考译文	原文例句	译文例句
421	租赁期限	lease term	第七百一十七条 承租人经出租人同意将租赁物转租给第三人，转租期限超过承租人剩余租赁期限的，超过部分的约定对出租人不具有法律约束力，但是出租人与承租人另有约定的除外。	Article 717 Where a lessee, upon consent of the lessor, subleases the leased object to a third person, if the term of the sublease exceeds the remaining term of the original lease, the sublease beyond the term of the original lease is not legally binding on the lessor unless otherwise agreed by the lessor and the lessee.
422	最高额	maximum amount	第四百二十二条 最高额抵押担保的债权确定前，抵押权人与抵押人可以通过协议变更债权确定的期间、债权范围以及最高债权额。但是，变更的内容不得对其他抵押权人产生不利影响。	Article 422 Before the claims secured by a maximum mortgage for floating claims are ascertained, the mortgagee and the mortgagor may change by agreement the period of time for the ascertainment of the claims, the scope of the claims, and the maximum amount of the claims, provided that such changes may not adversely affect other mortgagees.
423	实际……数额	the actual amount of	利息预先在本金中扣除的，应当按照实际借款数额返还借款并计算利息。	Where the interest is deducted from the principal in advance, the loan shall be repaid and the interest shall be calculated according to the actual amount of money provided.

后 记

这是一部在智能时代有关法律语言与翻译的著作。书中所提的"法概念"是个颇为哲学化的表达,甚至可以说有点玄妙。我的脑海中常常盘旋着《法的门前》中那位看门人和门内的"法",禁不住总想打开门看看"它"的模样。选用这个表达是希翼在法的语言表示中找寻它的面貌,发现它的精神,实现它的功能。朱尔斯·科尔曼和斯科特·夏皮罗在《牛津法理学与法哲学手册》第二十二章篇章页中有言,"语言的力量足以摧城拔寨"。毫无疑问,理解法的概念首先需要理解语言,而通过研究语言可以在一定程度上说明法的本质。

洛克、边沁、奥斯丁、哈特这些大名鼎鼎的哲学家、政治家、法学家,又何尝不是语言学家?尽管边沁对于语言问题的诸多看法都来自于其对洛克观点的理解,但仍可以毫不夸张地将其视为研究语言哲学的第一人。他创制了"Paraphrasis"(意译)这种方法,去解释抽象理论概念,包括权利、义务以及民生、法律等。继承边沁衣钵的奥斯丁则更加关注文字的"properly so called"(恰当称谓)——"能够明晰感知"便是恰当。这样的观点不免偏颇,却为后来深入研究法律语言留下了空间和启示。后来的哈特发扬了边沁的法理学观点,看重阐释(elucidate)。进一步对其研究语言的角度进行总结,不难得出:语境原则、多样性原则、模糊性原则和语言的具象化适用是讨论的四个重点。这里的语境原则恰是语言学研究的重要关切。维特根斯坦也曾断言,"除非作为句子的一部分,否则单字毫无意义可言"。超越小词的意义单位便由此而生,故此无论怎样的概念都是抽象的,需要通过语言承载、传递、扩散,并在语境中得到确认。既然概念是对客观事物的抽象概括,并以人所获得的概念为出发点赋予事物指称及意义,法概念便是具有法律意义的社会事实或社会现象,概括性表达而成的术语或其他意义单位。当法概念在一种语境中承载的意义单位,寻找在另一种语言中的对应单位,从而形成翻译单位的过程时,便是一种概念的旅行。在此过程中,涉及对语言层面的各级意义单位,包括术语、法律用语、篇章句式、语篇、话语的研究;在超语言层面,则涉及国家主义、历史主义、文化主义、本质主义等方面。

这部书稿历经了五年的思量和实践,脱胎于上海市哲学社会科学规划青年课题"语料库驱动下的汉英立法文本翻译单位研究"的结项报告,从语义单位、翻译单位出发,探索文字背后的法律"意思表示"和其跨语际实现。同时,在智能时代的观照下,利用语料库语言学的方法对法律中扩展意义单位进行梳理,探寻了法律与语言、翻译结合的未来方案,并以法律知识图谱构建为例释,希翼为法律解释学的发展提供新角度。

2022 年是我入职华东政法大学的第十年,日月穿梭,有如流水,我有幸见证了华政从六十华诞走到了七十华诞。感谢华东政法大学科研处在这部作品问世过程中的支持,著书立说是每个读书人的执念,如今虽谈不上"立说",但总算能把一段时间内的思考整理并出版,是令人愉悦的。感谢时任科研处处长屈文生教授,他也是国内法律翻译方向最重要的学者之一,学术造诣深厚,书中的很多观点深受屈老师启发。感谢外语学院全体领导班子,尤其是余素青院长、黄岳峥书记、王文胜副书记、曹嬿副院长的支持和鼓励。从 2021 年 10 月暂别学院驻外工作起，我原先分管的各项工作全部落在几位领导肩上，后遇上海疫情，学校、学院"全员皆兵"，几位领导和全体办公室人员、辅导员老师更是成为站在第一线的"排头兵"，他们的辛劳人所共知。感谢与我在工作中紧密合作的王文主任、詹继续博士和胡伊鹭老师，三位都是坚志而勇为的青年才俊，未可量也。我的硕士生艾佳婧（现已是公证员助理）完成了第四章第二节、第三节部分的撰写，方可则完成了第一节的资料整理和画图工作，没有两位的辛苦付出，按期完稿几乎是不可能的。此外，我和正在哈佛法学院访学的挚友李明倩，几乎同时出发分隔两地，但仍会在电话里打磨译稿、探讨研究课题、分享两地趣闻，不亦乐乎。

2022 年注定是不平凡的一年，全球疫情伴随局部战情，有关"正当性"的争论似乎无休无止，而身在海外则更加感到中国发展之艰，华人华侨之难。我于此感谢在驻外期间对我关怀备至的齐前进大使、李欣公参、杜鹤亭参赞、刘华博参赞、毕磊武官、赵辰主任、白鹏主任、赵丽华一秘、及智一秘、张达武官、王邦武官和刘宇辉、刘杰、赵亚男、胡淑萍、唐云云等可亲可爱的同志。这是一群平凡又极不凡的外交官，他们在遥远的异乡，守护着祖国安危。向他们致敬！希望在未来的外交路上，"法律话语"会更好地保护他们平安前行。

最后，我要感谢家人对我无私的包容和支持。短短四年间，我的外公、外婆相继离世，母亲重病生活不能自理，是父亲一个人担负起照顾母亲的重任，不分寒暑，不分昼夜。从小到大，我在他身上看到的都是坚若磐石的意志，虚心克己又休休有容。现在，我只盼能够在回国之后将二老接至身边，尽儿女之孝道。当然，还要感谢我的先生孟维亮，在那些数不清的我对着电脑愁眉不展的日子里，能闻到从厨房传来的饭菜香是踏踏实实的幸福，我也在他的熏陶下厨艺大增。小儿安迪时年八岁，对地图痴迷，会拉着我追问国际局势，我却时常语塞，深感学识有限，唯有力学笃行，不负光阴和爱。

　　是以为记。

宋丽珏

2022 年 8 月 5 日于萨格勒布

图书在版编目 (CIP) 数据

法概念的跨语际旅行 : 从意义单位到翻译单位 / 宋
丽珏著 . — 北京 : 商务印书馆 , 2022
（棠树文丛）
ISBN 978-7-100-21176-5

Ⅰ . ①法… Ⅱ . ①宋… Ⅲ . ①法律－英语－翻译
Ⅳ . ① D9

中国版本图书馆 CIP 数据核字（2022）第 081625 号

棠树文丛

法概念的跨语际旅行

从意义单位到翻译单位

宋丽珏　著

商 务 印 书 馆 出 版
（北京王府井大街 36 号　邮政编码 100710）
商 务 印 书 馆 发 行
南京新洲印刷有限公司印刷
ISBN　978-7-100-21176-5

2022 年 10 月第 1 版　　开本 880 × 1240　1/32
2022 年 10 月第 1 次印刷　印张　10

定价：59.00 元